RUSSIAN

A ROUGH GUIDE DICTIONARY PHRASEBOOK

Compiled by

LEXUS

Credits

Compiled by Lexus with Irina and Alistair MacLean
Lexus Series Editor: Sally Davies
Rough Guides Phrase Book Editor: Jonathan Buckley
Rough Guides Series Editor: Mark Ellingham

First edition published in 1997 by Rough Guides Ltd,
62–70 Shorts Gardens, London WC2H 9AB.
Revised in 2001.

Distributed by the Penguin Group.

Penguin Books Ltd, 27 Wrights Lane, London W8 5TZ
Penguin Books USA Inc., 375 Hudson Street, New York 10014, USA
Penguin Books Australia Ltd, 487 Maroondah Highway,
PO Box 257, Ringwood, Victoria 3134, Australia
Penguin Books Canada Ltd, Alcorn Avenue,
Toronto, Ontario, Canada M4V 1E4
Penguin Books (NZ) Ltd, 182–190 Wairau Road,
Auckland 10, New Zealand

Typeset in Minion Cyrillic, Bembo and Helvetica to an original design
by Henry Iles.
Printed in Spain by Graphy Cems.

British Library Cataloguing in Publication Data
A catalogue for this book is available from the British Library.

ISBN 1-85828-921-1

HELP US GET IT RIGHT

Lexus and Rough Guides have made great efforts to be accurate and
informative in this Rough Guide Russian phrasebook. However, if you feel
we have overlooked a useful word or phrase, or have any other
comments to make about the book, please let us know. All contributors
will be acknowledged and the best letters will be rewarded with a free
Rough Guide phrasebook of your choice. Please write to 'Russian
Phrasebook Update', at either Shorts Gardens (London) or Hudson Street
(New York) – for full addresses see above. Alternatively you can email us at
mail@roughguides.co.uk

Online information about Rough Guides can be found at our website
www.roughguides.com

CONTENTS

Introduction

The Rough Guide Russian phrasebook is a highly practical introduction to the contemporary language. Laid out in clear A-Z style, it uses key-word referencing to lead you straight to the words and phrases you want – so if you need to book a room, just look up 'room'. The Rough Guide gets straight to the point in every situation, in bars and shops, on trains and buses, and in hotels and banks.

The main part of the Rough Guide is a double dictionary: English-Russian then Russian-English. Before that, there's a section called The Basics, which sets out the fundamental rules of the language and its pronunciation, with plenty of practical examples. You'll also find here other essentials like numbers, dates, telling the time and basic phrases.

Forming the heart of the guide, the English-Russian section gives easy-to-use transliterations of the Russian words, and to get you involved quickly in two-way communication, the Rough Guide includes dialogues featuring typical responses on key topics – such as renting a car and asking directions. Feature boxes fill you in on cultural pitfalls as well as the simple mechanics of how to make a phone call, what to do in an emergency, where to change money and more. Throughout this section, cross-references enable you to pinpoint key facts and phrases, while asterisked words indicate where further information can be found in The Basics.

In the Russian-English dictionary, we've given not just the phrases you're likely to hear (starting with a selection of slang and colloquialisms), but also all the signs, labels, instructions and other basic words you might come across in print or in public places.

Finally the Rough Guide rounds off with an extensive Menu Reader. Consisting of food and drink sections (each starting with a list of essential terms), it's indispensable whether you're eating out, stopping for a quick drink or browsing through a local food market.

счастливого пути!
sh-chasl**ee**vava poot**ee**!
have a good trip!

Basics

Pronunciation

Throughout this book Russian words have been transliterated into romanized form (see the Cyrillic Alphabet on pages 10-11) so that they can be read as though they were English bearing in mind the notes on pronunciation given below:

a	as in **at**	iy	i as in b**i**t followed
ay	as in m**ay**		by y as in **y**es
e	as in m**e**t	J	like the s in mea**s**ure
g	hard g as in **g**et	o	as in n**o**t
H	a guttural ch as in the	s	as in mi**ss**
	Scottish word lo**ch**	y	as in **y**es
i	as in b**i**t	ye	as in **ye**s
I	i sound as in **I** or **eye**		

Letters given in bold type indicate the part of the word to be stressed.

Abbreviations

acc	accusative case	m	masculine
adj	adjective	n	neuter
dat	dative case	nom	nominative case
f	feminine	pl	plural
fam	familiar	pol	polite
gen	genitive case	prep	prepositional case
instr	instrumental case	sing	singular

Notes

When two forms of the verb are given in the dictionary sections, the first form is the imperfective aspect and the second is the perfective aspect (see The Basics page 33 for further information).

The Cyrillic Alphabet

Set out below is the Cyrillic alphabet, the names of the letters and the system of transliteration used in this book:

А, а	ah	a as in **at**
Б, б	beh	b
В, в	veh	v
Г, г	geh	g as in **g**et or v
Д, д	deh	d
Е, е	yeh	ye as in **ye**s
Ё, ё	yo	yo as in **yo**nder
Ж, ж	Jeh	J: pronounced like the s in mea**s**ure
З, з	zeh	z
И, и	ee	ee
Й, й	ee kratka-yeh	sometimes y as in bo**y**, but usually silent
К, к	ka	k
Л, л	el	l
М, м	em	m
Н, н	en	n
О, о	o	when stressed, o as in n**o**t; when unstressed, a as in **at**
П, п	peh	p
Р, р	er	r
С, с	es	s
Т, т	teh	t
У, у	oo	oo as in b**oo**t
Ф, ф	ef	f
Х, х	На	H: a guttural ch as in Scottish lo**ch**
Ц, ц	tseh	ts as in hat**s**
Ч, ч	cheh	ch as in **ch**urch
Ш, ш	sha	sh as in **sh**ip
Щ, щ	sh-cha	sh-ch
Ъ, ъ	tvyordi znak	hard sign: no sound, but indicates hardening of preceding consonant
Ы, ы	iy	i as in b**i**t followed by y as in **ye**s
Ь, ь	myaнkee znak	soft sign: no sound but softens the preceding letter

Э, э	eh	e as in **e**nd
Ю, ю	yoo	yoo
Я, я	ya	ya as in **ya**m

б, **в**, **г**, **д** and **з** may be pronounced p, f, k, t and s respectively, usually when they occur at the end of a word or when preceding certain consonants. For example:

выход	**вход**
ví**y**Hat	**f**Hot
exit	entrance

Combinations and Diphthongs

АЙ, ай	I: i sound as in **I** or **eye**; ee if unstressed
ЕЙ, ей	yay
ИЙ, ий	ee
ОЙ, ой	oy as in b**oy**; I: i sound as in **I** or **eye** if unstressed
ЫЙ, ый	i as in b**i**t

Russian Handwriting

Handwritten Russian does not always resemble the printed characters. The letters below are examples of actual Russian handwriting:

А, а	*А а а*	К, к	*К Ж к к*	Х, х	*Ж Х х х*
Б, б	*Б Б Б*	Л, л	*Л л*	Ц, ц	*Ц ц*
В, в	*В В в*	М, м	*М м*	Ч, ч	*Ч ч*
Г, г	*Г Г г*	Н, н	*Н н*	Ш, ш	*Ш ш*
Д, д	*Д Д д*	О, о	*О о*	Щ, щ	*Щ щ*
Е, е	*В е*	П, п	*П п*	Ъ, ъ	*ъ*
Ё, ё	*В ё/е*	Р, р	*Р Р р р*	Ы, ы	*ы ы*
Ж, ж	*Ж ж*	С, с	*С с*	Ь, ь	*ь*
З, з	*З з*	Т, т	*Т м т т*	Э, э	*Э э*
И, и	*И и*	У, у	*У у*	Ю, ю	*Ю Ю ю*
Й, й	*Й й*	Ф, ф	*Ф ф ф*	Я, я	*Я я*

11

Articles

There are no articles (a, an, the) in Russian:

окно	полотенце
akno	palatyentseh
window/a window/the window	towel/a towel/the towel

Context clarifies the equivalent English article:

вы не возражаете, если я открою окно ...?
viy nyeh vazraJa-yetyeh, **ye**slee ya atkr**o**-yoo akn**o**?
do you mind if I open the window?

дайте мне, пожалуйста, полотенце
d**i**tyeh mnyeh paJ**a**lsta, palaty**e**nseh
can I have a towel?

Nouns and Cases

Nouns

Russian nouns have one of three genders — masculine, feminine or neuter. The gender is determined by the noun ending. Most nouns ending in a consonant are masculine:

вагон	отец	дом
vagon	atyets	dom
carriage	father	house

Nouns ending in -й are also masculine:

музей	трамвай
moozyay	tramvi
museum	tram

Most nouns ending in -a or -я are feminine:

машина	сестра
mashiyna	syestra
car	sister

12

учительница
ooch**ee**tyelneetsa
teacher (**woman**)

тётя
t**yo**tya
aunt

спальня
sp**a**lnya
bedroom

гостья
g**o**stya
guest (**woman**)

Most nouns ending in a soft sign -**ь** are feminine, but some are masculine (indicated by **f** or **m** in the English-Russian section of this book):

мелочь f
m**ye**lach
small change

дверь f
dvyer
door

кровать f
krav**a**t
bed

рубль m
roobl
rouble

день m
dyen
day

картофель m
kart**o**fyel
potato

Most nouns ending in -**o** or -**e** are neuter:

блюдо
bl**yoo**da
dish

пиво
p**ee**va
beer

вино
veen**o**
wine

море
m**o**ryeh
sea

отделение
od-dyel**ye**nee-yeh
department

Nouns ending in -**мя** are neuter:

время
vr**ye**mya
time

имя
eemya
first name

Some nouns ending in -**a** or -**я** that refer to males are masculine:

мужчина
moosh-cheena
man

дядя
dya-dya
uncle

Cases

Russian has six cases: nominative, accusative, genitive, dative, instrumental and prepositional. Noun endings change depending on the case. The case endings used depend on the following factors:

whether the noun is masculine inanimate (objects), masculine animate (people or animals), feminine or neuter

whether the noun is singular or plural

whether the noun stem ends in г, к, х, ч, щ, ж or ш, in which case и is used instead of ы in the ending.

Nominative Case

The nominative is the case of the subject of a sentence. In the following examples, 'shop' and 'he' are in the nominative:

магазин открыт
magazeen atkriyt
the shop is open

он сегодня приехал
on syevodnya pree-yeHal
he arrived today

Accusative Case

The object of most verbs takes the accusative. In the following examples the objects (the sights, stamps and pen) are in the accusative:

мы хотим осмотреть достопримечательности
miy Hateem asmatryet dastapreemyechatyelnastee
we want to see the sights

вы продаёте марки?
viy prada-yotyeh markee?
do you sell stamps?

вы не одолжите ручку?
viy nyeh adaLJityeh roochkoo?
may I borrow your pen?

Some prepositions indicating motion or direction towards something are followed by the accusative:

<table>
<tr><td align="center">**в**
v
to; into</td><td align="center">**на**
na
to; onto</td></tr>
<tr><td align="center">**через**
chyeryes
through</td><td align="center">**в Москву**
vmaskvoo
to Moscow</td></tr>
<tr><td align="center">**мы едем на вокзал**
miy yedyem na vakzal
we're going to the station</td><td align="center">**я пройду через парк**
ya pridoo chyeryes park
I'll walk through the park</td></tr>
</table>

Genitive Case

The genitive is used to indicate possession:

машина Кати
mashiyna katee
Katya's car

There is no word for 'of' in Russian. The genitive is used to translate 'of':

<table>
<tr><td align="center">**бутылка водки**
bootiylka votkee
a bottle of vodka</td><td align="center">**плитка шоколада**
pleetka shakalada
a bar of chocolate</td></tr>
</table>

The genitive is also used after some prepositions, for example:

<table>
<tr><td align="center">**до**
do
until; to</td><td align="center">**у**
oo
by; at</td><td align="center">**около**
okala
near, by; beside; about</td></tr>
</table>

до Москвы	у Саши	около гостиницы
da maskv**iy**	oo s**a**shi	**o**kala gast**ee**neetsi
to Moscow	at Sasha's house	beside the hotel

Dative Case

The dative is used for indirect objects with verbs like 'to give' and 'to send'. It often corresponds to 'to' (as in 'to me') in English:

дайте мне ..., пожалуйста
d**i**tyeh mnyeh ..., pa**J**alsta
please give me ...

я дал ему это
ya dal yem**oo** **e**ta
I gave it to him

See the forms of personal pronouns on pages 30–31.

The dative is also used after some prepositions, for example:

к	по
k	pa
to, towards	on; along

к вокзалу	по улице
k vakz**a**loo	pa **oo**leetseh
to the station	along the street

Instrumental Case

The instrumental is used to show by whom or by what means an action is carried out. It is used to translate 'by' when referring to means of transport:

мы приехали поездом
miy pree-**ye**Halee p**o**-yezdam
we came by train

авиапочтой
avee-a-p**o**chti
by airmail

The instrumental is also used with some prepositions:

под	перед	с
pot	p**ye**ryet	s
under	before; in front of	with

под столом
pat stal**o**m
under the table

перед обедом
p**ye**ryed ab**ye**dam
before lunch

я пью чай с лимоном
ya pyoo chı sleem**o**nam
I take tea with lemon

Prepositional Case

The prepositional is used with most prepositions which indicate the position or location of something:

на
na
at; on

в
v
at; in

на самолёте
na samal**yo**tyeh
on the plane

в городе
vg**o**ratyeh
in the town

на улице
na **oo**leetseh
on the street

на вокзале
na vakz**a**lyeh
at the station

It is also used with the preposition **о [a]** about:

они говорили о фильме
an**ee** gavar**ee**lee a f**ee**lmyeh
they were talking about the film

Numbers and Cases

Numbers in Russian also determine the case of the noun. 1 and all numbers ending in 1 (eg 21, 31 and so on) are followed by a noun in the nominative singular; 2, 3, and 4 and all numbers ending in 2, 3, and 4 (except for 11, 12, 13 and 14) take the genitive singular; all other numbers (including 11, 12, 13 and 14) take the genitive plural:

одна бутылка
adn**a** boot**iy**lka
one bottle

две бутылки
dvyeh boot**iy**lkee
two bottles

три женщины	двадцать одна женщина
tree Jensh-cheeni	dvatsat adna Jensh-cheena
three women	21 women

один час	семь часов
adeen chas	syem chasof
one hour	seven hours

двадцать четыре часа
dvatsat chyetiyryeh chasa
24 hours

See Numbers on pages 45-46.

Noun Cases

In the following tables, when the noun stem ends in г, ж, к, х, ч, ш or щ, и is used instead of ы in the noun endings, for example:

язык/языки	марка/марки
yaziyk/yaziykee	marka/markee
language/languages	stamp/stamps

masculine singular inanimate

	carriage	museum	rouble
nom	вагон	музей	рубль
	vagon	moozyay	roobl
acc	вагон	музей	рубль
	vagon	moozyay	roobl
gen	вагона	музея	рубля
	vagona	moozyeh-ya	rooblya
dat	вагону	музею	рублю
	vagonoo	moozyeh-yoo	rooblyoo
instr	вагоном	музеем	рублем
	vagonam	moozyeh-yem	rooblyom
prep	вагоне	музее	рубле
	vagonyeh	moozyeh-yeh	rooblyeh

masculine singular animate

	artist	driver
nom	художник	водитель
	Hood**o**Jneek	vad**ee**tyel
acc	художника	водителя
	Hood**o**Jneeka	vad**ee**tyelya
gen	художника	водителя
	Hood**o**Jneeka	vad**ee**tyelya
dat	художнику	водителю
	Hood**o**Jneekoo	vad**ee**tyelyoo
instr	художником	водителем
	Hood**o**Jneekam	vad**ee**tyelyem
prep	художнике	водителе
	Hood**o**Jneekyeh	vad**ee**tyelyeh

feminine singular

	car	aunt	door
nom	машина	тётя	дверь
	mash**iy**na	t**yo**tya	dvyer
acc	машину	тётю	дверь
	mash**iy**noo	t**yo**tyoo	dvyer
gen	машины	тёти	двери
	mash**iy**ni	t**yo**tee	dv**ye**ree
dat	машине	тёте	двери
	mash**iy**nyeh	t**yo**tyeh	dv**ye**ree
instr	машиной	тётей	дверью
	mash**iy**nɪ	t**yo**tyay	dv**ye**ryoo
prep	машине	тёте	двери
	mash**iy**nyeh	t**yo**tyeh	dv**ye**ree

neuter singular

	dish	sea	first name	department
nom	блюдо	море	имя	отделение
	blyooda	moryeh	eemya	ad-dyelyenee-yeh
acc	блюдо	море	имя	отделение
	blyooda	moryeh	eemya	ad-dyelyenee-yeh
gen	блюда	моря	имени	отделения
	blyooda	morya	eemyenee	ad-dyelyenee-ya
dat	блюду	морю	имени	отделению
	blyoodoo	moryoo	eemyenee	ad-dyelyenee-yoo
instr	блюдом	морем	именем	отделением
	blyoodam	moryem	eemyenyem	ad-dyelyenee-yem
prep	блюде	море	имени	отделении
	blyoodyeh	moryeh	eemyenee	ad-dyelyenee-ee

masculine plural inanimate

	carriage	museum	rouble
nom	вагоны	музеи	рубли
	vagoni	moozyeh-ee	rooblee
acc	вагоны	музеи	рубли
	vagoni	moozyeh-ee	rooblee
gen	вагонов	музеев	рублей
	vagonaf	moozyeh-yef	rooblyay
dat	вагонам	музеям	рублям
	vagonam	moozyeh-yam	rooblyam
instr	вагонами	музеями	рублями
	vagonamee	moozyeh-yamee	rooblyamee
prep	вагонах	музеях	рублях
	vagoнaн	moozyeh-yaн	rooblyaн

masculine plural animate

	artist	driver
nom	художники	водители
	Hood**o**Jneekee	vad**ee**tyelee
acc	художников	водителей
	Hood**o**Jneekaf	vad**ee**tyelyay
gen	художников	водителей
	Hood**o**Jneekaf	vad**ee**tyelyay
dat	художникам	водителям
	Hood**o**Jneekam	vad**ee**tyelyam
instr	художниками	водителями
	Hood**o**Jneekamee	vad**ee**tyelyamee
prep	художниках	водителях
	Hood**o**JneekaH	vad**ee**tyelyaH

feminine plural

	car	aunt	door
nom	машины	тёти	двери
	mash**i**yni	t**yo**tee	dv**ye**ree
acc	машины	тётей	двери
	mash**i**yni	t**yo**tyay	dv**ye**ree
gen	машин	тётей	дверей
	mash**i**yn	t**yo**tyay	dvyer**yay**
dat	машинам	тётям	дверям
	mash**i**ynam	t**yo**tyam	dvyer**ya**m
instr	машинами	тётями	дверями
	mash**i**ynamee	t**yo**tyamee	dvyer**ya**mee
prep	машинах	тётях	дверях
	mash**i**ynaH	t**yo**tyaH	dvyer**ya**H

neuter plural

	dish	sea	first name	department
nom	блюда	моря	имена	отделения
	blyooda	marya	eemyena	ad-dyelyenee-ya
acc	блюда	моря	имена	отделения
	blyooda	marya	eemyena	ad-dyelyenee-ya
gen	блюд	морей	имён	отделений
	blyoot	maryay	eemyon	ad-dyelyenee
dat	блюдам	морям	именам	отделениям
	blyoodam	maryam	eemyenam	ad-dyelyenee-yam
instr	блюдами	морями	именами	отделениями
	blyoodamee	maryamee	eemyenamee	ad-dyelyenee-yamee
prep	блюдах	морях	именах	отделениях
	blyoodaн	maryaн	eemyenaн	ad-dyelyenee-yaн

Irregular Plurals

Several common nouns have irregular plurals:

дом/дома	[dom/dama]	house/houses
поезд/поезда	[poyest/payezda]	train/trains
город/города	[gorat/garada]	town/towns
номер/номера	[nomyer/namyera]	room/rooms; number/numbers
сестра/сёстры	[syestra/syostri]	sister/sisters
брат/братья	[brat/bratya]	brother/brothers
мать/матери	[mat/matyeree]	mother/mothers
сын/сыновья	[siyn/sinavya]	son/sons
дочь/дочери	[doch/dochyeree]	daughter/daughters
друг/друзья	[drook/droozya]	friend/friends

Some common Russian nouns do not change in the plural or according to case and are known as indeclinable nouns:

кафе	[kafeh]	cafe
кино	[keeno]	cinema
кофe	[kofyeh]	coffee
метро	[myetro]	underground, (US) subway
пальто	[palto]	overcoat
такси	[taksee]	taxi
фойе	[fi-yeh]	foyer

Prepositions

The following are some common prepositions and the cases they take (see also pages 15–17):

без [byes] (+ gen) without
в [v] (+ acc) to
в [v] (+ prep) in
для [dlya] (+ gen) for
до [do] (+ gen) before; until
за [za] (+ acc) behind; beyond; after; over
за [za] (+ instr) behind; beyond; at
между [myeJdoo] (+ instr) between; among
на [na] (+ acc) to
на [na] (+ prep) on
над [nat] (+ instr) above
напротив [naproteef] (+ gen) opposite
о [a] (+ prep) about
около [okala] (+ gen) about; near
от [ot] (+ gen) from
перед [pyeryed] (+ instr) in front of; before
по [po] (+ dat) on; along
под [pot] (+ instr) under
после [poslyeh] (+ gen) after
при [pree] (+ prep) by; at
с [s] (+ instr) with
через [chyeryes] (+ acc) through, via

Adjectives

Adjectives agree in case, gender and number with the nouns to which they refer.

Most Russian adjectives end in **-ый** and change as follows:

	singular			**plural**
	masculine	feminine	neuter	
красивый [kraseevi] beautiful				
nom	красивый	красивая	красивое	красивые
	kraseevi	kraseeva-ya	kraseeva-yeh	kraseevi-yeh
acc	красивый	красивую	красивое	красивые
	kraseevi	kraseevoo-yoo	kraseeva-yeh	kraseevi-yeh
gen	красивого	красивой	красивого	красивых
	kraseevava	kraseevi	kraseevava	kraseeviH
dat	красивому	красивой	красивому	красивым
	kraseevamoo	kraseevi	kraseevamoo	kraseevim
instr	красивым	красивой	красивым	красивыми
	kraseevim	kraseevi	kraseevim	kraseevimee
prep	красивом	красивой	красивом	красивых
	kraseevam	kraseevi	kraseevam	kraseeviH

Some adjectives ending in **-ий** (often preceded by **г, ж, к, х, ч, ш, щ**) change as follows:

	singular			**plural**
	masculine	feminine	neuter	
зимний [zeemnee] winter, winter's				
nom	зимний	зимняя	зимнее	зимние
	zeemnee	zeemnya-ya	zeemnyeh-yeh	zeemnee-yeh
acc	зимний	зимнюю	зимнее	зимние
	zeemnee	zeemnyoo-yoo	zeemnyeh-yeh	zeemnee-yeh
gen	зимнего	зимней	зимнего	зимних
	zeemnyeva	zeemnyay	zeemnyeva	zeemneeH
dat	зимнему	зимней	зимнему	зимним
	zeemnyemoo	zeemnyay	zeemnyemoo	zeemneem
instr	зимним	зимней	зимним	зимними
	zeemneem	zeemnyay	zeemneem	zeemneemee
prep	зимнем	зимней	зимнем	зимних
	zeemnyem	zeemnyay	zeemnyem	zeemneeH

		singular		plural
	masculine	feminine	neuter	
хороший Haroshi good				
nom	хороший	хорошая	хорошее	хорошие
	Haroshi	Harosha-ya	Harosheh-yeh	Haroshi-yeh
acc	хороший	хорошую	хорошее	хорошие
	Haroshi	Haroshoo-yoo	Harosheh-yeh	Haroshi-yeh
gen	хорошего	хорошей	хорошего	хороших
	Harosheva	Haroshay	Harosheva	HaroshiH
dat	хорошему	хорошей	хорошему	хорошим
	Haroshemoo	Haroshay	Haroshemoo	Haroshim
instr	хорошим	хорошей	хорошим	хорошими
	Haroshim	Haroshay	Haroshim	Haroshimee
prep	хорошем	хорошей	хорошем	хороших
	Haroshem	Haroshay	Haroshem	HaroshiH

Some adjectives ending in **-ой** (when the stress is on the ending) change as follows:

		singular		plural
	masculine	feminine	neuter	
большой [balshoy] big				
nom	большой	большая	большое	большие
	balshoy	balsha-ya	balsho-yeh	balshiy-yeh
acc	большой	большую	большое	большие
	balshoy	balshoo-yoo	balsho-yeh	balshiy-yeh
gen	большого	большой	большого	больших
	balshova	balshoy	balshova	balshiyH
dat	большому	большой	большому	большим
	balshomoo	balshoy	balsho-moo	balshiym
instr	большим	большой	большим	большими
	balshiym	balshoy	balshiym	balshiymee
prep	большом	большой	большом	больших
	balshom	balshoy	balshom	balshiyH

красивая картина
kraseeva-ya karteena
a beautiful picture

мне нравится русское пиво
mnyeh nraveetsa rooska-yeh peeva
I like Russian beer

это хорошая гостиница
eta нarosha-ya gasteeneetsa
it's a good hotel

Comparatives

The comparative of adjectives is generally formed by adding the words for 'more' or 'less' in front of the adjective and noun:

более
bolyeh-yeh
more

более интересный
bolyeh-yeh eentyeryesni
more interesting

менее
myenyeh-yeh
less

менее дорогой
myenyeh-yeh daragoy
less expensive

Some common adjectives have irregular comparatives:

большой [balshoy] big
больше [bolsheh] bigger
маленький [malyenkee] small
меньше [myensheh] smaller
старый [stari] old
старше [starsheh] older
дорогой [daragoy] dear
дороже [daroJeh] dearer
дешёвый [dyeshovi] cheap
дешевле [dyeshevlyeh] cheaper

'Than' is **чем** [chyem]:

это дешевле, чем я думал
eta dyeshevlyeh, chyem ya doomal
it's cheaper than I thought

Superlatives

To form the superlative, add the adverb **наиболее** [na-eeb**o**lyeh-yeh] or the particle **самый** [s**a**mi] in front of the adjective and noun:

наиболее удобный
na-eeb**o**lyeh-yeh ood**o**bni
the most convenient

самый популярный
s**a**mi papool**ya**rni
the most popular

Adverbs

To form the adverb, remove the final **-ый** or **-ий** from the adjective and add **-о**:

хороший	**хорошо**	**медленный**	**медленно**
Har**o**shi	Harash**o**	m**ye**dlyen-ni	m**ye**dlyen-na
good	well	slow	slowly

Demonstratives

The demonstratives are:

этот	**эти**	**тот**	**те**
this (one)	these	that (one)	those

In Russian, the demonstrative agrees with the gender and case of the noun to which it refers. **этот** and **эти** change as follows:

	masculine	feminine	neuter	plural
nom	**этот**	**эта**	**это**	**эти**
	etat	**e**ta	**e**ta	**e**tee
acc	**этот**	**эту**	**это**	**эти**
	etat	**e**too	**e**ta	**e**tee
gen	**этого**	**этой**	**этого**	**этих**
	etava	**e**tı	**e**tava	**e**teeн
dat	**этому**	**этой**	**этому**	**этим**
	etamoo	**e**tı	**e**tamoo	**e**teem
instr	**этим**	**этой**	**этим**	**этими**
	eteem	**e**tı	**e**teem	**e**teemee
prep	**этом**	**этой**	**этом**	**этих**
	etam	**e**tı	**e**tam	**e**teeн

я этого не заказывал
ya etava nyeh zakazival
I didn't order this

эти открытки, пожалуйста
etee atkriytkee, paJalsta
these cards please

тот and **те** change as follows:

	masculine	feminine	neuter	plural
nom	**тот**	**та**	**то**	**те**
	tot	ta	to	tyeh
acc	**тот**	**ту**	**то**	**те**
	tot	too	to	tyeh
gen	**того**	**той**	**того**	**тех**
	tavo	toy	tavo	tyeH
dat	**тому**	**той**	**тому**	**тем**
	tamoo	toy	tamoo	tyem
instr	**тем**	**той**	**тем**	**теми**
	tyem	toy	tyem	tyemee
prep	**том**	**той**	**том**	**тех**
	tom	toy	tom	tyeH

я зайду в тот магазин
ya zidoo ftot magazeen
I'll pop into that shop

можна взглянуть на ту книгу?
moJna vzglyanoot na too kneegoo?
can I see that book?

Possessives

Possessive adjectives and pronouns are as follows:

мой [moy] my; mine
твой [tvoy] your (fam); yours
его [yevo] his/its
её [yeh-**yo**] her; hers

наш [nash] our; ours
ваш [vash] your (sing pol or pl); yours
их [eeH] their; theirs

See pages 31–32 for more on the use of **твой** and **ваш**.

	masculine	feminine	neuter	plural
		my; mine		
nom	**мой**	**моя**	**моё**	**мои**
	moy	ma-**ya**	ma-**yo**	ma-**ee**
acc	**мой**	**мою**	**моё**	**мои**
	moy	ma-**yoo**	ma-**yo**	ma-**ee**
gen	**моего**	**моей**	**моего**	**моих**
	ma-yev**o**	ma-**yay**	ma-yev**o**	ma-**ee**н
dat	**моему**	**моей**	**моему**	**моим**
	ma-yem**oo**	ma-**yay**	ma-yem**oo**	ma-**ee**m
instr	**моим**	**моей**	**моим**	**моими**
	ma-**ee**m	ma-**yay**	ma-**ee**m	ma-**ee**mee
prep	**моём**	**моей**	**моём**	**моих**
	ma-**yo**m	ma-**yay**	ma-**yo**m	ma-**ee**н

твой [tvoy] (your; yours) declines in the same way as **мой**.

	masculine	feminine	neuter	plural
		our; ours		
nom	**наш**	**наша**	**наше**	**наши**
	nash	n**a**sha	n**a**sheh	n**a**shi
acc	**наш**	**нашу**	**наше**	**наши**
	nash	n**a**shoo	n**a**sheh	n**a**shi
gen	**нашего**	**нашей**	**нашего**	**наших**
	n**a**sheva	n**a**shay	n**a**sheva	n**a**shiн
dat	**нашему**	**нашей**	**нашему**	**нашим**
	n**a**shemoo	n**a**shay	n**a**shemoo	n**a**shim
instr	**нашим**	**нашей**	**нашим**	**нашими**
	n**a**shim	n**a**shay	n**a**shim	n**a**shimee
prep	**нашем**	**нашей**	**нашем**	**наших**
	n**a**shem	n**a**shay	n**a**shem	n**a**shiн

ваш [vash] (your; yours) declines in the same way as **наш**.

отнесите это в мой номер
atnyes**ee**tyeh **e**ta vmoy n**o**myer
take this to my room

вы не видели нашего гида?   **возвращаю вашу ручку**
viy nyeh **vee**dyelee **na**sheva **gee**da?   vazvrash-cha-yoo **va**shoo **roo**chkoo
have you seen our guide?   I'm returning your pen

The following possessives are invariable:

его [**ye**vo]	his/its
её [yeh-**yo**]	her; hers
их [eeн]	their; theirs

это её сумка	**я его друг**	**это их автобус**
eta yeh-**yo** **soo**mka	ya ye**vo** drook	eta eeн af**to**boos
it's her bag	I'm his friend	it's their bus

The possessive adjective **свой** [svoy] is used when the object
possessed relates directly to the subject of the sentence. It
declines like **мой**.

я потерял свой ключ
ya patyer**yal** svoy klyooch
I've lost my key

мы живём в своём собственном доме
miy Jiv**yom** fsva-**yom** **so**pstvyen-nam **do**myeh
we live in our own house

The possessives can be omitted when the object possessed
relates directly to the subject of the sentence:

я скучаю по родителям
ya skoocha-yoo pa rad**ee**tyelyam
I miss my parents

Pronouns

Personal Pronouns

я	[ya]	I		**мы**	[miy]	we
ты	[tiy]	you (fam)		**вы**	[viy]	you (sing pol or pl)
он	[on]	he				
она	[ana]	she		**они**	[anee]	they
оно	[ano]	it				

Personal pronouns change according to case as follows:

nom	я	ты	он/оно	она
	ya	tiy	on/ano	ana
acc	меня	тебя	его	её
	myenya	tyebya	yevo	yeh-yo
gen	меня	тебя	его	её
	myenya	tyebya	yevo	yeh-yo
dat	мне	тебе	ему	ей
	mnyeh	tyebyeh	yemoo	yay
instr	мной	тобой	им	ей
	mnoy	taboy	eem	yay
prep	мне	тебе	нём	ней
	mnyeh	tyebyeh	nyom	nyay

nom	мы	вы	они
	miy	viy	anee
acc	нас	вас	их
	nas	vas	eeн
gen	нас	вас	их
	nas	vas	eeн
dat	нам	вам	им
	nam	vam	eem
instr	нами	вами	ими
	namee	vamee	eemee
prep	нас	вас	них
	nas	vas	neeн

The third person singular and plural pronouns take the prefix **н-** after prepositions i.e.:

> для них
> dlya neeн
> for them

'You'

There are two words for 'you' in Russian: the polite/plural

form **вы** [viy] and the familiar/singular form **ты** [tiy]. **Вы** is used when you are addressing someone you do not know at all, do not know well enough to consider a friend, as a sign of respect to an elder, or if you are addressing more than one person. **Ты** is used when addressing a child or a friend. The corresponding possessives are: **ваш** for the singular polite or plural and **твой** for the familiar form (see pages 28-29).

Reflexive Pronouns

The reflexive pronoun **себя** can mean 'myself', 'yourself', 'himself', 'herself', 'itself', 'ourselves', 'yourselves' or 'themselves', depending on the context in which it is used. It changes according to case as follows:

acc	**себя** syeb**ya**	instr	**собой** sab**oy**
gen	**себя** syeb**ya**	prep	**себе** syeb**yeh**
dat	**себе** syeb**yeh**		

Interrogative Pronouns

кто (who) and **что** (what) decline as follows:

nom	**кто** kto	dat	**кому** kam**oo**
acc	**кого** kav**o**	instr	**кем** kyem
gen	**кого** kav**o**	prep	**ком** kom

nom	**что** shto	dat	**чему** chyem**oo**
acc	**что** shto	instr	**чем** chyem
gen	**чего** chyev**o**	prep	**чём** chom

Verbs

Verb Aspects

The basic form of the verb given in the dictionaries in this book is the infinitive (e.g. to do, to go, to read etc). Most Russian verbs have two forms known as the imperfective and perfective aspects. In the English-Russian and Russian-English sections of this book, where useful, the two aspects of common verbs are given in this order: imperfective/perfective. For example the verb 'to do' is:

делать [dyelat]/**сделать** [zdyelat]

The imperfective aspect is generally used to form what in English would be the present and imperfect (continuous) tenses and the future (with the future tense of **быть** to be). The perfective aspect is generally used to form what in English would be expressed by the perfect tense.

Russian regular verbs usually have one of two endings and are known as first conjugation and second conjugation verbs:

first conjugation
-ать   **делать** to do

second conjugation
-ить   **говорить** to speak, to say

To form the various tenses, the ending of the verb is removed and appropriate endings are added to the basic stem.

Present Tense

The present tense corresponds to 'I leave' and 'I am leaving' in English. Using the imperfective aspect of the verb, the conjugation patterns for the present tense are as follows:

first conjugation	second conjugation
делать	говорить
dyelat	gavareet
to do	to speak, to say
я читаю	я говорю
ya dyela-yoo	ya gavaryoo
ты делаешь	ты говоришь
tiy dyela-yesh	tiy gavareesh
он/она делает	он/она говорит
on/ana dyela-yet	on/ana gavareet
мы делаем	мы говорим
miy dyela-yem	miy gavareem
вы делаете	вы говорите
viy dyela-yetyeh	viy gavareetyeh
они делают	они говорят
anee dyela-yoot	anee gavaryat

Most verbs ending in -ать or -ять conjugate in the same way as делать. The following are some common exceptions:

слышать	спать
sliyshat	spat
to hear	to sleep
я слышу	я сплю
ya sliyshoo	ya splyoo
ты слышишь	ты спишь
tiy sliyshish	tiy speesh
он/она слышит	он/она спит
on/ana sliyshit	on/ana speet
мы слышим	мы спим
miy sliyshim	miy speem
вы слышите	вы спите
viy sliyshityeh	viy speetyeh
они слышат	они спят
anee sliyshat	anee spyat

ждать	брать
Jdat	brat
to wait	to take
я жду	я беру
ya Jdoo	ya byer**oo**
ты ждёшь	ты берёшь
tiy Jdyosh	tiy byer**yosh**
он/она ждёт	он/она берёт
on/on**a** Jdyot	on/on**a** byer**yot**
мы ждём	мы берём
miy Jdyom	miy byer**yom**
вы ждёте	вы берёте
viy Jd**yo**tyeh	viy byer**yo**tyeh
они ждут	берут
an**ee** Jdoot	an**ee** byer**oot**

Most verbs ending in **-ить** and **-еть** are conjugated in a similar way to **говорить**. However, the first person singular may change slightly in that there may also be consonant changes or the addition of an л between the verb stem and ending:

видеть	любить
veedyet	lyoob**eet**
to see	to like
я вижу	я люблю
ya **vee**Joo	ya lyoobl**yoo**
ты видишь	ты любишь
tiy **vee**deesh	tiy l**yoo**beesh
он/она видит	он/она любит
on/an**a vee**deet	on/an**a l**yoo**beet
мы видим	мы любим
miy **vee**deem	miy l**yoo**beem
вы видите	вы любите
viy **vee**deetyeh	viy l**yoo**beetyeh
они видят	они любят
an**ee vee**dyat	an**ee** l**yoo**byat

платить	просить
plat**eet**	pras**eet**
to pay for	to ask
я плачу	я прошу
ya plach**oo**	prash**oo**
ты платишь	ты просишь
tiy plat**ee**sh	tiy pr**o**seesh
он/она платит	он/она просит
on/an**a** plat**eet**	on/an**a** pr**o**seet
мы платим	мы просим
miy pl**a**teem	miy pr**o**seem
вы платите	вы просите
viy pl**a**teetyeh	viy pr**o**seetyeh
они платят	они просят
an**ee** pl**a**tyat	an**ee** pr**o**syat

сидеть [seed**yet**] (to sit) and all forms of the verb ходить
[Had**eet**] (to walk) are conjugated like видеть.

The following verbs are irregular in the present tense:

есть	хотеть
yest	Hat**yet**
to eat	to want
я ем	я хочу
ya yem	ya Hach**oo**
ты ешь	ты хочешь
tiy yesh	tiy H**o**chyesh
он/она ест	он/она хочет
on/an**a** yest	on/an**a** H**o**chyet
мы едим	мы хотим
miy yed**ee**m	miy Hat**ee**m
вы едите	вы хотите
viy yed**ee**tyeh	viy Hat**ee**tyeh
они едят	они хотят
an**ee** yed**ya**t	an**ee** Hat**ya**t

пить	**жить**
peet	jiyt
to drink	to live, to stay
я пью	**я живу**
ya pyoo	ya jivoo
ты пьёшь	**ты живёшь**
tiy pyosh	tiy jivyosh
он/она пьёт	**он/она живёт**
on/ana pyot	on/ana jivyot
мы пьём	**мы живём**
miy pyom	miy jivyom
вы пьёте	**вы живёте**
viy pyotyeh	viy jivyotyeh
они пьют	**они живут**
anee pyoot	anee jivoot

The Past Tense: Imperfective and Perfective Forms

There are two types of past tense formed by the imperfective and the perfective of the verb.

The imperfective form describes an action which is seen as continuing:

они покупали сувениры
anee pakoopalee soovyeneeri
they were buying souvenirs

The perfective form describes an action which is seen as completed:

они купили сувениры
anee koopeelee soovyeneeri
they bought souvenirs

Some perfective verbs can be formed by adding various prefixes to the imperfective form:

imperfective	perfective
делать	**сделать** to do
dy**e**lat	zd**ye**lat
платить	**заплатить** to pay for
plat**ee**t	zaplat**ee**t

Other perfective forms may be a different verb altogether:

imperfective	perfective
брать	**взять** to take
brat	vzyat
говорить	**сказать** to speak, to say
gavar**ee**t	skaz**a**t

Perfective verbs can sometimes be identified because they look like a simpler form of the imperfective, for example:

imperfective	perfective
открывать	**открыть** to open
atkr**i**vat	atkr**iy**t
давать	**дать** to give
dav**a**t	dat

To form the past tense of both the imperfective and perfective forms, remove the ending from the infinitive and add the appropriate ending for masculine, feminine, neuter or plural subjects:

masculine	feminine	neuter	plural
-л	-ла	-ло	-ли
-l	-la	-lo	-lee

вчера шёл дождь
fchy**e**ra shol dosht
it was raining yesterday

я только что поела (said by woman)
ya t**o**lka shto pa-**yeh**la
I've only just eaten

38

время пролетело очень быстро
vr**ye**mya pralyet**ye**la **o**chyen b**iy**stra
time flew by

мы побывали в Кремле
miy pabiv**a**lee fkryeml**yeh**
we visited the Kremlin

masculine	feminine	neuter	plural
идти [eet-**tee**] to go			
шёл	**шла**	**шло**	**шли**
shol	shla	shlo	shlee
нести [nyest**ee**] to carry			
нёс	**несла**	**несло**	**несли**
nyos	nyesl**a**	nyesl**o**	nyesl**ee**
вести [vyest**ee**] to lead			
вёл	**вела**	**вело**	**вели**
vyol	vyel**a**	vyel**o**	vyel**ee**

Future Tense

There are two ways of forming the future tense in Russian. The imperfective future is formed with the infinitive of the main verb (imperfective aspect) and the future tense of the verb 'to be' **быть** (see next page.)

он будет встречать нас в аэропорту
on b**oo**dyet fstryech**a**t nas va-erapart**oo**
he'll be meeting us at the airport

The future can also be expressed using the 'present' tense of perfective verbs. The conjugation patterns are the same as those for the present tense on page 34.

завтра мы поедем в Суздаль
z**a**ftra miy pa-**ye**dyem fs**oo**zdal
tomorrow we'll go to Suzdal

'To Be'

In Russian, there is no equivalent of the verb 'to be' in the present tense; it is not translated:

я уверен/уверена	он здесь?
ya oov**ye**ryen/oov**ye**ryena	on zdyes?
I'm sure (said by man/woman)	is he here?

The past tense of the verb 'to be' is as follows:

masculine	feminine	neuter	plural
был	была	было	были
biyl	bil**a**	bi**y**la	bi**y**lee

The future tense of the verb 'to be' is as follows:

я буду	мы будет
ya b**oo**doo	miy b**oo**dyem
ты будешь	вы будете
tiy b**oo**dyesh	viy b**oo**dyetyeh
он/она будет	они будут
on/ana b**oo**dyet	anee b**oo**doot

'To Have'

'To have' is translated in Russian using the preposition **y** followed by the genitive of the noun or pronoun; the object possessed is in the nominative:

у меня была простуда	у вас есть другие?
oo myen**ya** bila prast**oo**da	oo vas yest droog**ee**-yeh?
I had a cold	do you have any others?

у нас будет достаточно времени для покупок
oo nas b**oo**dyet dast**a**chna vr**ye**myenee dlya pak**oo**pak
we'll have enough time for shopping

Negatives

To form a negative sentence, insert **не** (not, no) in front of the verb:

In phrases, using 'have not', 'had not' or 'will not', **нет**, **не было** and **не будет** are used respectively as follows:

у меня нет талонов
oo men**ya** nyet tal**o**naf
I don't have any bus tickets

у меня не хватило денег на подарки
oo myen**ya** nyeh нvat**ee**la d**ye**nyek na pad**a**rkee
I hadn't enough money to buy presents

у меня не будет времени на это
oo myen**ya** nyeh b**oo**dyet vr**ye**myenee na **e**ta
I won't have time for that

Double negatives are common:

ничего	**я ничего не хочу**
neechyev**o**	ya neechyev**o** nyeh нach**oo**
nothing	I don't want anything

никогда	**я никогда там не был/была**
neekagd**a**	ya neekagd**a** tam nyeh biyl/bil**a**
never	I've never been there (said by man/woman)

Imperative

The imperative form of the verb is used to express a command such as 'come here!', 'sit down' etc. The imperative is formed by taking the second person (**ты** form) of the verb (either the imperfective or perfective depending on the context), removing the last three letters and adding the endings as follows:

	stem ending in consonant	stem ending in vowel
fam	-**и**, or -**ь**	-**й**
pol/pl	-**ите**, or **ьте**	-**йте**

иди сюда!	**идите сюда!**
eed**ee** sy**oo**d**a**!	eed**ee**tyeh sy**oo**d**a**!
come here!	come here!

41

открой дверь
atkroy dvyer
open the door

откройте дверь
atkroytyeh dvyer
open the door

перестань кричать
pyeryestan kreechat
stop shouting

перестаньте кричать
pyeryestantyeh kreechat
stop shouting

Reflexive Verbs

Reflexive verbs such as 'to wash oneself', 'to get dressed' etc are formed by adding -ся to verbs ending in a consonant or -сь to verbs ending in a vowel:

одевать
adyevat
to dress

одеваться
adyevatsa
to get dressed

The same endings are used for 'myself', 'yourself', 'himself', 'themselves' etc.

Some verbs only exist in the reflexive form:

бояться [ba-yatsa] to be afraid of
надеяться [nadyeh-yatsa] to hope
нравиться [nraveetsa] to like
смеяться [smyeh-yatsa] to laugh

Questions

A statement can be turned into a question by using a questioning intonation:

мы возвращаемся в гостиницу
miy vazvrash-cha-yemsya vgasteeneetsoo
we are returning to the hotel

мы возвращаемся в гостиницу?
miy vazvrash-cha-yemsya vgasteeneetsoo?
are we returning to the hotel?

Dates

Use the neuter form of the ordinal numbers on page 47 to express the date. These decline like adjectives (see pages 24–25).

второе ноября
ftaro-yeh na-yabrya
the second of November

тридцать первое января
treetsat pyerva-yeh yanvarya
the thirty-first of January

Days

Sunday воскресенье [vaskryesyenyeh]
Monday понедельник [panyedyelneek]
Tuesday вторник [ftorneek]
Wednesday среда [sryeda]
Thursday четверг [chyetvyerk]
Friday пятница [pyatneetsa]
Saturday суббота [soobota]

Months

January январь [yanvar]
February февраль [fyevral]
March март [mart]
April апрель [apryel]
May май [mI]
June июнь [ee-yoon]
July июль [ee-yool]
August август [avgoost]
September сентябрь [syentyabr]
October октябрь [aktyabr]
November ноябрь [na-yabr]
December декабрь [dyekabr]

Time

what time is it? который час? [ka**to**ri chas?]

(it's) one o'clock час [chas]

(it's) two o'clock два часа [dva cha**sa**]

(it's) three o'clock три часа [tree cha**sa**]

(it's) four o'clock четыре часа [chye**ti**yryeh cha**sa**]

(it's) five o'clock* пять часов [pyat cha**sof**]

* For numbers of five and above, use часов. See Numbers and Cases page 17.

five past one** пять минут второго [pyat mee**noot** fta**ro**va]

ten past two** десять минут третьего [**dye**syat mee**noot** **trye**tyeva]

quarter past one** чертверть второго [**chye**tvyert fta**ro**va]

quarter past two** чертверть третьего [**chye**tvyert **trye**tyeva]

half past one** половина второго [pala**vee**na fta**ro**va]

half past two** половина третьего [pala**vee**na **trye**tyeva]

** For time past the hour, refer to the next hour. половина второго 'half past one' literally means 'half of the second'.

twenty to ten без двадцати десять [byez dvatsa**tee dye**sat]

quarter to two без четверти два [byez **chye**tvyertee dva]

quarter to ten без четверти десять [byez **chye**tvyertee **dye**sat]

at one o'clock в час [fchas]

at two/three/four o'clock в два/три/четыре часа [v dva/tree/ chye**ti**yryeh cha**sa**]

at five o'clock в пять часов [fpyat cha**sof**]

at half past four в половине пятого [fpala**vee**nyeh **pya**tava]

14.00 hours четырнадцать ноль-ноль [chye**ti**yrnatsat nol-nol]

17.30 семнадцать тридцать [syem**na**tsat **tree**tsat]

noon полдень [**pol**dyen]

midnight полночь [**pol**nach]

am утра [**oo**tra]

pm (in the afternoon) дня [dnya]
   (in the evening) вечера [**vye**chyera]

hour час [chas]
minute минута [meenoota]
second секунда [syekoonda]
quarter of an hour четверть часа [chyetvyert chasa]
half an hour полчаса [polchasa]
three quarters of an hour сорок пять минут [sorak pyat meenoot]

Numbers

See Numbers and Cases page 17.

0	ноль [nol]
1	один m, одна f, одно n [adeen, adna, adno]
2	два m/n, две f [dva, dvyeh]
3	три [tree]
4	четыре [chyetiyryeh]
5	пять [pyat]
6	шесть [shest]
7	семь [syem]
8	восемь [vosyem]
9	девять [dyevyat]
10	десять [dyesyat]
11	одиннадцать [adeenatsat]
12	двенадцать [dvyenatsat]
13	тринадцать [treenatsat]
14	четырнадцать [chyetiyrnatsat]
15	пятнадцать [pyatnatsat]
16	шестнадцать [shesnatsat]
17	семнадцать [syemnatsat]
18	восемнадцать [vasyemnatsat]
19	девятнадцать [dyevyatnatsat]
20	двадцать [dvatsat]
21	двадцать один/одна/одно [dvatsat adeen/adna/adno]
22	двадцать два/две [dvatsat dva/dvyeh]
30	тридцать [treetsat]

40	сорок [**so**rak]
50	пятьдесят [pyadye**syat**]
60	шестьдесят [shesdye**syat**]
70	семьдесят [**syem**dyesyat]
80	восемьдесят [**vo**syemdyesyat]
90	девяносто [dyevyan**o**sta]
100	сто [sto]
101	сто один/одна/одно [sto ad**een**/adn**a**/adn**o**]
102	сто два/две [sto dva/dvyeh]
200	двести [**dvye**stee]
300	триста [**tree**sta]
400	четыреста [chye**tiy**ryesta]
500	пятьсот [pyat**sot**]
600	шестьсот [shes-s**ot**]
700	семьсот [syem**sot**]
800	восемьсот [vasyem**sot**]
900	девятьсот [dyevyat**sot**]
1,000	тысяча [**tiy**syacha]
2,000	две тысячи [dvyeh **tiy**syachi]
3,000	три тысячи [tree **tiy**syachi]
4,000	четыре тысячи [chye**tiy**ryeh **tiy**syachi]
5,000	пять тысяч [pyat **tiy**syach]
10,000	десять тысяч [**dye**syat **tiy**syach]
20,000	двадцать тысяч [**dva**tsat **tiy**syach]
100,000	сто тысяч [sto **tiy**syach]
1,000,000	миллион [meelee-**on**]

Ordinals

1st	первый	[**py**ervi]
2nd	второй	[ftar**oy**]
3rd	третий	[tr**ye**tee]
4th	четвёртый	[chyetv**yo**rti]
5th	пятый	[**py**ati]
6th	шестой	[shest**oy**]
7th	седьмой	[syedm**oy**]
8th	восьмой	[vasm**oy**]
9th	девятый	[dyev**ya**ti]
10th	десятый	[dyes**ya**ti]
11th	одиннадцатый	[ad**ee**natsati]
12th	двенадцатый	[dvyen**a**tsati]
13th	тринадцатый	[treen**a**tsati]
14th	четырнадцатый	[chyet**iy**rnatsati]
15th	пятнадцатый	[pyatn**a**tsati]
16th	шестнадцатый	[shesn**a**tsati]
17th	семнадцатый	[syemn**a**tsati]
18th	восемнадцатый	[vasyemn**a**tsati]
19th	девятнадцатый	[dyevyatn**a**tsati]
20th	двадцатый	[dvats**a**ti]
21st	двадцать первый	[dv**a**tsat p**ye**rvi]
22nd	двадцать второй	[dv**a**tsat ftar**oy**]
23rd	двадцать третий	[dv**a**tsat tr**ye**tee]
24th	двадцать четвёртый	[dv**a**tsat chyetv**yo**rti]
25th	двадцать пятый	[dv**a**tsat p**ya**ti]
26th	двадцать шестой	[dv**a**tsat shest**oy**]
27th	двадцать седьмой	[dv**a**tsat syedm**oy**]
28th	двадцать восьмой	[dv**a**tsat vasm**oy**]
29th	двадцать девятый	[dv**a**tsat dyev**ya**ti]
30th	тридцатый	[treets**a**ti]
31st	тридцать первый	[tr**ee**tsat p**ye**rvi]

Basic Phrases

yes
да
da

no
нет
nyet

OK
хорошо
Harasho

hello
здравствуйте
zdrasvooytyeh

good morning
доброе утро
dobra-yeh ootra

good evening
добрый вечер
dobri vyechyer

good night (when leaving)
до свидания
da sveedanya

good night (when going to bed)
спокойной ночи
spakoynı nochee

goodbye
до свидания
da sveedanya

hi!
привет!
preevyet!

cheerio!
пока!
paka!

see you!
пока!
paka!

please
пожалуйста
paJalsta

yes please
да, спасибо
da, spaseeba

thank you, thanks
спасибо
spaseeba

no, thank you
нет, спасибо
nyet, spaseeba

thank you very much
большое спасибо
balsho-yeh spaseeba

don't mention it
не за что
nyeh-za-shta

how do you do?
здравствуйте
zdr**a**svooytyeh

how are you?
как дела?
kak dyel**a**?

fine, thanks
хорошо, спасибо
Harash**o**, spas**ee**ba

nice to meet you
приятно познакомиться
pree-**ya**tna paznak**o**meetsa

excuse me (to get past, to say sorry)
извините
eezveen**ee**tyeh

excuse me! (to get attention)
простите!
prast**ee**tyeh!

excuse me (addressing someone with question)
извините, пожалуйста ...
eezveen**ee**tyeh, pa**J**alsta ...

(I'm) sorry
прошу прощения
prash**oo** prash-ch**ye**nee-ya

sorry?/pardon me? (didn't understand)
простите?
prast**ee**tyeh?

what?
что?
shto?

what did you say?
что вы сказали?
shto viy skaz**a**lee?

I see (I understand)
понятно
pan**ya**tna

I don't understand
я не понимаю
ya nyeh paneem**a**-yoo

do you speak English?
вы говорите
по-английски?
viy gavar**ee**tyeh pa-angl**ee**skee?

I don't speak Russian
я не говорю по-русски
ya nyeh gavar**yoo** pa-r**oo**skee

could you speak more slowly?
вы не могли бы говорить
помедленнее?
viy nyeh magl**ee**bi gavar**ee**t
pam**ye**dlyenyeh-yeh?

could you repeat that?
повторите, пожалуйста
paftar**ee**tyeh, pa**J**alsta

could you write it down?
запишите, пожалуйста
zapeesh**iy**tyeh, pa**J**alsta

I'd like ... (said by man/woman)
я бы хотел/хотела ...
ya biy наtyel/наtyela ...

can I have ...?
можно, пожалуйста ...?
moлna, paлalsta ...?

do you have ...?
у вас есть ...?
oo vas yest ...?

how much is it?
сколько это стоит?
skolka eta sto-eet?

cheers! (toast)
ваше здоровье!
vasheh zdarovyeh!

it is ...
это ...
eta ...

where is the ...?
где ...?
gdyeh ...?

is it far from here?
это далеко отсюда?
eta dalyeko atsyooda?

what's the time?
который час?
katori chas?

Conversion Tables

1 centimetre = 0.39 inches

1 metre = 39.37 inches = 1.09 yards

1 kilometre = 0.62 miles = 5/8 mile

1 inch = 2.54 cm

1 foot = 30.48 cm

1 yard = 0.91 m

1 mile = 1.61 km

km	1	2	3	4	5	10	20	30	40	50	100
miles	0.6	1.2	1.9	2.5	3.1	6.2	12.4	18.6	24.8	31.0	62.1

miles	1	2	3	4	5	10	20	30	40	50	100
km	1.6	3.2	4.8	6.4	8.0	16.1	32.2	48.3	64.4	80.5	161

1 gram = 0.035 ounces

g	100	250	500
oz	3.5	8.75	17.5

1 kilo = 1000 g = 2.2 pounds

1 oz = 28.35 g

1 lb = 0.45 kg

kg	0.5	1	2	3	4	5	6	7	8	9	10
lb	1.1	2.2	4.4	6.6	8.8	11.0	13.2	15.4	17.6	19.8	22.0

kg	20	30	40	50	60	70	80	90	100
lb	44	66	88	110	132	154	176	198	220

lb	0.5	1	2	3	4	5	6	7	8	9	10	20
kg	0.2	0.5	0.9	1.4	1.8	2.3	2.7	3.2	3.6	4.1	4.5	9.0

1 litre = 1.75 UK pints / 2.13 US pints

1 UK pint = 0.57 l

1 US pint = 0.47 l

1 UK gallon = 4.55 l

1 US gallon = 3.79 l

centigrade / Celsius $°C = (°F - 32) \times 5/9$

°C	-5	0	5	10	15	18	20	25	30	36.8	38
°F	23	32	41	50	59	64	68	77	86	98.4	100.4

Fahrenheit $°F = (°C \times 9/5) + 32$

°F	23	32	40	50	60	65	70	80	85	98.4	101
°C	-5	0	4	10	16	18	21	27	29	36.8	38.3

English

→

Russian

A

a, an*

about: about 20 около двадцати [**o**kala dvatsat**ee**]

it's about 5 o'clock около пяти часов [**o**kala pyat**ee** chas**of**]

a film about Russia фильм о России [**fee**lm a rass**ee**-ee]

above над [nad]

abroad за границей [za gran**ee**tsay]

absolutely! конечно! [kan**ye**shna!]

absorbent cotton вата [**v**ata]

accelerator акселератор [aksyely**e**ratar]

accept принимать/принять [preeneem**at**/preen**y**at]

accident несчастный случай [ny**e**sh-ch**a**sni sl**oo**chee]

there's been an accident произошёл несчастный случай [pra-eezash**o**l nyesh-ch**a**sni sl**oo**chee]

accommodation жильё [ji**lyo**]

 Private accommodation for tourists is best arranged in advance from abroad, as doing it through local bureaux may be a bit hit-or-miss. Most agencies offer bed and breakfast in a Russian home. Your hosts may volunteer to act as guides or drivers, and are often keen to offer insights into Russian life. Most people in the habit of renting rooms to foreigners speak some English or another foreign language.

The cost varies depending on factors such as location and whether you opt for bed and breakfast or full board, so it definitely pays to shop around. If possible, you should try to get the address of the flat and check how far it is from the centre and the nearest metro station.

see **room** and **hotel**

ache боль **f** [bol]

my back aches у меня болит спина [oo men**ya** bal**ee**t speen**a**]

across: across the road через дорогу [ch**ye**ryes dar**o**goo]

adaptor адаптер [ad**a**pter]

address адрес [**a**dryes]

what's your address? какой ваш адрес? [kak**oy** vash **a**dryes?]

 When addressing letters, Russians start with the country, followed by the town/city along with a six-digit postal code on the next line, then the street, block and apartment number, and finally the addressee's name; the sender's details are usually written at the bottom of the envelope. The number of the house, block or complex may be preceded

English → Russian

by дом (dom), abbreviated as д.
Two numbers separated by a
forward slash (for example, 16/21)
usually indicates a corner, the
second number being the address
on the smaller side street. Buildings
encompassing more than one
number are also written like this (for
example, 4/6). Floors are numbered
in the American fashion; the ground
floor is known as the first floor
(etash1).

One final oddity is that some names
are preceded by an ordinal number,
for example: 2-ой
Кадашевский пер.
1-ая or 1-ый (pronounced
'pyerva-ya' or 'pyervi') means '1st';
2-ая or 2-ой ('ftara-ya' or 'ftaroy')
'2nd', and so on. This usually applies
to a series of parallel lanes or side
streets.
Here is an address, as a Russian
would write it:

Россия
173060 г. Новгород
ул. Менделеева, д. 12,
корп. 2, кв. 126
Сидоров Б. А.

Russia
173060 Novgorod
12 Mendelayev Street, Block 2,
Flat 126
B. A. Sidorov

address book алфавитная
записная книжка
[alfaveetna-ya zapeesna-ya
kneeshka]

**admission charge: how much
is the admission charge?**
сколько стоит билет?
[skolka sto-eet beelyet?]

adult взрослый человек
[vzrosli chyelavyek]

advance: in advance заранее
[zaranyeh-yeh]

aeroplane самолёт [samalyot]

after после [poslyeh]
after you после вас [poslyeh
vas]
after lunch после обеда
[poslyeh abyeda]

afternoon: in the afternoon
днём [dnyom]
this afternoon сегодня
днём [syevodnya dnyom]

aftershave лосьон после
бритья [lasyon poslyeh breetya]

aftersun cream крем после
загара [kryem poslyeh zagara]

afterwards потом [patom]

again снова [snova]

against против [proteef]

age возраст [vozrast]

ago: a week ago неделю
назад [nyedyelyoo nazat]
an hour ago час назад [chas
nazat]

agree: I agree (said by
man/woman) я согласен/
согласна [ya saglasyen/
saglasna]

Aids СПИД [speed]

air воздух [vozdooh]
by air самолётом
[samalyotam]

air-conditioning: with air-conditioning с кондиционером [skandeetsi-an**ye**ram]

airline авиалиния [**a**vee-a-**lee**nee-ya]

airmail: by airmail авиапочтой [**a**vee-a-p**o**chtı]

airmail envelope международный конверт [myeJdoona**ro**dni kan**vye**rt]

airport аэропорт [a-era**po**rt]

to the airport, please в аэропорт, пожалуйста [va-era**po**rt, paJa**l**sta]

airport bus автобус-экспресс в аэропорт [aft**o**boos-eksp**re**s va-era**po**rt]

aisle seat место у прохода [m**ye**sto oo praH**o**da]

alcohol спиртное [speertn**o**-yeh]

alcoholic: is it alcoholic? это спиртное? [**e**ta speertn**o**-yeh?]

all* (things) всё [fs**yo**] (people) все [fs**ye**h]

all the children все дети [fs**ye**h d**ye**tee]

all of it всё [fs**yo**]

all of them все [fs**ye**h]

all day весь день [vyes dyen]

that's all, thanks это всё, спасибо [**e**ta fs**yo**, spas**ee**ba]

allergic: I'm allergic to ... у меня аллергия на ... [oo men**ya** alyerg**ee**-ya na ...]

allowed: is smoking allowed here? можно ли здесь курить? [m**o**Jnalee zdyes koor**ee**t?]

all right хорошо [Har**a**sho]

I'm all right со мной всё в порядке [sam**no**y fsyo fpar**ya**tkyeh]

are you all right? с вами всё в порядке? [sv**a**mee fsyo fpar**ya**tkyeh?]

almond миндаль **m** [meend**a**l]

almost почти [pacht**ee**]

alone (man/woman) один/одна [ad**ee**n/adn**a**]

alphabet алфавит [alfav**ee**t]

a ah	**р** er
б beh	**с** es
в veh	**т** teh
г geh	**у** oo
д deh	**ф** ef
е yeh	**х** Ha
ё yo	**ц** tseh
ж Jeh	**ч** chyeh
з zeh	**ш** sha
и ee	**щ** sh-chya
й ee kratka-yeh	**ъ** tv**yo**rdi znak
к ka	**ы** iy
л el	**ь** m**ya**Hkee znak
м em	**э** e
н en	**ю** yoo
о o	**я** ya
п peh	

already уже [ooJ**eh**]

also тоже [t**o**Jeh]

although хотя [Hat**ya**]

altogether всего [fsy**e**vo]

always всегда [fsyegd**a**]

am*: at seven am в семь часов утра [fsyem chas**o**f oot**ra**]

amazing (surprising)
удивительный
[oodeeveetyelni]
    (very good) потрясающий
[patrysa-yoosh-chee]
ambulance скорая помощь
[skora-ya pomash-ch]
    call an ambulance!
вызовите скорую
помощь! [viyzaveetyeh
skoroo-yoo pomash-ch!]

Public ambulances (dial
03) leave a lot to be
desired, but in many
places there is still no alternative. If
you are staying in Moscow or St
Petersburg, however, there are now
a number of private healthcare
companies which can provide
reliable fee-paying ambulance and
emergency services.

America Америка [amyereeka]
American (adj)
американский
[amyereekanskee]
    I'm American (man/woman) я
американец/американка
[ya amyereekanyets/
amyereekanka]
among среди [sryedee]
amount количество
[kaleechyestva]
    (money) сумма [soom-ma]
amp: 13-amp fuse
предохранитель на
тринадцать ампер
[predaнraneetyel na treenatsat

ampyer]
and и [ee]
angry сердитый [syerdeeti]
animal животное [Jivotna-yeh]
ankle лодыжка [ladiyshka]
anniversary (wedding) юбилей
[yoobeelyay]
annoy: this man's annoying
me этот человек мне
досаждает [etat chyelavyek
mnyeh dasaJda-yet]
annoying: it's annoying это
раздражает [eta razdraJa-yet]
another другой [droogoy]
can we have another room?
можно другой номер?
[moJna droogoy nomyer?]
    another beer, please ещё
одно пиво, пожалуйста
[yesh-cho adno peeva, paJalsta]
antibiotics антибиотики
[anteebee-oteekee]
antifreeze антифриз
[anteefrees]
antihistamine антигистамин
[anteegeestameen]
antique антиквариат
[anteekvaree-at]
antique shop антикварный
магазин [anteekvarni
magazeen]
antiseptic антисептическое
средство [anteesepteechyeska-
yeh sryetstva]
any: have you got any
bread/tomatoes? у вас есть
хлеб/помидоры? [oo vas yest
Hlyep/pameedori?]
do you have any ...? у вас

есть ...? [oo vas yest ...?]

sorry, I don't have any
извините, у меня нет
[eezveen**ee**tyeh, oo men**ya** nyet]

anybody кто-нибудь
[kt**o**-neeboot]

**does anybody speak
English?** кто-нибудь
говорит по-английски?
[kt**o**-neeboot gavar**ee**t pa-angl**ee**skee?]

there wasn't anybody there
там никого не было [tam
neek**a**vo n**ye**bila]

anything что-нибудь
[sht**o**-neeboot]

dialogues

anything else? что-
нибудь ещё? [sht**o**-neeboot
yesh-ch**o**?]

nothing else, thanks
больше ничего,
спасибо [b**o**lsheh neech**ye**vo,
spas**ee**ba]

**would you like anything to
drink?** вы хотите что-
нибудь выпить? [viy
нat**ee**tyeh sht**o**-neeboot
v**iy**peet?]

**I don't want anything,
thanks** спасибо, я
ничего не хочу [spas**ee**ba,
ya neech**ye**vo nyeh нach**oo**]

apart from кроме [kr**o**myeh]
apartment квартира

[kvart**ee**ra]

apartment block
многоквартирный дом
[mnogakvart**ee**rni dom]

aperitif аперитив [apyeree**tee**f]

apology извинение
[eezveen**ye**nee-yeh]

appendicitis аппендицит
[apyendeets**iy**t]

appetizer закуска [zak**oo**ska]

apple яблоко [**ya**blaka]

appointment приём [pree**yo**m]

dialogue

**good morning, how can I
help you?** доброе утро,
чем я могу вам
помочь? [d**o**bra-yeh **oo**tra,
chem ya mag**oo** vam pam**o**ch?]

**I'd like to make an
appointment** (said by man/
woman) я бы хотел/
хотела записаться на
приём [**ya** bi нat**ye**l/нat**ye**la
zapee**sa**tsa na pree**yo**m]

what time would you like?
какое время для вас
удобно? [kak**o**-yeh vr**ye**mya
dlya vas ood**o**bna?]

three o'clock в три часа
[ftree chas**a**]

**I'm afraid that's not
possible, is four o'clock all
right?** боюсь, что в три
часа не получится, в
четыре вас устроит?
[bay**oo**s, shto ftree chas**a** nyeh
pal**oo**cheetsa, fchyet**iy**ryeh vas

oostro-eet?]
yes, that will be fine да,
это меня устроит [da, **e**ta
myen**ya** oostro-eet]
the name was ...? ваше
имя ...? [**v**asheh **ee**mya ...?]

apricot абрикос [abreek**o**s]
April апрель **m** [apr**yel**]
area район [rı-**o**n]
area code междугородный
код [myeJdoogar**o**dni kod]
arm рука [r**oo**ka]
**arrange: will you arrange it for
us?** вы организуете это
для нас? [viy arganeez**oo**-yetyeh
eta dlya nas?]
arrival прибытие [preeb**y**itee-
yeh]
arrive приезжать/приехать
[pree-yeJJat/pree-**ye**Hat]
when do we arrive? когда
мы приезжаем? [kagda miy
pree-yeJ-J**a**-yem?]
has my fax arrived yet? ещё
не пришёл факс для
меня? [yesh-ch**o** nyeh preesh**o**l
faks dlya men**ya**?]
we arrived today мы
приехали сегодня [miy
pree-**ye**Halee syev**o**dnya]
art искусство [eesk**oo**stva]
art gallery картинная
галерея [kart**ee**n-na-ya
galyer**yeh**-ya]
artist художник [Hood**o**Jneek]
as: as big as такой же
большой как ... [tak**oy**Jeh
balsh**oy** kak ...]

as soon as possible как
можно быстрее [kak m**o**Jna
bistr**yeh**-yeh]
ashtray пепельница
[p**ye**pyelneetsa]
ask спрашивать/спросить
[spr**a**shivat/spras**ee**t]
I didn't ask for this (said by
man/woman) это не то, что я
заказал/заказала [**e**ta nyeh
to, shto ya zakaz**a**l/zakaz**a**la]
could you ask him to ...?
попросите его,
пожалуйста ... [papras**ee**tyeh
yevo, paJalsta ...]
asleep: she's asleep она
спит [an**a** speet]
aspirin аспирин [aspeer**ee**n]
asthma астма [**a**stma]
astonishing поразительный
[paraz**ee**tyelni]
at: at the hotel в гостинице
[vgast**ee**neetseh]
at the station на станции
[na st**a**ntsi-ee]
at six o'clock в шесть
часов [fshest chas**o**f]
at Sasha's у Саши [oo s**a**shi]
athletics атлетика [atl**ye**teeka]
ATM банкомат [bankam**a**t]
attractive привлекательный
[preevlyek**a**tyelni]
aubergine баклажан
[bakla**J**an]
August август [**a**vgoost]
aunt тётя [**tyo**tya]
Australia Австралия
[afstr**a**lee-ya]
Australian (adj)

автралийский

австралийский
[afstral**ee**skee]
I'm Australian (man/woman) я
австралиец/австралийка
[ya afstral**ee**-yets/afstral**ee**ka]
Austria Австрия [**a**fstree-ya]
automatic (adj)
автоматический
[aftamat**ee**chyeskee]
(noun: car) с
автоматической
коробкой передач
[saftamat**ee**chyeski kar**o**pkı
pyeryed**a**ch]
autumn осень f [**o**syen]
in the autumn осенью
[**o**senyoo]
avenue аллея [al**yeh**-ya]
average (not good)
посредственный
[pasr**ye**tstvyen-ni]
on average в среднем
[fsr**ye**dnyem]
awake: is he awake? он
проснулся? [on prasn**oo**lsya?]
away: go away! уходите!
[ooHad**ee**tyeh!]
is it far away? это далеко?
[eta dalyek**o**?]
awful ужасный [ooJ**a**sni]

B

baby ребёнок [ryeb**yo**nak]
baby food детское питание
[d**ye**tska-yeh peetanee-yeh]
baby's bottle бутылочка для
кормления ребёнка

[bootiylachka dlya karmlyenee-ya
ryeb**yo**nka]
baby-sitter няня [**n**yanya]
back (of body) спина [speena]
(back part) задняя часть
[z**a**dnya-ya chast]
at the back сзади [z-z**a**dee]
I'd like my money back (said
by man/woman) я хотел/
хотела бы получить
обратно деньги [ya
Hat**yel**/Hat**ye**la biy palooch**ee**t
abratna d**ye**ngee]
to come back
возвращаться/вернуться
[vazvrash-ch**a**tsa/vyern**oo**tsa]
to go back (by transport)
уезжать/уехать [oo-yeɀ-
Jat/oo-**ye**Hat]
(on foot)
возвращатьсвернуться
[vazvrash-ch**a**tsa/vyern**oo**tsa]
backache боль в спине [bol
fspeen**yeh**]
bacon бекон [byek**o**n]
bad плохой [plaH**o**y]
not bad неплохо [nyepl**o**Ha]
a bad headache сильная
головная боль [s**ee**lna-ya
galavn**a**-ya bol]
badly плохо [pl**o**Ha]
bag сумка [s**oo**mka]
(handbag) дамская сумка
[d**a**mska-ya s**oo**mka]
(suitcase) чемодан
[chyemod**a**n]
baggage багаж [bag**a**sh]
baggage checkroom
камера хранения

[ka**m**yera Hran**ye**nee-ya]
baggage claim выдача
багажа [**viy**dacha baga**Ja**]
bakery булочная
[**boo**lachna-ya]
balcony балкон [bal**kon**]
a room with a balcony
номер с балконом [**no**myer
zbal**ko**nam]
bald лысый [**liy**si]
ball мяч [myach]
ballet балет [bal**yet**]
ballpoint pen шариковая
ручка [sha**ree**kava-ya **roo**chka]
banana банан [ba**nan**]
band (orchestra) оркестр
[ar**kye**str]
bandage бинт [beent]
Bandaid® пластырь **m**
[**pla**stir]
bank (money) банк [bank]

As the exchange rate
(koors) is now set by
market forces and the
black market offers nothing but
risks, there's no reason to change
money anywhere other than in an
official bank or currency exchange
booth: **обмен валюты**
(ab**myen** val**yoo**ti). These are to be
found all over town and inside hotel
foyers, shops and restaurants (they
usually keep the same hours as the
shop or restaurant). Exchange rates
vary slightly from place to place and
most banks charge a maximum of a
few hundred roubles commission, if
anything at all. You should make

sure you have your passport with
you if you intend to change money.

bank account банковский
счёт [**ban**kofskee sh-chot]
banknote банкнота
[bank**no**ta]
bar бар [bar]

Although there are now a
good many bars and
particularly English/Irish-
style pubs in Moscow and St
Petersburg, watering holes in the
regional centres are still relatively
few and far between, and on the
whole tend to be frequented by the
local Mafia. Due to prohibitive prices
in Western-style bars, Russians
often buy from a kiosk/shop and
drink at home.
There are still the old Soviet-style
beer halls (peev**noy** bar, otherwise
known as peev**noo**shka) which are
fairly grim. Although you can find
bottled or canned imported beer in
cafés now, to drink a decent pint in
pleasant surroundings you really
need to go to a Western-run bar.
Nowadays you can buy alcohol
almost anywhere: in cafés,
restaurants, theatres, and street
kiosks. The kiosks sell vodka,
spirits, trashy brands of imported
spirits, and Moldovan, Crimean or
Bulgarian wines. More basically,
you'll just find someone dispensing
beer bottles from a pile of crates: it
costs a little more to take the stuff

away (s-saboy) than to drink it on the spot (na myestyeh). Many kiosks are open 24 hours.

a bar of chocolate плитка шоколада [pleetka shakalada]
barber's парикмахерская [pareeнмаnyerska-ya]
bargaining

dialogue

how much is this?
сколько это стоит?
[skolka eta sto-eet?]
100,000 roubles сто тысяч рублей [sto tiysyach rooblyay]
that's too expensive это слишком дорого [eta sleeshkam doraga]
how about 70,000? как насчёт семидесяти тысяч? [kak nash-chot syemeedyestee tiysyach?]
I'll let you have it for 90,000 отдам за девяносто тысяч [ad-dam za dyevyanosta tiysyach]
can you reduce it a bit more?/OK, it's a deal сбросьте ещё немного/ладно, идёт [sbrostyeh yesh-cho nyemnoga/ladna, eedyot]

basket корзина [karzeena]
bath ванна [van-na]
can I have a bath? можно ли принять ванну?
[moжnalee preenyat van-noo?]
bathhouse баня [banya]

The Russian bathhouse is as much a national institution as the sauna is in Scandinavia. Some bathhouses have separate floors for men and women, while others operate on different days for each sex but, whatever the set-up, there's no mixed bathing except in special deluxe saunas (available for private rental). Towels are provided; other things such as shampoo should be brought with you. At the entrance you can buy a 'vyeneek' – a leafy bunch of birch twigs – with which bathers flail themselves (and each other) in the steam room, to open up the pores and improve the circulation.

Hand your coat and valuables to the cloakroom attendant before going into the changing rooms. Beyond these lies a washroom with a cold plunge pool or bath; the metal basins are for soaking your 'vyeneek' to make it supple. Finally you enter the hot room (pareelka), with its tiers of benches – it gets hotter the higher you go. Novices shouldn't try to stick it out for more than five to seven minutes. After a dunk in the cold bath and a rest, you repeat the process all over again.

bathroom ванная [van-na-ya]

with a private bathroom с ванной [svan-nl]

bath towel банное полотенце [ban-na-yeh palat**yent**seh]

bathtub ванна [van-na]

battery (for radio) батарейка [batar**yay**ka]

(for car) аккумулятор [akoomool**ya**tar]

bay бухта [booHta]

be* быть [biyt]

beach пляж [plyash]

on the beach на пляже [na plyaJeh]

beach mat пляжная подстилка [plyaJna-ya patst**ee**lka]

beach umbrella пляжный зонт [plyaJni zont]

beans фасоль (f, sing) [fasol]

French beans фасоль [fasol]

broad beans бобы [bab**iy**]

beard борода [barada]

beautiful красивый [kras**ee**vi]

because потому что [patam**oo**shta]

because of из-за [eez-za]

bed кровать f [kravat]

I'm going to bed now я ложусь спать [ya laJoos spat]

bed and breakfast проживание и завтрак [praJiv**a**nee-yeh ee z**a**ftrak]

see accommodation and hotel

bedroom спальня [spalnya]

beef говядина [gav**ya**deena]

beer пиво [peeva]

two beers, please два пива, пожалуйста [dva peeva, paJalsta]

Beer can be good if it's fresh, but few cafés sell it and it's sold and drunk mostly at street kiosks. The most common brands are Очаковское (achakafska-yeh), Жигулёвское (Jigool-yofska-yeh) and Московское (mas-kofska-yeh), which is best described as light ale; the various Балтика (balteeka) beers come in dark, pale and now even alcohol-free varieties and are increasingly popular. The best readily available dark beer is Тверское (tversko-yeh).

see bar

before перед [pyeryet]

begin начинаться/начаться [nacheenatsa/nachatsa]

when does it begin? когда начало? [kagda nachala?]

beginner (man/woman) начинающий/начинающ ая [nacheena-yoosh-chee/ nacheena-yoosh-cha-ya]

beginning: at the beginning в начале [vnachalyeh]

behind за [za]

behind me за мной [za mnoy]

Belgium Бельгия [byelgee-ya]

believe верить/поверить [vyereet/pavyereet]

below под [pod]

belt ремень [ryemyen]

bend (in road) поворот

berth (on ship) койка [**koy**ka]

beside: beside the ... рядом
с ... [**rya**dam s ...]

best лучший [**looch**shi]

better лучше [**looch**sheh]

 are you feeling better? вам
лучше? [vam **looch**sheh?]

between между [**mye**Jdoo]

beyond за [za]

bicycle велосипед
[vyelaseep**yet**]

big большой [balsh**oy**]

 too big слишком большой
[**slee**shkam balsh**oy**]

 it's not big enough
недостаточно большой
[nyedast**a**tachna balsh**oy**]

bike велосипед
[vyelaseep**yet**]

 (motorbike) мотоцикл
[matats**iyk**l]

bill счёт [sh-chot]

 (US: banknote) банкнота
[bankn**o**ta]

 could I have the bill, please?
счёт, пожалуйста [sh-chot,
paJ**a**lsta]

bin мусорное ведро
[**moo**sarna-yeh vyedr**o**]

bird птица [pt**ee**tsa]

birthday день рождения
[dyen raJd**ye**nee-ya]

 happy birthday! с днём
рождения! [sdnyom
raJd**ye**nee-ya!]

biscuit печенье
[pyech**ye**nyeh]

bit: a little bit немножко

[nyeh-mn**o**shka]

 a big bit большой кусок
[balsh**oy** koos**ok**]

 a bit of ... кусочек ...
[koos**o**chyek ...]

 a bit expensive дороговато
[daragav**a**ta]

bite (by insect) укус
(насекомого) [ook**oo**s
(nasyek**o**mava)]

 (by dog) укус (собаки)
[ook**oo**s (sab**a**kee)]

bitter (taste) горький [**gor**kee]

black чёрный [**chor**ni]

black market чёрный
рынок [**chor**ni **riy**nak]

Black Sea Чёрное море
[**chor**na-yeh **mor**yeh]

blanket одеяло [adyeh-**ya**la]

bleach (for toilet) хлорка
[Hl**or**ka]

bless you! будьте здоровы!
[**boo**t-tyeh zdar**o**vi!]

blind слепой [slyep**oy**]

blinds шторы [**shtor**i]

blocked (road)
перегороженный
[pyeryegar**o**Jen-ni]

 (sink) засоренный [zas**o**ryen-
ni]

blond (adj) белокурый
[byelak**oo**ri]

blood кровь f [krof]

 high blood pressure
высокое давление
[vis**o**ka-yeh davl**ye**nee-yeh]

blouse блузка [bl**oo**ska]

blow-dry укладка феном
[ookl**a**tka f**ye**nam]

I'd like a cut and blow-dry
пожалуйста, постригите
и сделайте укладку
феном [paJalsta,
pastreegeetyeh ee sdyelityeh
ooklatkoo fyenam]

blue синий [seenee]

blue eyes голубые глаза
[galoobiy-yeh glaza]

blusher румяна pl [roomyana]

boarding pass
посадочный талон
[pasadachni talon]

boat лодка [lotka]
(for passengers) корабль m
[karabl]

when is the next boat to ...?
когда следующий рейс
в ...? [kagda slyedoo-sh-chee
ryays v ...?]

body тело [tyela]

**boil: do we have to boil the
water?** нужно ли
кипятить воду? [nooJnalee
keepyateet vodoo?]

boiled egg варёное яйцо
[varyona-yeh yltso]

boiled water кипячёная
вода [keepyachona-ya vada]

boiler кипятильник
[keepyateelneek]

bone кость [kost]

bonnet (of car) капот [kapot]

book (noun) книга [kneega]
(verb) заказывать/заказать
[zakazivat/zakazat]

can I book a seat? могу ли
я заказать билет [magoolee
ya zakazat beelyet?]

dialogue

**I'd like to book a table for
two** (said by man/woman) я
хотел/хотела бы
заказать столик на
двоих [ya Hatyel/Hatyela biy
zakazat stoleek na dva-eeн]
**what time would you like it
booked for?** на какое
время? [na kako-yeh
vryemya?]
half past seven на
половину восьмого [na
palaveenoo vasmova]
that's fine хорошо
[Harasho]
and your name? ваше
имя? [vasheh eemya?]

bookshop, bookstore
книжный магазин [kneeJni
magazeen]

boot (footwear) ботинок
[bateenak]
(of car) багажник
[bagaJneek]

border (of country) граница
[graneetsa]

bored: I'm bored мне скучно
[mnyeh skooshna]

boring скучный [skooshni]

**born: I was born in
Manchester** (said by
man/woman) я родился/
родилась в Манчестере
[ya radeelsa/radeelas
vmanchyesteryeh]

I was born in 1960 (said by

man/woman) я родился/
родилась в тысяча
девятьсот шестидесятом
году [ya rad**ee**lsa/rad**ee**las
ft**iy**syacha dyevyats**ot**
shest**ee**dyes**ya**tam gad**oo**]
borrow занимать/занять
[zaneem**at**/zan**ya**t]
  may I borrow ...? вы не
  одолжите ...? [viy nyeh
  adalJ**iy**teh ...?]
both оба [**o**ba]
bother: sorry to bother you
извините за
беспокойство [eezveen**ee**tyeh
za byespak**oy**stva]
bottle бутылка [boot**iy**lka]
  a bottle of vodka бутылка
  водки [boot**iy**lka v**o**tkee]
bottle-opener открывалка
[atkriv**al**ka]
bottom (of person) зад [zat]
  at the bottom of ... (street etc)
  в конце ... (улицы)
  [fkants**eh** (**oo**leetsi)]
  (hill) у подножия ... [oo
  padn**o**Ji-ya ...]
bouncer вышибала [vishib**a**la]
bowl тарелка [tar**ye**lka]
box коробка [kar**o**pka]
box office театральная
касса [tyeh-atr**a**lna-ya k**a**s-sa]
boy мальчик [**ma**lcheek]
boyfriend друг [drook]
bra бюстгальтер
[byoostg**a**lter]
bracelet браслет [brasl**ye**t]
brake тормоз [**to**rmas]
brandy коньяк [kan**ya**k]

bread хлеб [Hlyep]
  white bread белый хлеб
  [b**ye**li Hlyep]
  brown bread чёрный хлеб
  [ch**o**rni Hlyep]
  rye bread ржаной хлеб
  [rJan**oy** Hlyep]
  wholemeal bread хлеб из
  непросеянной муки [Hlyep
  eez nyepras**yeh**-yani mook**ee**]

Bread (Hlyep) is available
from bakeries
булочная (boolachna-
ya), and is one of Russia's culinary
strong points. 'Black' bread (known
as 'chorni' or 'rJanoy') is the
traditional rye bread. French-style
baguettes **батон** (baton) are also
popular. On the whole, you still have
to queue at the 'kas-sa' to pay and
then queue again for the bread.

break (verb) ломать/сломать
[lam**at**/slam**at**]
  I've broken the ... (said by
  man/woman) я сломал/
  сломала ... [ya slam**al**/slam**a**la]
  I think I've broken my wrist
  (said by man/woman) кажется,
  я сломал/сломала
  запястье [k**a**Jetsa, ya
  slam**al**/slam**a**la zap**ya**styeh]
break down ломаться/
сломаться [lam**a**tsa/slam**a**tsa]
  I've broken down у меня
  сломалась машина [oo
  men**ya** slam**a**las mash**iy**na]
breakdown поломка

[palomka]

breakdown service экстренная техпомощь [**e**kstryen-na-ya tyeнp**o**mosh-ch]

breakfast завтрак [**za**ftrak]

break-in: I've had a break-in мою комнату обокрали [ma-**yoo** k**o**mnatoo abakral**ee**]

breast грудь **f** [grood]

breathe дышать [dish**a**t]

breeze ветерок [vyetyer**o**k]

bribe взятка [vz**ya**tka]

bridge (over river) мост [mosst]

brief краткий [kr**a**tkee]

briefcase портфель **m** [partf**ye**l]

bright (light etc) яркий [**ya**rkee]

bright red ярко-красный [**ya**rka-kr**a**sni]

brilliant (idea, person) блестящий [blyesty**a**sh-chee]

bring приносить/принести [preenas**ee**t/preenyest**ee**]

I'll bring it back later я верну это позже [ya vyern**oo** eta p**oJ**-Jeh]

Britain Великобритания [vyeleeka-breet**a**nee-ya]

British британский [breet**a**nskee]

brochure брошюра [brash**oo**ra]

broken сломанный [sl**o**man-ni]

bronchitis бронхит [branh**ee**t]

brooch брошь **f** [brosh]

broom метла [myetl**a**]

brother брат [brat]

brother-in-law (husband's brother)

деверь [d**ye**vyer] (wife's brother) шурин [sh**oo**reen]

brown коричневый [kar**ee**chnyevi]

brown hair каштановые волосы [kasht**a**navi-yeh v**o**lasi]

brown eyes карие глаза [k**a**ree-yeh glaz**a**]

bruise синяк [seeny**a**k]

brush щётка [sh-ch**o**tka] (artist's) кисть **f** [keest]

bucket ведро [vyedr**o**]

buffet (on train etc) буфет [boof**ye**t] (in restaurant) шведский стол [shv**e**tskee stol]

buggy (for child) детская коляска [d**ye**tska-ya kaly**a**ska]

building здание [zd**a**nee-yeh]

bulb (light bulb) лампочка [l**a**mpachka]

Bulgaria Болгария [balg**a**ree-ya]

bumper бампер [b**a**mpyer]

bunk койка [k**o**yka]

bureau de change обмен валюты [abm**ye**n val**yoo**ti] see **bank**

burglary ограбление [agrabl**ye**nee-yeh]

burn (noun) ожог [aJ**o**k] (verb) гореть/сгореть [gar**ye**t/sgar**ye**t] **this is burnt** это горелое [eta gar**ye**la-yeh]

burst: a burst pipe лопнувшая труба [l**o**pnoofsha-ya troob**a**]

bus автобус [aftoboos]
 what number bus is it to ...?
 какой автобус идёт до ...?
 [kakoy aftoboos eedyot da ...?]
 when is the next bus to ...?
 когда следующий
 автобус до ...? [kagda
 slyedoosh-chee aftoboos da ...?]
 what time is the last bus?
 когда приходит
 последний автобус? [kagda
 preeHodeet paslyednee aftoboos?]

Tickets (taloni) for buses,
trams and trolley buses
are available from some
street kiosks and vendors, or from
the driver of the vehicle, who sells
them in batches of ten. You must
use a separate 'talon' each time you
board, punching it on one of the
archaic gadgets mounted inside the
vehicle. Roaming plain-clothes
inspectors will issue on-the-spot
fines to anyone caught without a
ticket.
To save money, most Russians buy a
monthly travel pass (yedeeni
beelyet), which goes on sale in
metro stations and kiosks towards
the end of the calendar month (in
Moscow, from the 20th). This covers
all forms of transport, although it is
possible to buy a pass just for the
metro or for surface transport. On
buses, trams and trolley buses, you
only need to produce the pass at the
request of an inspector.
Stops tend to be few and far

between, so getting off at the wrong
one can mean a lengthy walk. Bus
stops are marked with an 'A' (for
aftoboos) and trolley bus stops with
a 'T' (for tralyayboos). The signs for
tram stops (bearing a 'T' for tramvi)
are suspended from the overhead
cables.
In addition to the services outlined
above, there are special express
buses (ekspres) on certain routes.
These are not to be confused with
minibuses, which Russians call
'marshrootna-yeh taksee'. The latter
tend to leave from metro or mainline
stations and serve outlying
destinations, like the airports, with
limited stops. On both, you pay the
driver instead of using a 'talon', and
the fares are a lot higher than on
regular buses.

dialogue

 does this bus go to ...?
 идёт ли этот автобус
 до ...? [eedyotlee etat aftoboos
 da ...?]
 no, you need a number ...
 нет, вам нужен
 номер ... [nyet, vam nooJen
 nomyer ...]

business бизнес [beeznes]
bus station автобусная
 станция [aftoboosna-ya stantsi-
 ya]
bus stop остановка
 автобуса [astanofka aftoboosa]

bust бюст [byoost]

busy (restaurant etc)
оживлённый [aJivlyon-ni]

I'm busy tomorrow (said by
man/woman) я буду
занят/занята завтра [ya
boodoo zanyat/zanyata zaftra]

but но [no]

butcher's мясной магазин
[myasnoy magazeen]

butter масло [masla]

button пуговица [poogaveetsa]

buy покупать/купить
[pakoopat/koopeet]

where can I buy ...? где
можно купить ...? [gdyeh
moJna koopeet ...?]

by: by train/by car/by plane
на поезде/на машине/на
самолёте [na po-yezdyeh/na
mashiynyeh/na samalyotyeh]

the book is written by ...
книга написана ... [kneega
napeesana ...]

by the window около окна
[okala akna]

by the sea у моря [oo morya]

by Thursday к четвергу
[kchyetvyergoo]

bye! пока! [paka]

C

cabaret кабаре [kabareh]

cabbage капуста [kapoosta]

cabin (on ship) каюта
[ka-yoota]

cable car фуникулёр

[fooneekoolyor]

café кафе [kafeh]

Cafés always serve some
sort of food, at much
lower prices than full-
blown restaurants, and seldom
require bookings. Most cafés, like
restaurants, sell vodka and cognac,
which usually come in large
measures of 100 grams (sto gram),
as well as beer.
see bar

cagoule куртка от дождя
[koortka ad-daJdya]

cake торт [tort]

a piece of cake кусок торта
[koosok torta]

cake shop кондитерская
[kandeetyerska-ya]

call (verb) звать/позвать
[zvat/pazvat]
(verb: to phone) звонить/
позвонить [zvaneet/
pazvaneet]

what's it called? как это
называется? [kak eta
naziva-yetsa?]

he/she is called ... его/её
зовут ... [yevo/ye-yo zavoot ...]

please call the doctor
вызовите, пожалуйста,
врача [viyzaveetyeh, paJalsta,
vracha]

please give me a call at 7.30
am tomorrow позвоните
мне, пожалуйста, завтра
в семь тридцать утра

[pazvan**ee**tyeh mnyeh, pa**J**a**l**sta,
za**f**tra fs**y**em tr**ee**tsat oo**tra**]
please ask him to call me
пожалуйста, попросите
его мне позвонить
[pa**J**alsta, papras**ee**tyeh ye**vo** mnyeh
pazvan**ee**t]

call back: I'll call back later я
вернусь позже [ya vyern**oo**s
p**o**J-Jeh]
(phone back) я перезвоню
попозже [ya pyeryezvan**yoo**
pap**o**J-Jeh]

**call round: I'll call round
tomorrow** я зайду завтра
[ya zid**oo** z**a**ftra]

camcorder видеокамера
[veedyeh-ok**a**myera]

camera фотоаппарат [f**o**ta-
apar**at**]

camera shop магазин кино-
и фотоаппаратуры
[magaz**ee**n keena-ee-f**o**ta-
aparat**oo**ri]

camp (verb) жить в
палатках [J**i**yt fpal**a**tkah]
can we camp here? можно
ли здесь разбить лагерь?
[m**o**Jnalee zdyes razb**ee**t l**a**gyer?]
see **hotel**

camping gas газовый
баллончик [g**a**zavi
bal**o**ncheek]

campsite кемпинг
[k**ye**mpeeng]

can банка [b**a**nka]
a can of beer банка пива
[b**a**nka p**ee**va]

can*: can you ...? вы

можете ...? [viy m**o**Jetyeh ...?]
can you show me ...? вы
можете показать мне ...?
[viy m**o**Jetyeh pakaz**at** mnyeh ...?]
can I have ...? можно мне,
пожалуйста ... [m**o**Jna mnyeh,
pa**J**alsta ...]
I can't ... я не могу ... [ya
nyeh mag**oo** ...]

Canada Канада [kan**a**da]

Canadian канадский
[kan**a**tskee]
I'm Canadian (man/woman) я
канадец/канадка [ya
kan**a**dyets/kan**a**tka]

canal канал [kan**a**l]

cancel отменять/отменить
[atmyen**yat**/atmyen**eet**]

candies конфеты [kanf**ye**ti]

candle свеча [svy**e**cha]

can-opener открывалка
[atkriv**a**lka]

cap (hat) шапка [sh**a**pka]
(of bottle) крышка [kr**i**yshka]

car машина [mash**i**yna]
by car на машине [na
mash**i**ynyeh]

carafe графин [graf**ee**n]
a carafe of white wine, please
графин белого вина,
пожалуйста [graf**ee**n b**ye**lava
v**ee**na, pa**J**alsta]

card (birthday etc) открытка
[atkr**i**ytka]
here's my (business) card
моя карточка,
пожалуйста [ma-**ya** k**a**rtachka,
pa**J**alsta]

cardigan кофта [k**o**fta]

cardphone телефон, принимающий карточки [tyelyefon, preeneema-yoosh-chee kartachkee]

cards карты [karti]

careful осторожный [astaroJni]

be careful! осторожно! [astaroJna!]

caretaker (man/woman) сторож [storash]

car ferry автопаром [aftaparom]

car park стоянка [sta-yanka]

carpet ковёр [kavyor]

car rental прокат автомобилей [prakat aftamabeelyay]

A growing number of car rental agencies offer Western models, with or without a driver. You should seriously consider hiring a driver: it could spare you a lot of anxiety, and may not cost a lot more than straightforward car rental. Most rental agencies prefer payment by credit card and require the full range of documentation for self-drive rental. Most places tend to charge about the same after you take all the hidden charges into account, so you might as well go for a well-known firm rather than an obscure one, where possible.

carriage (of train) вагон [vagon]

carrier bag сумка [soomka]

carrot морковь f [markof]

carry нести [nyestee]

carry-cot переносная кроватка [pyeryenasna-ya kravatka]

carton пакет [pakyet]

case (suitcase) чемодан [chyemadan]

cash наличные деньги [naleechni-yeh dyengee]

will you cash this for me? (travellers' cheque) обменяйте, пожалуйста, на наличные [abmyenyaytyeh, paJalsta, na naleechni-yeh]

cash desk касса [kas-sa]

cash dispenser банкомат [bankamat]

cassette кассета [kas-syeta]

cassette recorder кассетный магнитофон [kas-syetni magneetafon]

castle замок [zamak]

casualty department палата скорой помощи [palata skori pomash-chee]

cat кошка [koshka]

catch (verb: ball) ловить/поймать [laveet/pimat]

where do we catch the bus to ...? откуда идёт автобус до ...? [atkooda eedyot aftoboos da ...?]

cathedral собор [sabor]

Catholic (adj) католический [kataleechyeskee]

cauliflower цветная капуста [tsvyetna-ya kapoosta]

cave пещера [pyesh-chyera]

caviar икра [eekra]
  red caviar красная икра
  [krasna-ya eekra]
  black caviar чёрная икра
  [chorna-ya eekra]
ceiling потолок [patalok]
celery сельдерей [syeldyer**yay**]
cemetery кладбище
  [kladbeesh-chyeh]
centigrade по Цельсию [pa
  tselsee-yoo]
centimetre сантиметр
  [santeem**yetr**]
central центральный
  [tsentralni]
central heating центральное
  отопление [tsentralna-yeh
  ataplyenee-yeh]
centre центр [tsentr]
  how do we get to the city
  centre? как попасть в
  центр города? [kak papast
  ftsentr gorada?]
cereal сухой завтрак [sooнoy
  zaftrak]
certainly да, конечно [da,
  kanyeshna]
  certainly not ни в коем
  случае [nee fko-yem sloocha-
  yeh]
chair стул [stool]
champagne шампанское
  [shampanska-yeh]

 Russian champagne,
some of which is good if
served chilled, is
extremely cheap compared with the
French variety. The two types to go
for are 'sooнo-yeh' and 'bryoot',
which are both reasonably dry;
'poloosooнo-yeh' or 'medium dry' is
actually very sweet, and 'slatka-yeh'
extremely sweet.

change (noun: money) мелочь
  [myelach]
  (verb: money) обменивать/
  обменять [abmyeneevat/
  abmyenyat]
  can I change this for ...?
  можно обменять это
  на ...? [moжna abmyenyat eta
  na ...?]
  I don't have any change у
  меня нет мелочи [oo menya
  nyet myelachee]
  can you give me change for a
  10,000 rouble note? вы не
  могли бы разменять
  десять тысяч? [viy nyeh
  magleebi razmyenyat dyesyat
  tiysyach?]

dialogue

do we have to change
(trains)? нужно ли нам
сделать пересадку?
[nooжnalee nam zdyelat
pyeryesatkoo?]
yes, change at St
Petersburg/no, it's a direct
train да, сделайте
пересадку в Санкт-
Петербурге/нет, это
прямой поезд [da,
zdyelityeh pyeryesatkoo

fsankt-peetyerboorgyeh/nyet, eta
pryamoy po-yest]

changed: to get changed
переодеваться/переодеть
ся [pyeryeh-adyevatsa/pyeryeh-
adyetsa]
charge (noun) цена [tsena]
(verb) назначать/
назначить цену
[naznachat/naznacheet tsenoo]
cheap дешёвый [dyeshovi]
**do you have anything
cheaper?** у вас нет ничего
подешевле? [oo vas nyet
neechyevo padyeshevlyeh?]
check (US: bill) счёт
[sh-chyot]
(US: cheque) чек [chyek]
check (verb) проверять/
проверить [pravyeryat/
pravyereet]
**could you check the ...,
please?** проверьте ...,
пожалуйста [pravyertyeh ...,
paJalsta]
check in регистрироваться/
зарегистрироваться
[ryegeestreeravatsa/
zaryegeestreeravatsa]
**where do we have to check
in?** где проходит
регистрация? [gdyeh
praHodeet ryegeestratsi-ya?]
check-in регистрация
[ryegeestratsi-ya]
cheek щека [sh-chyeka]
cheerio! пока! [paka!]
cheers! (toast) ваше

здоровье! [vasheh zdarovyeh!]
cheese сыр [siyr]
chemist's аптека [aptyeka]
see **pharmacy**
cheque чек [chyek]
do you take cheques? вы
принимаете чеки? [viy
preeneema-yetyeh chyekee?]
cheque book чековая
книжка [chyekava-ya
kneeshka]
cheque card чековая
карточка [chyekava-ya
kartachka]
cherry вишня [veeshnya]
chess шахматы [shaHmati]
chest грудь f [grood]
chewing gum жвачка
[Jvachka]
chicken цыплёнок
[tsiplyonak]
chickenpox ветрянка
[vyetryanka]
child ребёнок [ryebyonak]
children дети [dyetee]

 Disposable nappies are
now available in many
supermarkets, which
usually also stock baby food, but it's
best to bring a small supply to tide
you over, particularly if you're
travelling outside the big cities. Note
that breast-feeding in public is
totally unacceptable. Children up to
the age of seven ride free on all
forms of transport.

child minder няня [nyanya]

children's pool бассейн для детей [bas**ay**n dlya dyet**yay**]
children's portion детская порция [**dye**tska-ya p**o**rtsi-ya]
chin подбородок [padbar**o**dak]
China Китай [K**ee**tɪ]
Chinese (adj) китайский [keetɪskee]
chips картофель фри [kart**o**fyel free]
  (US: crisps) чипсы [**chee**psi]
chocolate шоколад [shakal**a**t]
  milk chocolate молочный шоколад [mal**o**chni shakal**a**t]
  plain chocolate шоколад [shakal**a**t]
  hot chocolate горячий шоколад [gar**ya**chee shakal**a**t]
choose выбирать/выбрать [vibeer**a**t/v**i**ybrat]
Christian name имя [**ee**mya]
Christmas Рождество [raJdyestv**o**]
  Christmas Eve канун рождества [kan**oo**n raJdyestv**a**]
  merry Christmas! счастливого Рождества! [sh-chasl**ee**vava raJdyestv**a**!]
church церковь f [ts**e**rkaf]

During Soviet times, many places of worship were converted into museums or workshops or simply left to fall into ruin. Though the majority have now reverted to their original function, many are only open for services.

Visitors are expected to dress modestly; women should wear headscarves and men remove their hats in church.

cider сидр [**see**dr]
cigar сигара [seeg**a**ra]
cigarette сигарета [seegar**ye**ta]
  (Russian non-filter) папироса [papeer**o**sa]

Nearly all Western cigarette brands are available, though many of the packets sold from kiosks are made under licence (or counterfeited) in Russia or Turkey; Marlboro kiosks and beer shops are likely to stock the genuine article. Traditional Soviet brands like **беломор** (byelam**o**r) are what are called 'papeer**o**si', with an inch of tobacco at the end of a long cardboard tube that is twisted to make a crude filter. It is not unusual to be approached by strangers asking for a light (sp**ee**chka nyeh nid**yo**tsa?) or a cigarette (oo vas nyeh nidyotsa zakoor**e**et?). While museums and public transport are no-smoking zones, Russians smoke everywhere else.

cigarette lighter зажигалка [zaJig**a**lka]
cinema кино [keen**o**]
circle круг [krook]

(in theatre) ярус [**ya**roos]

CIS СНГ [es-en-**geh**]

city город [**go**rat]

city centre центр города [tsentr **go**rada]

clean (adj) чистый [**chee**sti]

  can you clean these for me? вы можете почистить это [viy **mo**zhetyeh pach**ee**steet **e**ta?]

cleaning solution (for contact lenses) раствор для линз [rast**vo**r dlya leenz]

cleansing lotion очищающий лосьон [acheesh-cha-yoosh-chee las**yon**]

clear (obvious) ясный [**ya**sni]

clever умный [**oo**mni]

cliff скала [ska**la**]

climbing альпинизм [alpeen**ee**zm]

clinic клиника [k**lee**neeka]

cloakroom (for coats) гардероб [gardye**ro**p]

clock часы [chas**iy**]

close (verb) закрывать/закрыть [zakri**va**t/zak**riyt**]

dialogue

  what time do you close? когда вы закрываетесь? [kagd**a** viy zakri**va**-yetyes?]

  we close at 8pm on weekdays and 6pm on Saturdays мы закрываемся в восемь в будние дни и в шесть по субботам [miy zak**ri**va-yemsya v**vo**syem vb**oo**dnee-yeh dnee ee fshest pa soob**o**tam]

  do you close for lunch? у вас есть обеденный перерыв? [oo vas yest ab**ye**dyen-ni pyeryer**iy**f?]

  yes, between 1 and 2pm да, с часу до двух [da, sch**a**soo da dv**oo**H]

closed закрыто [zak**riy**ta]

cloth (fabric) ткань f [tkan] (for cleaning etc) тряпка [t**rya**pka]

clothes одежда [ad**ye**jda]

cloud облако [**o**blaka]

cloudy облачный [**o**blachni]

clutch сцепление [stsepl**ye**nee-yeh]

coach междугородный автобус [myeJd**oo**-gar**o**dni aft**o**boos] (on train) вагон [vag**o**n]

coach trip автобусная экскурсия [aft**o**boosna-ya eksk**oo**rsee-ya]

coast берег [**bye**ryek] on the coast на побережье [na pabyer**ye**Jeh]

coat пальто [pal**to**] (jacket) куртка [**koo**rtka]

coathanger вешалка [**vye**shalka]

cockroach таракан [tara**ka**n]

cocoa какао [kak**a**-o]

code (for phoning) код [kod] what's the (dialling) code for

Moscow? какой код для Москвы? [kak**oy** kod dlya maskv**iy**?]
coffee кофе **m** [k**o**fyeh]
 two coffees, please две чашки кофе, пожалуйста [dvyeh ch**a**shkee k**o**fyeh, pa**J**alsta]

Coffee is readily available and often of reasonable quality. Many places offer imported espresso brands like Lavazza and occasionally you will be served an approximation of an espresso or, better still, a Turkish coffee – both served strong and black. Note that coffee is usually served with sugar already added, so you should make it clear when you order if you don't want sugar (byes s**a**Hara, pa**J**alsta).

coin монета [man**ye**ta]
Coke® Кока-кола [k**o**ka-k**o**la]
cold холодный [H**a**l**o**dni]
 (noun) простуда [prast**oo**da]
 I'm cold мне холодно [mnyeh H**o**ladna]
 I have a cold у меня простуда [oo men**ya** prast**oo**da]
collapse: he's collapsed он потерял сознание [on patyer**ya**l sazn**a**nee-yeh]
collar воротник [varatn**ee**k]
collect: I've come to collect ... (said by man/woman) я пришёл/пришла за ... [ya preesh**o**l/preeshl**a** za ...]
collect call звонок с

оплатой вызываемым абонентом [zvan**o**k sapl**a**ti visiv**a**-yemim aban**ye**ntam]
college колледж [k**a**ledJ]
colour цвет [tsvyet]
 do you have this in other colours? у вас есть это другого цвета? [oo vas yest **e**ta droog**o**va tsvy**e**ta?]
colour film цветная плёнка [tsvyetn**a**-ya pl**yo**nka]
comb расчёска [rash-ch**o**ska]
come приходить/прийти [preeH**a**d**ee**t/preet**ee**]

dialogue

 where do you come from? вы откуда? [viy atk**oo**da?]
 I come from Edinburgh я из Эдинбурга [ya eez edeenb**oo**rga]

come back возвращаться/вернуться [vazvrash-ch**a**tsa/vyern**oo**tsa]
 I'll come back tomorrow я вернусь завтра [ya vyern**oo**s z**a**ftra]
come in входить/войти [fH**a**d**ee**t/vit**ee**]
comfortable удобный [ood**o**bni]
communism коммунизм [kamoon**ee**zm]
communist (adj) коммунистический [kamooneest**ee**chyeskee]
Communist party

коммунистическая партия [kamooneesteechyeska-ya partee-ya]
compact disc компакт-диск [kampakt-deesk]
company (business) компания [kampanee-ya]
compartment (on train) купе [koopeh]
complain жаловаться/пожаловаться [Jalavatsa/paJalavatsa]
complaint жалоба [Jalaba]
I have a complaint у меня есть жалоба [oo myenya yest Jalaba]
completely совершенно [savyershen-na]
computer компьютер [kampyooter]
concert концерт [kantsert]
concierge (in hotel) дежурная [dyeJoorna-ya]
see hotel
conditioner (for hair) опаласкиватель m [apalaskeevatyel]
condom презерватив [pryezyervateef]
conference конференция [kanfyeryentsi-ya]
confirm подтверждать/подтвердить [patvyerJdat/patverdeet]
congratulations! поздравляю! [pazdravlya-yoo!]
connecting flight

стыковочный рейс [stikovachni ryays]
connection (transport) пересадка [pyeryesatka]
conscious в сознании [fsaznanee-ee]
constipation запор [zapor]
consulate консульство [konsoolstva]
contact (verb) связаться с [svyazatsa s]
contact lenses контактные линзы [kantaktni-yeh leenzi]
contraceptive противозачаточное средство [proteevazachatachna-yeh sryetstva]
convenient удобный [oodobni]
that's not convenient это не удобно [eta nyeh oodobna]
cook (verb) готовить/приготовить [gatoveet/preegatoveet]
the meat is not cooked мясо не прожарено [myasa nyeh praJaryena]
cooker плита [pleeta]
cookie печенье [pyechyenyeh]
cooking utensils кухонная посуда [kooнan-na-ya pasooda]
cool прохладный [praнladni]
cork пробка [propka]
corkscrew штопор [shtopar]
corner: on the corner на углу [na oogloo]
in the corner в углу [voogloo]
cornflakes кукурузные

CO

хлопья [kookooroozni-yeh Hlopya]

correct (right) правильный [praveelni]

corridor коридор [kareedor]

cosmetics косметика [kasmyeteeka]

cost (noun) стоимость f [sto-eemast]

  how much does it cost? сколько это стоит? [skolka eta sto-eet?]

cot детская кроватка [dyetska-ya kravatka]

cottage (in the country) дача [dacha]

cotton хлопок [Hlopak]

cotton wool вата [vata]

couch (sofa) диван [deevan]

couchette спальное место [spalna-yeh myesta]

cough (noun) кашель m [kashel]

cough medicine средство от кашля [sryedstva at kashlya]

could: could you ...? вы не могли бы ..? [viy nyeh magleebi ...?]

  could I have ...? можно мне ...? [moJna mnyeh ...?]

country страна [strana]

  (countryside) деревня [dyeryevnya]

  in the country за городом [zagaradam]

countryside деревня [dyeryevnya]

couple (two people) пара [para]

  a couple of hours пару

часов [paroo chasof]

courgette кабачок [kabachok]

courier курьер [kooryer]

course (main course etc) блюдо [blyooda]

  of course конечно [kanyeshna]

  of course not конечно, нет [kanyeshna, nyet]

cousin (male/female) кузен/кузина [koozen/koozeena]

cow корова [karova]

cracker крекер [krekyer]

craft shop художественный салон [HoodoJestvyen-ni salon]

crash (noun) авария [avaree-ya]

  I've had a crash (said by man/woman) я попал/попала в аварию [ya papal/papala vavaree-yoo]

crazy сумасшедший [soomashetshi]

cream (in coffee etc) сливки pl [sleefkee]

  (in cake, lotion) крем [kryem]

  (colour) кремовый [kryemavi]

  soured cream сметана [smyetana]

creche ясли pl [yaslee]

credit card кредитная карточка [kryedeetna-ya kartachka]

  do you take credit cards? вы принимаете кредитные карточки? [viy preeneema-yetyeh kryedeetni-yeh kartachkee?]

Credit cards are becoming more widely accepted in restaurants and shops in Moscow and St Petersburg, but are still not accepted in the majority of outlets in regional towns and cities. Many places only take one or two types of card – mostly Visa, Mastercard or Amex (in that order). You will usually need to show your passport or some other form of identification. Always make sure that the transaction is properly recorded, keep the receipt and check that the carbons are destroyed.

Holders of Visa or Amex cards can obtain cash advances in Moscow and St Petersburg (in dollars or roubles) at several venues, notably Dialogbank and Credobank. Alternatively, in these cities, you can use cash dispensers/ATMs that accept Eurocard, Mastercard and bankcards on the Cirrus network, and pay out in dollars or roubles.

dialogue

can I pay by credit card? могу ли я заплатить кредитной карточкой? [mag**oo**lee ya zaplat**eet** kryed**ee**tnı kartachkı?]

which card do you want to use? какой карточкой вы хотите заплатить? [kak**oy** kartachkı viy нat**ee**tyeh zaplat**eet**?]

Mastercard/Visa

yes, sir да, пожалуйста [da, paлalsta]

what's the number? какой номер? [kak**oy** n**o**myer?]

and the expiry date? когда истекает срок действия? [kagd**a** eestyek**a**-yet srok d**yey**stvee-ya?]

crime
Moscow, in particular, is often viewed as a city overrun by gangsters, with shootings on every corner. Although such dangers are exaggerated by the Western media, visitors should certainly observe obvious precautions like not flashing money or cameras around, or going off with strangers. At night, stick to the well-lit and busier parts of town. Try to blend in whenever possible: the less you look like a tourist, the smaller the risk of trouble.

The main targets of crime are rich Russian businessmen, compared with whom foreign tourists are considered small fry. The Mafia is less of a hazard than petty crime (mostly thefts from cars and hotel rooms).

If you are unlucky enough to have something stolen, you will need to go to the police to report it. It's unlikely that there'll be anyone who speaks English, and even less likely that your belongings will be retrieved, but at the very least you should get a statement detailing what you've lost for your insurance claim.

Crimea Крым [kriym]

crisps хрустящий картофель [Hroost**ya**sh-chee kart**o**fyel]

crockery посуда [pas**oo**da]

crossing (by sea, across river) переправа [pyeryepr**a**va]

crossroads перекрёсток [pyeryekr**yo**stak]

crowd толпа [talp**a**]

crowded переполненный [pyeryep**o**lnyen-ni]

crown (on tooth) коронка [kar**o**nka]

cruise круиз [kroo-**ee**s]

crutches костыли [kastil**ee**]

cry (verb) плакать/заплакать [pl**a**kat/zapl**a**kat]

cucumber огурец [agoor**ye**ts]

pickled cucumber солёный огурец [sal**yo**ni agoor**ye**ts]

cup чашка [ch**a**shka]

a cup of tea, please чашку чая, пожалуйста [ch**a**shkoo ch**a**-ya, pa**ja**lsta]

cupboard шкаф [shkaf]

cure (verb) лечить/вылечить [lyech**ee**t/v**ee**lyecheet]

curly кудрявый [koodr**ya**vi]

current (electrical) ток [tok]

curtains занавески [zanav**ye**skee]

cushion подушка [pad**oo**shka]

custom обычай [ab**i**ychee]

Customs таможня [tam**o**jnya]

Over the last couple of years, border controls have relaxed considerably. However, all foreigners entering Russia still have to fill in a currency declaration form stating exactly how much money they are bringing into the country. The form will be stamped at Customs. When leaving the country, you must fill in a duplicate form stating how much currency you are taking out of Russia and submit it to the Customs officer along with the form you filled out on entry, the aim being to prevent you taking out more than you took in. The entry form is probably as important as your passport, since without it you will have serious problems getting through Customs, so it should be kept in a safe place at all times. As a tourist, you can take out, tax-free, goods worth up to fifty times the minimum wage; on anything over this amount, you'll have to pay sixty per cent tax on the difference. You can expect to encounter serious problems if you try to export any artwork, military souvenirs, electrical goods or antique samovars.

Customs form таможенная декларация [tam**o**Jen-na-ya dyeklar**a**tsi-ya]

cut (noun) порез [par**ye**s] (verb) резать/разрезать [r**ye**zat/razr**ye**zat]

I've cut myself (said by man/woman) я порезался/ порезалась [ya par**ye**zalsa/ par**ye**zalas]

cutlery столовые приборы [st**a**lovi-yeh preeb**o**ri]

cycling велоспорт [vyelasp**o**rt]

cyclist (man/woman) велосипедист/ велосипедистка [vyelaseepyed**ee**st/ vyelaseepyed**ee**stka]

Czech Republic Чешская республика [ch**ye**shska-ya ryesp**oo**bleeka]

D

dad папа [p**a**pa]

daily ежедневно [yeJedn**ye**vna] (adj) ежедневный [yeJedn**ye**vni]

damage (verb) повреждать/повредить [pavryeJd**a**t/pavryed**ee**t] it's damaged это повреждено [eta pavryeJd**ye**no] I'm sorry, I've damaged this (said by man/woman) извините, я повредил/ повредила это [eezveen**ee**tyeh, ya pavryed**ee**l/ pavryed**ee**la eta]

damn! чёрт! [chort!]

damp сырой [sir**oy**]

dance (noun) танец [t**a**nyets] (verb) танцевать [tantsev**a**t]

would you like to dance? можно пригласить вас на танец? [m**o**Jna preeglas**ee**t vas na t**a**nyets?]

dangerous опасный [ap**a**sni]

Danish (adj) датский [d**a**tskee]

dark (adj: colour) тёмный [t**yo**mni]

dark green тёмно-зелёный [t**yo**mna-zyel**yo**ni]

it's getting dark темнеет [tyemn**ye**-yet]

date*: what's the date today? какое сегодня число? [kak**o**-yeh syev**o**dnya chees**lo**?]

let's make a date for next Monday договоримся на следующий понедельник [dagavar**ee**msya na sl**ye**doosh-chee panyed**ye**lneek]

You may wonder why the Great October Revolution always used to be celebrated in November. The reason is that at the time of the Revolution the Russians were still using the Julian calendar, which lagged behind the Gregorian calendar (used by the rest of Europe) by a good two weeks. The Bolsheviks switched to the Gregorian calendar in February 1918, leaping straight forward from January 31 to February 14.

dates (fruit) финики [f**ee**neekee]

daughter дочь [doch]

daughter-in-law невестка
[nyev**ye**stka]

dawn рассвет [ras-s**vye**t]

at dawn на рассвете [na ras-
s**vye**tyeh]

day день **m** [dyen]

the day before накануне
[nakan**oo**nyeh]

the day after tomorrow
послезавтра [**p**oslyeh-z**a**ftra]

the day before yesterday
позавчера [pazafchyer**a**]

next day на следующий
день [na sl**ye**doosh-chee dyen]

every day каждый день
[k**a**Jdi dyen]

all day весь день [vyes dyen]

in two days' time через два
дня [ch**ye**ryes dva dnya]

have a nice day всего
хорошего! [fsyev**o** Har**o**sheva!]

day trip однодневная
экскурсия [adnadn**ye**vna-ya
eksk**oo**rsee-ya]

dead мёртвый [m**yo**rtvi]

deaf глухой [gloo**Hoy**]

deal (business) сделка [zd**ye**lka]

it's a deal (said by man/woman)
согласен/согласна
[sagl**a**syen/sagl**a**sna]

death смерть **f** [smyert]

decaffeinated coffee кофе
без кофеина [**k**ofyeh byes
kafyeh-**ee**na]

December декабрь **m**
[d**ye**kabr]

decide решать/решить
[ryesh**a**t/ryesh**i**yt]

we haven't decided yet мы

ещё не решили [miy yesh-
ch**o** nyeh ryesh**i**ylee]

decision решение [ryeshenee-
yeh]

deck (on ship) палуба [p**a**looba]

deckchair шезлонг [shezl**o**ng]

deep глубокий [gloob**o**kee]

definitely: we'll definitely come
мы обязательно придём
[miy abyaz**a**telna preed**yo**m]

it's definitely not possible это
совершенно невозможно
[**e**ta savyershen-na nyevazm**o**Jna]

degree (qualification) диплом
[deepl**o**m]

delay (noun) задержка
[zad**ye**rshka]

delay: the flight was delayed
рейс задержался [ryays
zadyerJ**a**lsa]

deliberately умышленно
[oom**i**yshlen-na]

delicatessen кулинария
[kooleenar**ee**-ya]

delicious вкусный [fk**oo**sni]

deliver доставлять/
доставить [dastavl**ya**t/
dast**a**veet]

delivery (of mail) доставка
[dast**a**fka]

democratic
демократический
[dyemakrat**ee**chyeskee]

Denmark Дания [d**a**nee-ya]

dental floss нитка для
чистки зубов [**ne**etka dlya
ch**ee**stkee zoob**o**f]

dentist зубной врач [zoobn**oy**
vrach]

dialogue

it's this one here вот этот
[vot etat]
this one? этот? [etat?]
no that one нет, вот этот
[nyet, vot etat]
here здесь [zdyes]
yes да [da]

dentures зубной протез
[zoobnoy prates]
deodorant дезодорант
[dyezadarant]
department отдел [ad-dyel]
department store универмаг
[ooneevyermak]
departure (train)
отправление [atpravlyenee-
yeh]
(plane) вылет [viylyet]
departure lounge зал
ожидания [zal aJidanee-ya]
depend: it depends как
сказать [kak skazat]
it depends on ... это
зависит от ... [eta zaveeseet
at ...]
deposit (as security) задаток
[zadatak]
(as part payment) взнос
[vznos]
dessert десерт [dyesyert]
destination: what's your
destination? куда вы едете?
[kooda viy yedeetyeh?]
develop проявлять/
проявить [pra-yavlyat/pra-
yaveet]

dialogue

could you develop these
films? вы можете
проявить эти плёнки?
[viy moJetyeh pra-yaveet etee
plyonkee?]
yes, certainly да, конечно
[da, kanyeshna]
when will they be ready?
когда они будут
готовы? [kagda anee
boodoot gatovi?]
tomorrow afternoon
завтра днём [zaftra dnyom]
how much is the four-hour
service? сколько стоит
проявить за четыре
часа? [skolka sto-eet pra-
yaveet za chyetiyryeh chasa?]

diabetic (noun) диабетик
[dee-abyeteek]
dial (verb)
набирать/набрать номер
[nabeerat/nabrat nomyer]
dialling code код [kod]

 To ring abroad from
Russia, dial 8, wait for the
tone, then dial 10 plus the
following country codes:

Australia	61	UK	44
Ireland	353	US & Canada	1
New Zealand	64		

diamond бриллиант
[breelee-ant]
diaper пелёнка [pyelyonka]

diarrhoea понос [panos]
  **do you have something for
  diarrhoea?** у вас есть
  что-нибудь от поноса? [oo
  vas yest shto-neeboot at panosa?]
diary (for personal experiences)
  дневник [dnyevneek]
  (business) записная книжка
  [zapeesna-ya kneeshka]
dictionary словарь **m** [slavar]
didn't*
  see **not**
die умирать/умереть
  [oomeerat/oomeryet]
diesel дизельное топливо
  [deezyelna-yeh topleeva]
diet диета [dee-yeta]
  I'm on a diet я на диете [ya
  na dee-yetyeh]
  I have to follow a special diet
  (said by man/woman) я
  должен/должна
  соблюдать особую диету
  [ya dolJen/dalJna sablyoodat
  asoboo-yoo dee-yetoo]
difference разница [razneetsa]
  what's the difference? в чём
  разница? [fchom razneetsa?]
different разный [razni]
  they are different они
  разные [anee razni-yeh]
  a different table другой
  столик [droogoy stoleek]
difficult трудный [troodni]
difficulty трудность **f**
  [troodnast]
dining room столовая
  [stalova-ya]
dinner (evening meal) ужин

[ooJin]
  to have dinner
  ужинать/поужинать
  [ooJinat/paooJinat]
direct (adj) прямой [pryamoy]
  is there a direct train? есть
  ли прямой поезд? [yestlee
  pryamoy po-yest?]
direction направление
  [napravlyenee-yeh]
  which direction is it? в
  каком это направлении?
  [fkakom eta napravlyenee-ee?]
  is it in this direction? это в
  этом направлении? [eta
  vetam napravlyenee-ee?]
directory enquiries
  справочная [spravachna-ya]
dirt грязь **f** [gryas]
dirty грязный [gryazni]
disabled инвалид [eenvaleet]
  **is there access for the
  disabled?** есть ли доступ
  для инвалидов? [yestlee
  dostoop dlya eenvaleedaf?]
disappear исчезать/
  исчезнуть [eeschyezat/
  eeschyeznoot]
  my watch has disappeared
  мои часы пропали [ma-ee
  cha-siy prapalee]
**disappointed: I am
  disappointed** (said by
  man/woman) я разочарован/
  разочарована [ya
  razacharovan/razacharovana]
disappointing неважный
  [nyevaJni]
disaster катастрофа

[katastrofa]

disco дискотека [deeskatyeka]

discount скидка [skeetka]

 is there a discount? нет ли
 скидки? [nyetlee skeetkee?]

disease болезнь [balyezn]

disgusting отвратительный
 [atvrateetyelni]

dish блюдо [blyooda]

dishcloth кухонное
 полотенце [kooHan-na-yeh
 palatyentseh]

disinfectant
 дезинфицирующее
 средство [dyezeen-feetsiyroo-
 yoosh-chyeh-yeh sryetstva]

disk (for computer) диск [deesk]

disposable diapers/nappies
 одноразовые пелёнки
 [adnarazavi-yeh pyelyonkee]

distance расстояние
 [rasta-yanee-yeh]

 in the distance на
 расстоянии [na rasta-yanee-
 ee]

district район [r-on]

disturb беспокоить
 [byespako-eet]

diversion (detour) объезд
 [abyest]

divorced: I'm divorced (said by
 man/woman) я разведён/
 разведена [ya razvyedyon/
 razvyedena]

dizzy: I feel dizzy у меня
 кружится голова [oo
 myenya krooJitsa galava]

do делать/сделать [dyelat/
 sdyelat]

what shall we do? что нам
делать? [shto nam dyelat?]

how do you do it? как это
делается? [kak eta
dyela-yetsa?]

will you do it for me?
пожалуйста, сделайте это
для меня [paJalsta, zdyelityeh
eta dlya menya]

dialogues

how do you do?
здравствуйте!
[zdrastvooytyeh!]

nice to meet you приятно
познакомиться [pree-
yatna paznakomeetsa]

what do you do? (work)
кем вы работаете? [kyem
viy rabota-yetyeh?]

I'm a teacher, and you?
(said by man/woman) я
учитель/учительница,
а вы? [ya oocheetyel/
oocheetyelneetsa, aviy?]

I'm a student (said by
man/woman) я студент/
студентка [ya stoodyent/
stoodyentka]

what are you doing this
evening? что вы делаете
сегодня вечером? [shto
viy dyela-yetyeh syevodnya
vyechyeram?]

we're going out for a drink,
do you want to join us?
мы идём куда-нибудь
выпить, не хотите

пойти с нами? [miy eed**yo**m koo**da**-nee**boot viy**peet, nyeh нa**tee**tyeh pi**tee** sna**mee**?]

do you want cream? вы хотите сливки? [viy нa**tee**tyeh slee**f**kee?]
I do, but she doesn't я да, а она нет [ya da, a a**na** nyet]

doctor врач [vrach]
(title) доктор [**do**ktar]
we need a doctor нам нужен врач [nam **noo**Jen vrach]
please call a doctor вызовите, пожалуйста, врача [**viy**zaveetee, pa**Ja**lsta, vra**cha**]

 The standard of doctors varies enormously so seek recommendations before consulting one. If your condition is serious, public hospitals will provide free emergency treatment to foreigners on production of a passport (but may charge for medication). Standards of hygiene and expertise can be low by Western standards.
If you don't want to go to a Russian hospital, then the only option is a private clinic charging US rates, which means that it's vital to take out travel insurance before you leave home. Ideally this should also cover you for medical evacuation if you require it.

dialogue

where does it hurt? где у вас болит? [gdyeh oo vas ba**leet**?]
right here здесь [zdyes]
does that hurt now? а теперь больно? [atye**pyer bol**na?]
yes да [da]
take this to the chemist получите это в аптеке [paloo**chee**tyeh eta vapt**yek**yeh]

document документ [dakoom**yent**]
dog собака [sab**a**ka]
doll кукла [**kook**la]
domestic flight внутренний рейс [v**noo**tryen-nee ryays]
don't!* (to adult/child) перестаньте/перестань! [pyeryest**an**tyeh/pyeryestan!]
don't do that! (to adult/child) не делайте/делай этого! [nyeh d**yel**ityeh/d**yel**i etava!]
door дверь f [dvyer]
doorman швейцар [shvyayts**ar**]
double двойной [dvin**oy**]
double bed двуспальная кровать [dvoospa**l**na-ya krav**at**]
double room двухместный номер [dvooнm**yes**ni n**o**myer]
doughnut пончик [**pon**cheek]
down вниз [vnees]
put it down over there положите там [palaJ**iy**tyeh tam]

it's down there on the right это там, справа [**e**ta tam, sprava]

it's further down the road это дальше по дороге [**e**ta dalsheh pa dar**o**gyeh]

downmarket (restaurant etc) дешёвый [dyesh**o**vi]

downstairs внизу [vneez**oo**]

dozen дюжина [d**yoo**Jina]

half a dozen полдюжины [poldy**oo**Jini]

draught beer бочковое пиво [bachk**o**va-yeh p**ee**va]

draughty: it's draughty дует [d**oo**-yet]

drawer ящик [**ya**sh-cheek]

drawing рисунок [rees**oo**nak]

dreadful ужасный [ooJ**a**sni]

dream сон [son]

(aspiration) мечта [mye**ch**ta]

dress (noun) платье [pl**a**tyeh]

dressed: to get dressed одеваться/одеться [adyev**a**tsa/ad**ye**tsa]

dressing (for cut) перевязка [pyeryev**ya**ska]

(for salad) приправа [preepr**a**va]

dressing gown халат [нal**a**t]

drink (noun) напиток [nap**ee**tak]

(verb) пить/выпить [peet/v**iy**peet]

a cold drink прохладительный напиток [praнlad**ee**tyelni nap**ee**tak]

can I get you a drink? не

хотите ли что-нибудь выпить? [nyeh наt**ee**tyehlee sht**o**-neeboot v**iy**peet?]

what would you like (to drink)? что бы вы хотели (выпить)? [sht**o**bi viy наt**ye**lee (v**iy**peet)?]

no thanks, I don't drink спасибо, я не пью [spas**ee**ba, ya nyeh pyoo]

I'll just have a drink of water стакан воды, пожалуйста [stak**a**n vad**iy**, paJ**a**lsta]

see bar

drinking water питьевая вода [peetyev**a**-ya vad**a**]

is this drinking water? это питьевая вода? [**e**ta peetyev**a**-ya vad**a?**]

drive водить машину [vad**ee**t mash**iy**noo]

we drove here мы приехали сюда на машине [miy pree-**ye**нalee syood**a** na mash**iy**nyeh]

I'll drive you home я отвезу вас домой [ya atvyez**oo** vas dam**oy**]

driver водитель **m** [vad**ee**tyel]

driving licence водительские права [vad**ee**tyelskee-yeh prav**a**]

drop: just a drop, please (of drink) чуть-чуть, пожалуйста [choot-ch**oo**t, paJ**a**lsta]

drug (medical) лекарство [lyek**a**rstva]

drugs (narcotics) наркотики

[narkoteekee]

drunk (adj) пьяный [pyani]

dry (adj) сухой [sooHoy]

dry-cleaner's химчистка [Heemcheestka]

duck утка [ootka]

due: he was due to arrive yesterday он должен был приехать вчера [on dolJen biyl pree-yeнat fchyera]

when is the train due? когда приходит поезд? [kagda preeнodeet po-yest?]

dull (pain) тупой [toopoy] (weather) пасмурный [pasmoorni]

dummy (baby's) пустышка [poostiyshka]

during в течение [ftyechyenee-yeh]

dust пыль [piyl]

dustbin мусорный ящик [moosarni yash-cheek]

dusty пыльный [piylni]

duty-free беспошлинный [byesposhleen-ni]

duty-free shop магазин беспошлинной торговли [magazeen byesposhleen-ni targovlee]

Duty-free allowances from Russia into EU countries are currently 250 cigarettes, two litres of wine or champagne, and one litre of spirits; into the US and Australia, allowances are 200 cigarettes, one litre of wine or spirits, and goods up to the value of $400. These allowances may change in the future, so check with Customs before you leave the country.

duvet одеяло [adye-yala]

E

each (every) каждый [kaJdi]

how much are they each? сколько стоит каждый? [skolka sto-eet kaJdi?]

ear ухо [ooнa]

earache: I have earache у меня болит ухо [oo menya baleet ooнa]

early рано [rana]

early in the morning рано утром [rana ootram]

I called by earlier (said by man/woman) я заходил/ заходила раньше [ya zaнadeel/zaнadeela ransheh]

earrings серьги [syergee]

east восток [vastok]

in the east на востоке [na vastokyeh]

Easter Пасха [pasнa]

eastern восточный [vastochni]

Eastern Europe Восточная Европа [vastochna-ya yevropa]

easy лёгкий [lyoнkee]

eat есть/поесть [yest/pa-yest]

we've already eaten, thanks мы уже поели, спасибо [miy ooJeh pa-yelee, spaseeba]

eating habits

At home, most Russians take breakfast (za**f**trak) seriously, tucking into buckwheat pancakes (bleen**iy**) or porridge (k**a**sha), with curd cheese (tv**o**rok) and sour cream (smet**a**na) – though some simply settle for a cup of tea and a slice of bread. Hotels usually serve an approximation of the Continental breakfast, probably just fried egg, bread, butter and jam; however, ritzier hotels in the big cities may provide a buffet and offer a Western-style brunch on Sundays. Savoury pies (peerashk**ee**) are often sold on the streets from late morning – the best are filled with cabbage, curd cheese or rice; steer clear of the meat ones.

Russians are very fond of cakes (tort). There are over sixty varieties, but the main ingredients are fairly standard: a sponge dough, a good deal of honey and a distinctive spice like cinnamon or ginger or lots of buttery cream and jam. Russians eat ice cream (mar**o**Jena-yeh) whatever the season; it's sold from kiosks in most towns.

Despite the increasing popularity of fast food and foreign cuisine, most Russians remain loyal to their culinary heritage – above all, to 'zak**oo**skee'. These small dishes are consumed before a big meal, as an accompaniment to vodka, or on their own as a light snack at any time of day. Salted fish, like sprats or

herring, are a firm favourite, as are gherkins, assorted cold meats and salads. Hard-boiled eggs or 'bleen**iy**', both served with caviar (eekr**a**), are also available.

At the weekends and when on holiday, many Russians eat their main meal of the day at lunchtime (ab**y**et), between 1 and 4 pm, and have only 'zak**oo**skee' and tea for supper (**oo**Jin), although restaurants concentrate on evening meals and may close for part of the afternoon. Most menus start with a choice of soup or 'zak**oo**skee'. Soup has long played an important role in Russian cuisine. Cabbage soup (sh-chee), served with sour cream, and beetroot soup (borsh-ch) are common.

Main courses are overwhelmingly based on meat (m**ya**sa), usually beef, mutton or pork, sometimes accompanied by a simple sauce (mushroom, sour cream or cheese). Meat may also make its way into 'pyelm**ye**ni', which are dumplings similar in form to ravioli, and often served in a broth.

eau de toilette туалетная
вода [too-al**ye**tna-ya vad**a**]
economy class
экономический класс
[ekanam**ee**chyeskee klass]
Edinburgh Эдинбург
[ed**ee**nboork]
egg яйцо [y**itso**]
eggplant баклажан [baklaJan]

either: either ... or ... или ...
или ... [**ee**lee ... **ee**lee ...]
either of them любой из
них [lyoob**oy** eez neen]
elastic (noun) резинка
[ryez**ee**nka]
elastic band резинка
[ryez**ee**nka]
elbow локоть m [**lo**kat]
electric электрический
[elyektr**ee**chyeskee]
electrical appliances
электрические приборы
[elyektr**ee**chyeskee-yeh preeb**o**ri]
electric fire электрокамин
[elyektrakam**ee**n]
electrician электрик
[el**ye**ktreek]
electricity электричество
[elyektr**ee**chyestva]
see **voltage**
elevator лифт [leeft]
else: something else что-то
другое [sht**o**-ta droog**o**-yeh]
somewhere else где-нибудь
в другом месте
[gd**yeh**-neeboot vdroog**o**m
m**ye**styeh]

dialogue

> **would you like anything
> else?** вы хотите ещё
> что-нибудь? [viy Hat**ee**tyeh
> yesh-ch**o** sht**o**-neeboot?]
> **no, nothing else, thanks**
> нет, спасибо, больше
> ничего [nyet, spas**ee**ba,
> b**o**lsheh neechyev**o**]

e-mail (noun) электронная
почта [elyektr**o**nnaya p**o**chta]
embassy посольство
[pas**o**lstva]
emergency критическая
ситуация [kreet**ee**chyeska-ya
seetoo-**a**tsi-ya]
this is an emergency!
требуется неотложная
помощь! [**try**eboo-yetsa
nyeh-atl**o**Jna-ya p**o**mash-ch!]
emergency exit запасной
выход [zapasn**oy** viy**н**at]
empty пустой [poost**oy**]
end (noun) конец [kan**yets**]
at the end of the street в
конце улицы [fkants**eh**
ooleetsi]
when does it end? когда это
заканчивается? [kagd**a** **e**ta
zak**a**ncheeva-yetsa?]
engaged (toilet/telephone)
занято [z**a**nyata]
(to be married: man/woman)
помолвлен/помолвлена
[pam**o**lvlyen/pam**o**lvlyena]
engine (car) двигатель m
[dv**ee**gatyel]
England Англия [**a**nglee-ya]
English (adj) английский
[angl**ee**skee]
(language) английский язык
[angl**ee**skee yaz**i**k]
I'm English (man/woman) я
англичанин/англичанка
[ya angleech**a**neen/angleech**a**nka]
do you speak English? вы
говорите по-английски?
[vi gavar**eet**-yeh pa-angl**ee**skee?]

91

enjoy: to enjoy oneself
хорошо проводить/
провести время [Harasho
pravadeet/pravyestee vryemya]

dialogue

how did you like the film?
вам понравился
фильм? [vam panraveelsya
feelm?]
I enjoyed it very much, did
you enjoy it? мне очень
понравился, а вам?
[mnyeh ochyen panraveelsa, a
vam?]

enjoyable приятный
[pree-yatni]
enlargement (of photo)
увеличение
[oovyeleechyenee-yeh]
enormous огромный
[agromni]
enough достаточно
[dastatachna]
that's enough достаточно
[dastatachna]
that's not enough этого
недостаточно [etava
nyedastatachna]
it's not big enough это не
достаточно большое [eta
nyeh dastatachna balsho-yeh]
entrance вход [fHot]
(to house) подъезд [padyest]
envelope конверт
[kanvyert]
epileptic эпилептик

[epeelyepteek]
equipment оборудование
[abaroodavanee-yeh]
(for climbing etc) снаряжение
[snaryaJenee-yeh]
(for photography)
фотоаппаратура [fota-ap-
paratoora]
error ошибка [ashiypka]
escalator эскалатор
[eskalatar]
especially особенно
[asobyen-na]
essential основной
[asnavnoy]
it is essential that ...
необходимо, чтобы ...
[nyeh-apHadeema, shtobi ...]
ethnic (restaurant, dress etc)
национальный [natsi-analni]
EU Европейский Союз
[yevrapyayskee sa-yoos]
Europe Европа [yevropa]
European (adj) европейский
[yevrapyayskee]
even даже [daJeh]
even if ... даже если [daJeh
yeslee]
evening вечер [vyechyer]
this evening сегодня
вечером [syevodnya
vyechyeram]
in the evening вечером
[vyechyeram]
evening meal ужин [ooJin]
eventually в конце концов
[fkantseh kantsof]
ever когда-нибудь
[kagda-neeboot]

dialogue

have you ever been to Novgorod? вы когда-нибудь были в Новгороде? [viy kagda-neeboot biylee vnovgaradyeh?]

yes, I was there two years ago (said by man/woman) да, я там был/была два года назад [da, ya tam biyl/bila dva goda nazat]

every каждый [kaJdi]
  every day каждый день [kaJdi dyen]
everyone все [fsyeh]
everything всё [fsyo]
everywhere везде [vyezdyeh]
exactly! совершенно верно [savyershen-na vyerna]
exam экзамен [ekzamyen]
example пример [preemyer]
  for example например [napreemyer]
excellent отличный [atleechni]
  excellent! отлично! [atleechna!]
except кроме [kromyeh]
excess baggage излишек багажа [eezleeshek bagaJa]
exchange rate обменный курс [abmyen-ni koors]
exciting увлекательный [oovlyekatyelni]
excuse me (to get past, to say sorry) извините! [eezveeneetyeh!]

(to get attention) простите! [prasteetyeh!]
(addressing someone with question) извините, пожалуйста ... [eezveeneetyeh, paJalsta ...]
exhausted: I'm exhausted (said by man/woman) я очень устал/устала [ya ochyen oostal/oostala]
exhaust pipe выхлопная труба [viHlapna-ya trooba]
exhibition выставка [viystafka]
exit выход [viyHat]
  where's the nearest exit? где ближайший выход? [gdyeh bleeJishi viyHat?]
expect ожидать [aJidat]
expensive дорогой [daragoy]
experienced опытный [opitni]
explain объяснять/объяснить [abyasnyat/abyasneet]
  can you explain that? вы можете это объяснить? [viy moJetyeh eta abyasneet?]
express (mail) срочное письмо [srochna-yeh peesmo]
  (train, bus) экспресс [ekspres]
extension (telephone) добавочный (номер) [dabavachni (nomyer)]
  extension 221, please добавочный двести двадцать один, пожалуйста [dabavachni dvyestee dvatsat adeen, paJalsta]

extension lead удлинитель [oodleen**ee**tyel]

extra: can we have an extra one? можно ещё один? [m**o**Jna yesh-ch**o** ad**ee**n?]

do you charge extra for that? вы берёте дополнительную плату за это? [viy byer**yo**tyeh dapaln**ee**tyelnoo-yoo pl**a**too za **e**ta?]

extraordinary удивительный [oodeev**ee**tyelni]

extremely крайне [kr**i**nyeh]

eye глаз [glas]

will you keep an eye on my suitcase for me? присмотрите, пожалуйста, за моим чемоданом [preesmatr**ee**tyeh, paJ**a**lsta, za ma-**ee**m chyemad**a**nam]

eyebrow pencil карандаш для бровей [karand**a**sh dlya brav**yay**]

eye drops глазные капли [glazn**i**y-yeh k**a**plee]

eyeglasses очки [achk**ee**]

eyeliner карандаш для глаз [karand**a**sh dlya glas]

eye shadow тени для век pl [t**ye**nee dlya vyek]

F

face лицо [leets**o**]

factory фабрика [f**a**breeka]

faint (verb) падать/упасть в обморок [p**a**dat/oop**a**st v**o**bmarak]

she's fainted она упала в обморок [an**a** oop**a**la v**o**bmarak]

I feel faint мне дурно [mnyeh d**oo**rna]

fair (funfair) парк аттракционов [park at-traktsi-on**a**f]

(trade) выставка [v**i**ystafka]

(adj: just) справедливый [spravyedl**ee**vi]

fairly довольно [dav**o**lna]

fake подделка [pad-d**ye**lka]

fall (verb) падать/упасть [p**a**dat/oop**a**st]

she's had a fall она упала [an**a** oop**a**la]

fall (US: autumn) осень f [**o**syen]

in the fall осенью [**o**syenyoo]

false ложный [l**o**Jni]

family семья [syem**ya**]

famous знаменитый [znamyen**ee**ti]

fan (electrical) вентилятор [vyenteel**ya**tar]

(sport: man/woman) любитель/любительница [lyoob**ee**tyel/lyoob**ee**tyelneetsa]

fantastic замечательный [zamyech**a**tyelni]

far далеко [dalyek**o**]

dialogue

is it far from here? это далеко отсюда? [**e**ta dalyek**o** ats**yoo**da?]

no, not very far нет, не
очень далеко [nyet, nyeh
ochyen dalyek**o**]
well how far? как далеко?
[kak dalyek**o**?]
it's about 20 kilometres
примерно двадцать
километров [preem**y**erna
dvatsat keelam**y**etraf]

fare стоимость **f** проезда
[st**o**-eemast pra-**ye**zda]
farm ферма [**f**yerma]
fashionable модный [**mo**dni]
fast быстрый [**bi**ystri]
fat (person) толстый [**to**lsti]
(on meat) жир [Jir]
father отец [at**ye**ts]
father-in-law (wife's father)
тесть [tyest]
(husband's father) свёкор
[sv**yo**kar]
faucet кран [kran]
fault (mechanical)
неисправность **f** [nyeh-
eespr**a**vnast]
sorry, it was my fault
извините, это моя вина
[eezveen**ee**tyeh, eta ma-**ya** veena]
it's not my fault это не моя
вина [**e**ta nyeh ma-**ya** veena]
faulty: this is faulty это не
работает [**e**ta nyeh rab**o**ta-yet]
favourite любимый
[lyoob**ee**mi]
fax (noun) факс [faks]
(verb) посылать/послать
по факсу [pasil**a**t/pasl**a**t pa
faks**oo**]

I want to send a fax Я хочу
послать факс [ya Hach**oo**
pasl**a**t faks]

Given the inadequacy of
the postal system, it's
better to use fax, telex,
telegram or electronic mail.
Most large hotels, even those in the
regional towns and cities, now have
a business centre offering an
immediate fax-sending service, via
satellite link. Otherwise, it is usually
possible to send a fax from the main
post office. For a fee you can also
arrange to receive faxes; if you leave
your number, the post office should
notify you when a fax arrives.

fax (machine) факс [faks]
February февраль **m** [fyevr**a**l]
feel чувствовать/
почувствовать [ch**oo**stvavat/
pach**oo**stvavat]
I feel hot мне жарко [mnyeh
Jarka]
I feel unwell мне нехорошо
[mnyeh nyeh-Harash**o**]
I feel like going for a walk
мне хочется прогуляться
[mnyeh H**o**chyetsa pragool**ya**tsa]
how are you feeling? как вы
себя чувствуете? [kak viy
syeb**ya** ch**oo**stvoo-yetyeh?]
I'm feeling better мне
лучше [mnyeh l**oo**chsheh]
felt-tip (pen) фломастер
[flam**a**styer]
fence забор [zab**o**r]

fender (of car) бампер
[bampyer]

ferry паром [parom]

festival фестиваль **m**
[fyesteeval]

fetch: I'll fetch him я схожу
за ним [ya sнaJoo za neem]

will you come and fetch me
later? вы зайдёте за мной
попозже? [viy zidyotyeh za
mnoy papoJ-Jeh?]

feverish: I'm feverish меня
лихорадит [myenya
leeнaradeet]

few: a few несколько
[nyeskalka]

a few days несколько дней
[nyeskalka dnyay]

fiancé жених [Jeneeн]

fiancée невеста [nyevyesta]

field поле [polyeh]

fight (noun) драка [draka]

figs инжир [eenJiyr]

fill in заполнять/заполнить
[zapalnyat/zapolneet]

do I have to fill this in? мне
нужно это заполнить?
[mnyeh nooJna eta zapolneet?]

fill up наполнять/
наполнить [napalnyat/
napolneet]

fill it up, please полный
бак, пожалуйста [polni bak,
paJalsta]

filling (in cake, sandwich)
начинка [nacheenka]
(in tooth) пломба [plomba]

film (movie) фильм [feelm]
(for camera) плёнка [plyonka]

dialogue

do you have this kind of
film? у вас есть такая
плёнка? [oo vas yest taka-ya
plyonka?]

yes, how many exposures?
да, на сколько кадров?
[da, na skolka kadraf?]

36 тридцать шесть
[treetsat shest]

film processing проявление
плёнки [pra-yavlyenee-yeh
plyonkee]

filthy грязный [gryazni]

find (verb) находить/найти
[naнadeet/niitee]

I can't find it я не могу это
найти [ya nyeh magoo eta nitee]

I've found it (said by
man/woman) я нашёл/нашла
это [ya nashol/nashla eta]

find out узнавать/узнать
[ooznavat/ooznat]

could you find out for me?
вы не могли бы узнать
для меня [viy nyeh magleebi
ooznat dlya myenya?]

fine (weather) хороший
[нaroshi]
(punishment) штраф [shtraf]

dialogues

how are you? как у вас
дела? [kak oo vas dyela?]

I'm fine thanks хорошо,
спасибо [нarasho, spaseeba]

is that OK? так хорошо?
[tak Harasho?]
that's fine thanks
хорошо, спасибо
[Harasho, spaseeba]

finger палец [palyets]
finish (verb) заканчивать/
закончить [zakancheevat/
zakoncheet]
I haven't finished yet (said by
man/woman) я ещё не
закончил/закончила [ya
yesh-cho nyeh zakoncheel/
zakoncheela]
when does it finish? когда
это заканчивается? [kagda
eta zakancheeva-yetsa?]
Finland Финляндия
[feenlyandee-ya]
fire (in hearth) огонь **m** [agon]
(campfire) костёр [kastyor]
(blaze) пожар [paJar]
fire! пожар! [paJar!]
can we light a fire here?
здесь можно разложить
костёр? [zdyes moJna razlaJiyt
kastyor?]
my room is on fire! в моём
номере пожар! [vma-yom
nomyeryeh paJar!]
fire alarm пожарная
тревога [paJarna-ya tryevoga]
fire brigade пожарная
команда [paJarna-ya kamanda]

To call out the fire brigade
dial 01.

fire escape пожарная
лестница [paJarna-ya
lyesneetsa]
fire extinguisher
огнетушитель **m**
[agnyetooshiytyel]
first первый [pyervi]
I was first (said by man) я был
первым [ya biyl pyervim]
(said by woman) я была
первой [ya biyla pyervi]
at first сначала [snachala]
the first time первый раз
[pyervi ras]
first turn on the left первый
поворот налево [pyervi
pavarot nalyeva]
first aid первая помощь **f**
[pyerva-ya pomash-ch]
first-aid kit походная
аптечка [paHodna-ya
aptyechka]
first class (travel etc) первым
классом [pyervim klasam]
first floor второй этаж
[ftaroy etash]
(US) первый этаж [pyervi
etash]
first name имя [eemya]
fish (noun) рыба [riyba]
fit (attack) приступ [preestoop]
fit: it doesn't fit me это мне
не по размеру [eta mnyeh
nyeh pa razmyeroo]
fitting room примерочная
[pryemyerachna-ya]
fix (verb: arrange) чинить/
починить [cheeneet/
pacheeneet]

can you fix this? (repair) вы можете это починить? [viy moJetyeh eta pacheeneet?]

fizzy газированный [gazeerovan-ni]

flag флаг [flag]

flash (for camera) вспышка [fspIyshka]

flat (noun: apartment) квартира [kvarteera]
(adj) плоский [ploskee]

I've got a flat tyre у меня спустила шина [oo menya spoosteela shIyna]

flavour вкус [fkoos]

flea блоха [blaHa]

flight рейс [ryays]

flight number номер рейса [nomyer ryaysa]

flood наводнение [navadnyenee-yeh]

floor (of room) пол [pol]
(storey) этаж [etash]

on the floor на полу [na paloo]

florist цветочный магазин [tsvyetochni magazeen]

flour мука [mooka]

flower цветок [tsvyetok]

flu грипп [greep]

fluent: he speaks fluent Russian он бегло говорит по-русски [on byegla gavareet pa-rooskee]

fly (noun) муха [mooHa]
(verb) лететь/полететь [lyetyet/palyetyet]

can we fly there? туда можно полететь? [tooda

moJna palyetyet?]

fog туман [tooman]

foggy туманный [tooman-ni]

folk dancing народные танцы pl [narodni-yeh tantsi]

folk music народная музыка [narodna-ya moozika]

follow следовать/последовать [slyedavat/paslyedavat]

follow me следуйте за мной [slyedooytyeh za mnoy]

food еда [yeda]

food poisoning пищевое отравление [peesh-chyevo-yeh atravlyenee-yeh]

food shop/store гастроном [gastranom]

foot (of person) ступня [stoopnya]

on foot пешком [pyeshkom]

football (game) футбол [footbol]
(ball) футбольный мяч [footbolni myach]

football match футбольный матч [footbolni match]

for: do you have something for a headache/diarrhoea? у вас есть что-то от головной боли/поноса? [oo vas yest shto-ta at galavnoy bolee/panosa?]

dialogues

who's the chicken Kiev for? для кого котлеты по-Киевски? [dlya kavo katlyeti pa-kee-yefskee?]

that's for me это для меня [**eta** dlya men**ya**]
and this one? а это? [a **eta**?]
that's for her это для неё [**eta** dlya nyeh-**yo**]

where do I get the bus for Belorussky station? откуда идёт автобус до Белорусского вокзала? [atk**oo**da eed**yot** aft**o**boos da byelar**oo**skava vakz**a**la?]
the bus for the railway station leaves from Tverskaya street автобус до вокзала идёт с Тверской улицы [aft**o**boos da vakz**a**la eed**yot** stvyersk**oy oo**leetsi]

how long have you been here? вы давно приехали? [viy davn**o** pree-**ye**Halee?]
I've been here for two days, how about you? я здесь уже два дня, а вы? [ya zdyes ooJ**eh** dva dnya, a viy?]
I've been here for a week я здесь уже неделю [ya zdyes ooJ**eh** nyed**ye**lyoo]

forehead лоб [lop]
foreign иностранный [eenastr**an**-ni]
foreigner (man/woman) иностранец/иностранка [eenastr**a**nyets/eenastr**a**nka]
forest лес [lyes]
forget забывать/забыть [zabiv**at**/zab**iy**t]
I forget, I've forgotten (said by man/woman) я забыл/забыла [ya zab**iy**l/zab**iy**la]
fork (for eating) вилка [**vee**lka]
form (document) бланк [blank]
formal (dress) вечерний [vyech**ye**rnee]
fortnight две недели [dvyeh nyed**ye**lee]
fortunately к счастью [ksh-ch**a**styoo]
forward: could you forward my mail? вы не могли бы переслать мне мою почту [viy nyeh magl**ee**bi pyeryesl**a**t mnyeh ma-**yoo** pochtoo]
forwarding address адрес для пересылки [**a**dryes dlya pyeryes**iy**lkee]
foundation (make-up) тональный крем [tan**a**lni kryem]
fountain фонтан [fant**an**]
foyer (hotel, theatre) фойе [fay-**yeh**]
fracture перелом [pyeryel**om**]
France Франция [fr**a**ntsi-ya]
free (no charge) бесплатный [byespl**a**tni]
is it free (of charge)? это бесплатно? [eta byespl**a**tna?]
freeway автострада [aftastr**a**da]
freezer морозилка [maraz**ee**lka]

French (adj, language)
французский [frantsooskee]
French fries картофель фри
[kartofyel free]
frequent частый [chasti]
how frequent is the bus to
Suzdal? как часто ходят
автобусы в Суздаль? [kak
chasta Hodyat aftoboosi fsoozdal?]
fresh (weather, breeze)
прохладный [praHladni]
(fruit etc) свежий [svyeЈi]
fresh orange juice свежий
апельсиновый сок [svyeЈi
apyelseenavi sok]
Friday пятница [pyatneetsa]
fridge холодильник
[Haladeelneek]
fried жареный [Јaryeni]
fried egg яичница
[ya-eeshneetsa]
friend (male/female)
друг/подруга
[drook/padrooga]
friendly дружеский
[drooЈeskee]
from: when does the next train
from Yaroslavl arrive? когда
приходит следующий
поезд из Ярославля?
[kagda preeHodeet slyedoosh-chee
po-yest eez yaraslavlya?]
from Monday to Friday с
понедельника до
пятницы [spanyedyelneeka da
pyatneetsi]
from Moscow to Tver от
Москвы до Твери [at
maskviy da tvyeree]

dialogue

where are you from? вы
откуда? [viy atkooda?]
I'm from England я из
англии [ya eez anglee-ee]

front передняя часть
[pyeryednya-ya chast]
in front впереди [fpyeryedee]
in front of the hotel перед
гостиницей [pyeryed
gasteeneetsay]
at the front спереди
[spyeryedee]
frost мороз [maros]
frozen замёрзший
[zamyorshi]
frozen food замороженные
продукты [zamaroЈeni-yeh
pradookti]
fruit фрукты [frookti]
fruit juice фруктовый сок
[frooktovi sok]
frying pan сковородка
[skavarotka]
FSS ФСБ (Федеральная
Служба Безопасности)
[ef-es-beh (fyedyeralna-ya slooЈba
byezapasnastee)]
full полный [polni]
this fish is full of bones в
этой рыбе одни кости
[veti riybyeh adnee kostee]
I'm full (said by man/woman) я
наелся/наелась [ya
na-yelsya/na-yelas]
full board полный пансион
[polni pansee-on]

fun: it was fun было весело
[b**i**yla v**ye**syela]

funeral похороны pl
[p**o**Harani]

funny (strange) странный
[str**a**n-ni]
(amusing) забавный [zab**a**vni]

fur мех [myeн]
fur hat меховая шапка
[myeн**a**va-ya sh**a**pka]

furniture мебель f [m**ye**byel]

further дальше [d**a**lsheh]
it's further down the road это
дальше по улице [**e**ta
d**a**lsheh pa **oo**leetseh]

dialogue

how much further is it to
Klin? далеко ли ещё до
Клина? [dalyek**o**lee yesh-ch**o**
da kl**ee**na?]
about 5 kilometres около
пяти километров [**o**kala
pyat**ee** keelam**ye**traf]

fuse предохранитель m
[pryedaнran**ee**tyel]
the lights have fused свет
перегорел [svyet pyeryegar**ye**l]
fuse wire проволока для
предохранителя [pr**o**valaka
dlya pryedaнran**ee**tyelya]

future будущее
[b**oo**doosh-chyeh-yeh]
in future в будущем
[vb**oo**doosh-chyem]

G

game (cards etc) игра [eegr**a**]
(match) матч [match]
(meat) дичь f [deech]

garage (for fuel)
бензоколонка
[byenzakal**o**nka]
(for repairs) станция
техобслуживания
[st**a**ntsi-ya tyeнapsl**oo**Jivanee-ya]
(for parking) гараж [gar**a**sh]

garden сад [sat]

garlic чеснок [chyesn**o**k]

gas газ [gas]
(US: petrol) бензин [byenz**ee**n]

gas cylinder (camping gas)
газовый баллон [g**a**zavi
bal**o**n]

gas-permeable lenses
газопроницаемые линзы
[gazapraneets**a**-yemi-yeh l**ee**nzi]

gas station бензоколонка
[byenzakal**o**nka]

gate ворота [var**o**ta]
(at airport) выход [v**i**yнat]

gay гомосексуалист
[gomaseksoo-al**ee**est]

gay bar бар для
гомосексуалистов [bar dlya
gomaseksoo-al**ee**estaf]

gear передача [pyeryed**a**cha]

gearbox коробка передач
[kar**o**pka pyeryed**a**ch]

general (adj) общий
[**o**psh-chee]

general delivery до
востребования

[da vastryebavanee-ya]

gents' toilet мужской
туалет [mooshskoy too-alyet]

genuine (antique etc)
подлинный [podleen-ni]

German (adj) немецкий
[nyemyetskee]

Germany Германия
[gyermanee-ya]

get (fetch) приносить/
принести [preenaseet/
preenyestee]

could you get me another
one, please? принесите,
пожалуйста, ещё один
[preenyeseetyeh, paJalsta, yesh-cho
adeen]

how do I get to ...? как
попасть в ...? [kak papast
v ...?]

do you know where I can get
them? вы не знаете, где я
могу их достать [viy nyeh
zna-yetyeh, gdyeh ya magoo eeн
dastat?]

dialogue

can I get you a drink??
что вы будете пить?
[shto viy boodyetyeh peet?]
no, I'll get this one, what
would you like? нет,
позвольте мне, что бы
вы хотели? [nyet, pazvoltyeh
mnyeh, shto biy viy нatyelee?]
a glass of red wine бокал
красного вина [bakal
krasnava veena]

get back (return)
возвращаться/вернуться
[vazvrash-chatsa/vyernootsa]

get in (arrive) приезжать/
приехать [pree-yeJ-
Jat/pree-yeнat]

get off выходить/выйти
[viнadeet/viytee]

where do I get off? где мне
выходить? [gdyeh mnyeh
viнadeet?]

get on (to train etc) садиться/
сесть [sadeetsa/syest]

get out (of car etc) выходить/
выйти [viнadeet/viytee]

get up (in the morning)
вставать/встать [fstavat/
fstat]

gift подарок [padarak]

gift shop магазин
сувениров [magazeen
soovyeneeraf]

gin джин [djin]

a gin and tonic, please джин
с тоником, пожалуйста
[djin stoneekam, paJalsta]

girl (child) девочка [dyevachka]
(young woman) девушка
[dyevooshka]

girlfriend подруга [padrooga]

give давать/дать [davat/dat]

can you give me some
change? вы не
разменяете? [viy nyeh
razmyenya-yetyeh?]

I gave it to him (said by
man/woman) я отдал/отдала
ему это [ya ad-dal/ad-dala
yemoo eta]

will you give this to ...?
передайте это,
пожалуйста, ... [pyeryedItyeh
eta, пaлalsta, ...]

dialogue

**how much do you want for
this?** сколько вы хотите
за это? [sk**o**lka viy нat**ee**tyeh
za **e**ta?]

40,000 roubles сорок
тысяч рублей [s**o**rak
t**i**ysyach roobl**ya**y]

I'll give you 30,000 я
дам вам тридцать
тысяч [ya dam vam tr**ee**tsat
t**i**ysyach]

give back возвращать/
вернуть [vazvrash-ch**a**t/
vyern**oo**t]

glad: I'm glad (said by
man/woman) я рад/рада [ya
rat/r**a**da]

glass (material) стекло
[sty**e**klo]
(for drinking) стакан [stak**a**n]

a glass of wine бокал вина
[bak**a**l v**ee**na]

glasses очки [ach**ee**]

gloves перчатки [pyerch**a**tkee]

glue (noun) клей [kly**a**y]

go (on foot) идти/пойти [eet-
t**ee**/p**ee**tee]
(by transport) ехать/поехать
[y**e**нat/pa-y**e**нat]

we'd like to go to the Kremlin
мы хотели бы сходить в

Кремль [miy нat**ye**leebi sнad**ee**t
fkr**ye**ml]

where are you going? куда
вы идёте? [k**oo**da viy
eed**yo**tyeh?]

where does this bus go?
куда идёт этот автобус?
[k**oo**da eed**yo**t **e**tat aft**o**boos?]

let's go! пойдемте!
[pid**yo**mtyeh!]

she's gone (left) она ушла
[an**a** oosh**la**]

where has he gone? куда он
ушёл? [k**oo**da on oosh**o**l?]

I went there last week (said by
man/woman) я там был/была
на прошлой неделе [ya tam
biyl/bil**a** na pr**o**shli nyed**ye**lyeh]

hamburger to go гамбургер
на вынос [gamb**oo**rgyer na
v**iy**nas]

go away уходить/уйти
[ooнad**ee**t/ooyt**ee**]

go away! уходите!
[ooнad**ee**tyeh!]

go back (return)
возвращаться/вернуться
[vazvrash-ch**a**tsa/vyern**oo**tsa]

go down (the stairs etc)
спускаться/спуститься
[spoosk**a**tsa/spoost**ee**tsa]

go in входить/войти
[fнad**ee**t/vit**ee**]

**go out: do you want to go out
tonight?** вы не хотите
куда-нибудь пойти
сегодня вечером? [viy nyeh
нat**ee**tyeh kooda-neeb**oo**d pit**ee**
syev**o**dnya v**ye**chyeram?]

go through проходить/
пройти [praHadeet/pritee]
go up (the stairs etc)
подниматься/подняться
[padneematsa/padnyatsa]
goat коза [kaza]
God бог [boH]
goggles защитные очки
[zash-cheetni-yeh achkee]
gold золото [zolata]
good хороший [Haroshi]
good! хорошо! [Harasho!]
it's no good это не годится
[eta nyeh gadeetsa]
goodbye до свидания [da
sveedanya]
good evening добрый вечер
[dobri vyechyer]
Good Friday Страстная
Пятница [strasna-ya
pyatneetsa]
good morning доброе утро
[dobra-yeh ootra]
good night (leaving) до
свидания [da sveedanya]
(when going to bed)
спокойной ночи [spakoyni
nochee]
goose гусь m [goos]
got: we've got to leave нам
нужно идти [nam nooJna eet-
tee]
have you got any ...? у вас
есть ... [oo vas yest ...]
government правительство
[praveetyelstva]
gradually постепенно
[pastyepyen-na]
gram(me) грамм [gram]

grammar грамматика [gram-
mateeka]
granddaughter внучка
[vnoochka]
grandfather дедушка
[dyedooshka]
grandmother бабушка
[babooshka]
grandson внук [vnook]
grapefruit грейпфрут
[gryaypfroot]
grapefruit juice
грейпфрутовый сок
[gryaypfrootavi sok]
grapes виноград [veenagrat]
grass трава [trava]
grateful благодарный
[blagadarni]
gravy соус [so-oos]
great (excellent)
замечательный
[zamyechatyelni]
that's great! здорово!
[zdorava!]
a great success большой
успех [balshoy oospyeH]
Great Britain
Великобритания
[vyeleekabreetanee-ya]
Greece Греция [gryetsi-ya]
greedy жадный [Jadni]
green зелёный [zyelyoni]
greengrocer's овощной
магазин [avash-chnoy
magazeen]
grey серый [syeri]
grilled жареный на
рашпере [Jaryeni na
rashpyeryeh]

grocer's бакалейный магазин [bakal**yay**ni maga**zeen**]

ground: on the ground на земле [na zyeml**yeh**]

ground floor первый этаж [p**y**ervi e**tash**]

group группа [gr**oo**p-pa]

guarantee (noun) гарантия [garan**tee**-ya]

guest (man/woman) гость/ гостья [gost/g**o**stya]

guesthouse дом для приезжих [dom dlya pree-**ye**J-JiH]
see hotel

guide (noun: man/woman) гид [geet]

guidebook путеводитель m [pooteeva**dee**tyel]

guided tour экскурсия с гидом [eks**koor**see-ya z**gee**dam]

guitar гитара [gee**ta**ra]

gum (in mouth) десна [dyes**na**]

gun (pistol) пистолет [peesta**lyet**]
(rifle) ружье [rooj**yo**]

gym спортзал [sport**zal**]

gymnastics гимнастика [geem**na**steeka]

H

hair волосы pl [**vo**lasi]

hairbrush щётка для волос [sh-ch**o**tka dlya va**los**]

haircut стрижка [**stree**shka]

hairdresser's парикмахерская

[pareeH**ma**Hyerska-ya]

hairdryer фен [fyen]

hair gel гель для волос m [gyel dlya va**los**]

hair grips шпильки [sh**peel**kee]

hairspray лак для волос [lak dlya va**los**]

half* половина [pala**vee**na]

half an hour полчаса [pol-cha**sa**]

half a litre пол-литра [pol-**lee**tra]

about half that примерно половина от этого [preem**yer**na pala**vee**na at **e**tava]

half board полупансион [**po**loo-pansee-**on**]

half-bottle полбутылки [polboo**tyl**kee]

half fare половинный тариф [pala**veen**-ni ta**reef**]

half-price полцены [pol-tsen**iy**]

ham ветчина [vyet**chee**na]

hamburger гамбургер [**gam**boorger]

hand рука [roo**ka**]

handbag сумочка [**soo**machka]

handbrake ручной тормоз [rooch**noy to**rmas]

handkerchief носовой платок [nasa**voy** pla**tok**]

handle (on door, suitcase etc) ручка [**roo**chka]

hand luggage ручная кладь f [rooch**na**-ya klat]

hangover похмелье [paH**myel**yeh]

I've got a hangover я с похмелья [ya sранmyelya]

happen случаться/ случиться [sloochatsa/ sloocheetsa]

what's happening? что нового? [shto novava?]

what has happened? что случилось? [shto sloocheelas?]

happy счастливый [sh-chastleevi]

I'm not happy about this мне это не нравится [mnyeh eta nyeh nraveetsa]

harbour порт [port]

hard твёрдый [tvyordi] (difficult) трудный [troodni]

hard-boiled egg яйцо вкрутую [yitso fkrootoo-yoo]

hard currency валюта [valyoota]

hard lenses жёсткие линзы [Joskee-yeh leensi]

hardly едва [yedva]

hardly ever очень редко [ochyen ryetka]

hardware shop хозяйственный магазин [Hazyıstvyen-ni magazeen]

hat шляпа [shlyapa] (with flaps) шапка [shapka]

hate (verb) ненавидеть [nyenaveedyet]

have* иметь [eemyet]

can I have ...? можно, пожалуйста ...? [moJna, paJalsta ...?]

do you have ...? у вас есть ...? [oo vas yest ...?]

what'll you have? что бы вы хотели? [shto biy viy Hatyelee?]

I have to leave now мне нужно идти [mnyeh noojna eet-tee]

do I have to ...? нужно ли мне ...? [nooJnalee mnyeh ...?]

can we have some ...? можно, пожалуйста ...? [moJna, paJalsta ...?]

hayfever сенная лихорадка [syen-naya leeнaratka]

hazelnuts фундук [foondook]

he* он [on]

head голова [galava]

headache головная боль f [galavna-ya bol]

headlights фары [fari]

healthy здоровый [zdarovi]

hear слышать/услышать [sliyshat/oosliyshat]

dialogue

can you hear me? вы меня слышите? [viy myenya sliyshityeh?]

I can't hear you, could you repeat that? я вас не слышу, повторите, пожалуйста [ya vas nyeh sliyshoo, paftareetyeh, paJalsta]

hearing aid слуховой аппарат [slooнavoy aparat]

heart сердце [syertseh]

heart attack сердечный приступ [syerdyechni

preestoop]

heartburn изжога [eezJoga]

heat жара [Jara]

heater (in room, car)
обогреватель [abagryevatyel]

heating отопление
[ataplyenee-yeh]

heavy тяжёлый [tyeJoli]

heel (of foot) пятка [pyatka]
(of shoe) каблук [kablook]
please could you heel these?
вы можете поставьте
сюда набойки? [viy moJetyeh
pastaveet syooda naboykee?]

heelbar мастерская по
ремонту обуви [mastyerska-
ya pa ryemontoo oboovee]

height (of person) рост [rost]
(of mountain, building etc)
высота [visata]

helicopter вертолёт
[vyertalyot]

hello здравствуйте
[zdrastvooytyeh]
(answer on phone) алло [allo]

helmet (for motorcycle) шлем
[shlyem]

help (noun) помощь f
[pomash-ch]
(verb) помогать/помочь
[pamagat/pamoch]
help! помогите!
[pamageetyeh!]
can you help me? вы
можете мне помочь? [viy
moJetyeh mnyeh pamoch?]
**thank you very much for your
help** большое спасибо за
помощь [balsho-yeh spaseeba

za pomash-ch]

helpful полезный [palyezni]

hepatitis гепатит [gyepateet]

her*: I haven't seen her (said by
man/woman) я её не
видел/видела [ya yeh-**yo** nyeh
veedyel/veedyela]
to her ей [yay]
with her с ней [snyay]
for her для неё [dlya nyeh-**yo**]
that's her это она [eta ana]
that's her towel это её
полотенце [eta yeh-**yo**
palatyentseh]

herbal tea травяной чай
[travyan**oy** chi]

herbs кухонные травы
[**koo**Han-ni-yeh travi]

here здесь [zdyes]
here is/are ... вот ... [vot...]
here you are вот,
пожалуйста [vot, paJalsta]

hers* её [yeh-**yo**]
that's hers это её [eta yeh-**yo**]

hey! эй! [ay!]

hi! (hello) привет! [preevyet!]

hide (verb) прятаться/
спрятаться [pryatatsa/
spryatatsa]

high высокий [visokee]

highchair высокий детский
стул [visokee dyetskee stool]

highway (US) автострада
[aftastrada]

hill холм [Holm]

him*: I haven't seen him (said
by man/woman) я его не
видел/видела [ya yevo nyeh
veedyel/veedyela]

to him ему [yem**oo**]

with him с ним [sneem]

for him для него [dlya ny**e**vo]

that's him это он [**e**ta on]

hip бедро [byedr**o**]

hire брать/взять напрокат [brat/vzyat naprak**a**t]

for hire напрокат [naprak**a**t]

where can I hire a bike? где я могу взять напрокат велосипед? [gdyeh ya mag**oo** vzyat naprak**a**t vyelaseep**ye**t?]

see rent

his*: it's his car это его машина [**e**ta yevo mash**ee**na]

that's his это его [**e**ta yev**o**]

hit (verb) ударять/ударить [oodar**ya**t/oodar**ee**t]

hitch-hike путешествовать автостопом [pootyesh**e**stvavat aftast**o**pam]

hobby хобби n [H**o**b-bee]

hockey хоккей m [Hak**ya**y]

hold (verb) держать/подержать [dyerJ**a**t/padyerJ**a**t]

hole дыра [dir**a**]

holiday праздник [pr**a**zneek]

on holiday в отпуске [v**o**tpooskyeh]

Holland Голландия [gal**a**ndee-ya]

home дом [dom]

at home (in my house etc) дома [d**o**ma]

(in my country) на родине [na r**o**deenyeh]

we go home tomorrow мы едем домой завтра [miy yedyem dam**oy** z**a**ftra]

honest честный [ch**ye**sni]

honey мёд [myot]

honeymoon медовый месяц [myed**o**vi m**ye**syats]

hood (US: of car) капот [kap**o**t]

hope (verb) надеяться [nad**ye**h-yatsa]

I hope so надеюсь, что да [nad**ye**h-yoos, shto da]

I hope not надеюсь, что нет [nad**ye**h-yoos, shto nyet]

hopefully надо надеяться [nada nad**ye**h-yatsa]

horn (of car) гудок [good**o**k]

horrible ужасный [ooJ**a**sni]

horse лошадь f [l**o**shat]

horse riding верховая езда [vyerH**a**va-ya yezd**a**]

hospital больница [balnee**tsa**]

hospitality гостеприимство [gastyepree-**ee**mstva]

thank you for your hospitality спасибо за ваше гостеприимство [spas**ee**ba za v**a**sheh gastyepree-**ee**mstva]

hot (water, food) горячий [gary**a**chee]

(weather) жаркий [J**a**rkee]

(spicy) острый [**o**stri]

I'm hot мне жарко [mnyeh J**a**rka]

it's hot today сегодня жарко [syev**o**dnya J**a**rka]

hotel гостиница [gast**ee**neetsa]

Most hotels are still unused to coping with people just turning up without booking. That's not to say that they won't have a room for you, but the price will in all likelihood be far above the rate charged to package tourists. While joint-venture hotels are comparable to their Western four-and five-star counterparts, wholly Russian places tend to have lower standards than suggested by the Intourist system of two to four stars, which should be taken with a pinch of salt. Four-star hotels tend to date from the 1980s and come closest to matching the standards (and prices) of their Western counterparts. When checking in you should receive a 'propoosk' or guest card that enables you to get past the doorman and claim your room key. Most hotels have a service bureau, which can obtain theatre tickets, arrange tours, rental cars and the like. Each floor is monitored by a 'dyeʤoorna-ya' or concierge, who will keep your key while you are away and can arrange to have your laundry done. A small gift to her on arrival should help resolve any ensuing problems, but her presence is no guarantee of security. Many hotels do not include breakfast in the price, so it's always wise to check beforehand. As hotels are expensive, anyone on a tight budget will be limited to the dingiest, dodgiest ones, and will almost certainly do better by opting for a hostel or private accommodation instead. Forget about campsites, which are miles outside the city, have poor facilities and security, and only function over the summer. In summer, it's wise to reserve hostel accommodation in advance.

hotel room номер [**no**myer]
hour час [chas]
house дом [dom]
hovercraft судно на воздушной подушке [**soo**dna na vaz**doo**shni pad**oo**shkyeh]
how как [kak]
  how many? сколько? [sk**o**lka?]
  how do you do? здравствуйте [zdr**a**stvooytyeh]

dialogue

  how are you? как дела? [kak dyel**a**?]
  fine, thanks, and you? хорошо, спасибо, а у вас? [Harash**o**, spas**ee**ba, a oo vas?]

  how much is it? сколько это стоит? [sk**o**lka **e**ta st**o**-eet?]
  10,500 roubles десять тысяч пятьсот рублей [d**ye**syat t**iy**syach pyats**o**t

 Но

roob**lyay**]
I'll take it я возьму это
[ya vaz**moo** eta]

humid влажный [vla**j**ni]
Hungary Венгрия
[**vye**ngree-ya]
hungry голодный [ga**lo**dni]
 are you hungry? вы
 голодны? [viy g**o**ladni?]
hurry (verb) спешить
 [spyesh**iyt**]
 I'm in a hurry я спешу [ya
 spyesh**oo**]
 there's no hurry это не к
 спеху [eta nyeh ksp**ye**Hoo]
 hurry up! быстрее!
 [bistr**yeh**-yeh]
hurt (verb) причинять/
 причинить боль
 [preecheen**yat**/preecheen**eet** bol]
 it hurts больно [**bo**lna]
 it really hurts очень больно
 [**o**chyen b**o**lna]
husband муж [moosh]
hydrofoil судно на
 подводных крыльях
 [**soo**dna na padv**o**dniH kr**iy**lyaн]

I

I* я [ya]
ice лёд [lyot]
 with ice со льдом [sald**o**m]
 no ice, thanks безо льда,
 пожалуйста [byezald**a**,
 pa**j**alsta]
ice cream мороженое

[mar**o**jena-yeh]
ice-cream cone рожок [raj**o**k]
ice lolly эскимо [eskee**mo**]
ice rink каток [kat**o**k]
ice skates коньки [kankee]
ice skating катание на
 коньках [kat**a**nee-yeh na
 kank**a**н]
icon икона [eek**o**na]
icy ледяной [lyedyan**oy**]
idea идея [eed**yeh**-ya]
idiot идиот [eedee-**o**t]
if если [**ye**slee]
ignition зажигание
 [za**j**ig**a**nee-yeh]
ill: he/she is ill он болен/она
 больна [on b**o**lyen/ona b**a**lna]
 I feel ill мне плохо [mnyeh
 pl**o**нa]
illness болезнь f [bal**ye**zn]
imitation (leather)
 искусственный
 [eeskoo**st**vyen-ni]
 (jewellery) подделка [pad-
 d**ye**lka]
immediately немедленно
 [nyemy**e**dlyen-na]
important важный [**va**jni]
 it's very important это очень
 важно [eta **o**chyen v**a**jna]
 it's not important это не
 важно [eta nyeh v**a**jna]
impossible: it's impossible
 это невозможно [eta
 nyevazm**o**jna]
impressive впечатляющий
 [fpyechatl**ya**-yoosh-chee]
improve улучшать/
 улучшить

110

[ooloochsh**at**/ool**oo**chshit]

in: it's in the centre это в центре [eta fts**e**ntryeh]

in my car в моей машине [vma-**yay** mash**iy**nyeh]

in Moscow в Москве [vmaskv**yeh**]

in two days from now через два дня [ch**ye**ryez dva dnya]

in five minutes через пять минут [ch**ye**ryes pyat meen**oot**]

in May в мае [vma-**yeh**]

in English по-английски [pa-angl**ee**skee]

in Russian по-русски [pa-**roo**skee]

include включать/включить [fklyooch**at**/fklyooch**ee**t]

does that include meals? в это входит стоимость питания? [**ve**ta fH**o**deet st**o**-eemast peet**a**nee-ya?]

is that included? это включено в стоимость? [**e**ta fklyoochyen**o** fst**o**-eemast?]

inconvenient неудобный [nyeh-ood**o**bni]

incredible поразительный [paraz**ee**tyelni]

Indian (adj) индийский [eend**ee**skee]

indicator указатель **m** [ookaz**a**tyel]

indigestion несварение [nyesvar**ye**nee-yeh]

indoor pool закрытый бассейн [zakr**iy**ti bass**yay**n]

indoors в помещении

[fpamyesh-ch**ye**nee-ee]

inexpensive дешёвый [dyesh**o**vi]

infection инфекция [eenf**ye**ktsi-ya]

infectious инфекционный [eenfyektsi-**o**n-ni]

inflammation воспаление [vaspal**ye**nee-yeh]

informal неофициальный [nyeh-afeetsi-**a**lni]

information информация [eenfarm**a**tsi-ya]

do you have any information about ...? у вас есть какая-то информация о ...? [oo vas yest kak**a**-ya-ta eenfarm**a**tsi-ya a...?]

information desk справочный стол [spr**a**vachni stol]

injection инъекция [een**ye**ktsi-ya]

injured раненый [**r**anyeni]

she's been injured она ранена [an**a r**anyena]

innocent: I'm innocent (said by man/woman) я не виновен/виновна [ya nyeh veen**o**vyen/veen**o**vna]

insect насекомое [nasyek**o**ma-yeh]

insect bite укус насекомого [ook**oo**s nasyek**o**mava]

do you have anything for insect bites? у вас есть что-то от укусов насекомых? [oo vas yest sht**o**-ta at ook**oo**saf nasyek**o**miH?]

insect repellent средство от насекомых [sryetstva at nasyekomih]

inside внутри [vnootree]
  inside the hotel в гостинице [vgasteeneetseh]
  let's sit inside давайте сядем внутри [davuytyeh syadyem vnootree]

insist настаивать [nasta-eevat]
  I insist я настаиваю [ya nasta-eeva-yoo]

instant coffee растворимый кофе m [rastvareemi kofyeh]

instead вместо [vmyesta]
  give me that one instead дайте мне это взамен [duytyeh mnyeh eta vzamyen]
  instead of ... вместо ... [vmyesta ...]

insurance страховка [strahofka]

intelligent умный [oomni]

interested: I'm interested in ... меня интересует ... [myenya eentyeryesoo-yet ...]

interesting интересный [eentyeryesni]
  that's very interesting это очень интересно [eta ochyen eentyeryesna]

international международный [myeJdoonarodni]

Internet Интернет [eenternet]

interpreter (man/woman) переводчик/переводчица [pyeryevotcheek/pyeryevotcheetsa]

intersection перекрёсток [pyeryekryostak]

interval (at theatre) антракт [antrakt]

into в [v]
  I'm not into ... я не увлекаюсь ... [ya nyeh oovlyeka-yoos ...]

Intourist Интурист [eentooreest]

introduce знакомить/познакомить [znakomeet/paznakomeet]
  may I introduce ...? разрешите представить ... [razryeshuytyeh pryetstaveet...]

invitation приглашение [preeglashenee-yeh]

invite приглашать/пригласить [preeglashat/preeglaseet]

Ireland Ирландия [eerlandee-ya]

Irish ирландский [eerlantskee]
  I'm Irish (man/woman) я ирландец/ирландка [ya eerlandyets/eerlantka]

iron (for ironing) утюг [ootyook]
  can you iron these for me? вы не могли бы погладить это? [viy nyeh magleebi pagladeet eta?]

island остров [ostraf]

it* это [eta]
  it is ... это ... [eta ...]
  is it ...? это ...? [eta ...?]
  where is it? где это? [gdyeh eta?]

it's him это он [**e**ta on]
Italian (adj) итальянский [eetal**ya**nskee]
Italy Италия [ee**ta**lee-ya]
itch: it itches чешется [ch**ye**shetsa]

J

jack (for car) домкрат [damk**ra**t]
jacket куртка [**koo**rtka]
  (tailored) пиджак [peed**ja**k]
jam варенье [var**ye**nyeh]
jammed: it's jammed заело [za-**ye**la]
January январь m [yanvar]
jar (noun) банка [**ba**nka]
jaw челюсть f [ch**ye**lyoost]
jazz джаз [**dja**z]
jealous ревнивый [ryevn**ee**vi]
jeans джинсы [**dji**nsi]
jellyfish медуза [myed**oo**za]
jersey джерси n [**dje**rsee]
jetty пристань f [**pree**stan]
jeweller's ювелирный магазин [yoovel**ee**rni magaz**ee**n]
jewellery ювелирные изделия pl [yoovel**ee**rni-yeh eezd**ye**lee-ya]
Jewish еврейский [yevr**ya**yskee]
job работа [rab**o**ta]
jogging бег трусцой [byek troosts**oy**]
  to go jogging бегать трусцой [b**ye**gat troosts**oy**]

joke шутка [sh**oo**tka]
journey путешествие [pootyesh**e**stvee-yeh]
  have a good journey! счастливого пути! [sh-chasl**ee**vava poot**ee**!]
jug кувшин [koofsh**i**yn]
  a jug of water кувшин воды [koofsh**i**yn vad**i**y]
juice сок [s**o**k]
July июль m [ee-**yoo**l]
jump (verb) прыгать/прыгнуть [**pri**ygat/**pri**ygnoot]
jumper джемпер [d**je**mpyer]
junction (of roads) перекрёсток [pyeryekr**yo**stak]
  (on motorway) развилка [razv**ee**lka]
June июнь m [ee-**yoo**n]
just (only) только [**to**lka]
  just two только два [**to**lka dva]
  just for me только для меня [**to**lka dlya myen**ya**]
  just here именно здесь [**ee**myen-na zdyes]
  not just now не сейчас [nyeh syech**a**s]
  we've just arrived мы только что приехали [miy **to**lka shto pree-**ye**Halee]

K

keep (verb) оставлять/оставить [astavl**ya**t/ast**a**veet]

keep the change сдачи не
надо [zdachee nyeh nada]
can I keep it? я могу
оставить это себе? [ya
magoo astaveet eta seebyeh?]
please keep it пожалуйста,
оставьте это себе [paJalsta,
astaftyeh eta seebyeh]
ketchup кетчуп [kyetchoop]
kettle чайник [chineek]
key ключ [klyooch]
the key for room 201, please
ключ от номера двести
один, пожалуйста [klyooch
at nomyera dvyestee adeen,
paJalsta]
keyring кольцо для ключей
[kaltso dlya klyoochyay]
kidneys почки [pochkee]
kill (verb) убивать/убить
[oobeevat/oobeet]
kilo килограмм [keelagram]
kilometre километр
[keelamyetr]
how many kilometres is it
to ...? сколько
километров до ... [skolka
keelamyetraf da ...]
kind (generous) добрый [dobri]
that's very kind вы очень
любезны [viy ochyen
lyoobyezni]

dialogue

which kind do you want?
какой именно вы
хотите? [kakoy eemyen-na
viy Hateetyeh?]

I want this/that kind вот
этот/тот, пожалуйста
[vot etat/tot, paJalsta]

kiosk киоск [kee-osk]
kiss (noun) поцелуй m
[patselooy]
(verb) целовать/
поцеловать [tselavat/
patselavat]
kitchen кухня [kooHnya]
Kleenex® бумажный
носовой платок [boomaJni
nasavoy platok]
knee колено [kalyena]
knickers трусики [trooseekee]
knife нож [nosh]
knock (verb) стучать/
постучать [stoochat/
pastoochat]
knock down сбивать/сбить
[zbeevat/zbeet]
he's been knocked down by a
car его сбила машина
[yevo zbeela mashiyna]
knock over (object)
опрокидывать/
опрокинуть [aprakeedivat/
aprakeenoot]
(pedestrian) сбивать/сбить с
ног [zbeevat/zbeet snok]
know (somebody, something, a
place) знать [znat]
I don't know я не знаю [ya
nyeh zna-yoo]
I didn't know that (said by
man/woman) я этого не
знал/знала [ya etava nyeh
znal/znala]

do you know where I can find ...? вы не знаете, где я могу найти ...? [viy nyeh zna-yetyeh, gdyeh ya magoo nitee ...?]

Kremlin Кремль **m** [kryeml]

L

label ярлык [yarliyk]

ladies' room, ladies' toilets женский туалет [Jenskee too-alyet]

ladies' wear женская одежда [Jenska-ya adyeJda]

lady дама [dama]

lager светлое пиво [svyetla-yeh peeva]

see **beer**

lake озеро [ozyera]

lamb (meat) баранина [baraneena]

lamp лампа [lampa]

lane (narrow street) переулок [pyeryeh-oolak]

(country road) дорожка [daroshka]

(motorway) ряд [ryat]

language язык [yaziyk]

language course курсы иностранного языка [koorsi eenastran-nava yazika]

large большой [balshoy]

last последний [paslyednee]

last week на прошлой неделе [na proshli nyedyelyeh]

last Friday в прошлую

пятницу [fproshloo-yoo pyatneetsoo]

last night (evening) вчера вечером [fchyera vyechyeram]

what time is the last train to Omsk? когда отходит последний поезд в Омск? [kagda atHodeet paslyednee po-yest vomsk?]

late: sorry I'm late извините за опоздание [eezveeneetyeh za apazdanee-yeh]

the train was late поезд опоздал [po-yest apazdal]

we must go, we'll be late нам нужно идти, а то опоздаем [nam nooJna eet-tee, a to apazda-yem]

it's getting late становится поздно [stanoveetsa pozna]

later позже [poJ-Jeh]

I'll come back later я вернусь попозже [ya vyernoos papoJ-Jeh]

see you later пока! [paka!]

later on потом [patom]

latest последний [paslyednee]

by Wednesday at the latest не позднее среды [nyeh paznyeh-yeh sryediy]

laugh (verb) смеяться/ засмеяться [smyeh-yatsa/ zasmyeh-yatsa]

launderette, laundromat прачечная самообслуживания [prachyechna-ya sama-apslooJivanee-ya]

laundry (clothes) бельё [byelyo]

(place) прачечная
[pr**a**chyechna-ya]

Russians generally wash their clothes at home in the bathtub, and few would risk their garments at municipal laundries, which take a week (or longer) to return clothing. If you're staying in a hotel where there aren't any formal laundry services available it's usually possible, for a small fee, to do a deal with your concierge (дуе**J**oorna-ya) or cleaner. If you're staying in Moscow or St Petersburg you can get your washing done at the growing number of private laundries – the various free English-language newspapers provide information on these.

lavatory туалет [too-al**ye**t]
law закон [zak**o**n]
lawn газон [gaz**o**n]
lawyer юрист [yoor**ee**st]
laxative слабительное
  [slab**ee**tyelna-yeh]
lazy ленивый [lyen**ee**evi]
lead (electrical) провод
  [pr**o**vat]
  (verb) вести/привести
  [vyest**ee**/preeveest**ee**]
  where does this lead to?
  куда это ведёт? [kood**a** eta
  vyed**yo**t?]
leaf лист [l**ee**st]
leaflet брошюрка
  [brash**oo**rka]

leak течь f [tyech]
  the roof leaks крыша течёт
  [kr**i**ysha tyech**o**t]
learn учиться [ooch**ee**etsa]
least: not in the least
  нисколько [neesk**o**lka]
  at least по крайней мере
  [pa kr**i**nyay m**ye**ryeh]
leather кожа [k**o**Ja]
leave (verb: by transport)
  уезжать/уехать [oo-yeJ-
  J**a**t/oo-**ye**Hat]
  (on foot) уходить/уйти
  [ooHad**ee**t/ooyt**ee**]
  I am leaving tomorrow я
  уезжаю завтра [ya
  oo-yeJJ**a**-yoo z**a**ftra]
  he left yesterday он уехал
  вчера [on oo-**ye**Hal fchyer**a**]
  may I leave this here?
  можно это здесь
  оставить? [m**o**Jna eta zdyes
  ast**a**veet?]
  I left my coat in the bar (said
  by man/woman) я оставил/
  оставила пальто в баре
  [ya ast**a**veel/ast**a**veela palt**o**
  vb**a**ryeh]
  when does the bus for
  Vladimir leave? когда
  отходит автобус во
  Владимир? [kagd**a** atH**o**deet
  aft**o**boos va vlad**ee**meer?]
leek лук-порей m
  [look-par**ay**]
left-handed левша [lyefsh**a**]
left левый [l**ye**vi]
  on the left слева [sl**ye**va]
  to the left налево [nal**ye**va]

turn left поверните налево
[pavyern**ee**tyeh nal**ye**va]

there's none left ничего не
осталось [neechyev**o** nyeh
ast**a**las]

left luggage (office) камера
хранения [k**a**myera
нran**ye**nee-ya]

Most train stations have
lockers and/or a 24-hour
left luggage office, but
you would be tempting fate to use
them.

leg нога [nag**a**]
lemon лимон [leem**o**n]
lemonade лимонад
[leeman**a**t]
lemon tea чай с лимоном m
[chі sleem**o**nam]
lend одолжить [adal**J**iyt]
will you lend me your pen?
одолжите, пожалуйста,
вашу ручку [adal**J**iytyeh,
pa**J**alsta, v**a**shoo r**oo**chkoo]
lens (of camera) объектив
[abyekt**ee**f]
lesbian лесбиянка
[lyezbee-**ya**nka]
less меньше [m**ye**nsheh]
less than меньше, чем
[m**ye**nsheh, chyem]
less expensive менее
дорогой [m**ye**nyeh-yeh
darag**oy**]
lesson урок [oor**o**k]
let (allow) позволять/
позволить [pazval**ya**t/

pazvol**ee**t]
will you let me know? вы
мне дадите знать? [viy
mnyeh dad**ee**tyeh znat?]
I'll let you know я дам вам
знать [ya dam vam znat]
let's go for something to eat
пойдёмте поедим
[pіd**yo**mtyeh pa-yed**ee**m]
to let сдаётся [sda-**yo**tsa]
let off высаживать/
высадить [vis**a**Jivat/v**iy**sadeet]
let me off at the corner я
выйду на углу [ya v**iy**doo na
oogl**oo**]
letter письмо [peesm**o**]
**do you have any letters for
me?** есть ли для меня
письма? [**ye**stlee dlya myen**ya**
p**ee**sma?]
letterbox почтовый ящик
[pacht**o**vi **ya**sh-cheek]

Letterboxes come in the
form of small blue-painted
metal boxes, usually fixed
to walls and embossed with the
word **почта** (mail).

lettuce салат [sal**a**t]
lever (noun) рычаг [rich**a**k]
library библиотека
[beeblee-at**ye**ka]
licence (driver's)
водительские права pl
[vad**ee**tyelskee-yeh prav**a**]
(permit) лицензия
[leets**e**nzee-ya]
lid крышка [kr**iy**shka]

Li:

lie (verb: tell untruth) лгать/
солгать [lgat/salgat]
lie down лежать/лечь
[lyeJat/lyech]
life жизнь f [Jizn]
lifebelt спасательный пояс
[spasatyelni po-yas]
lifeguard (man/woman)
спасатель [spasatyel]
life jacket спасательный
жилет [spasatyelni Jilyet]
lift (in building) лифт [leeft]
could you give me a lift? вы
не могли бы меня
подвезти? [viy nyeh magleebi
menya padvyestee?]
would you like a lift? вас
подвезти? [vas padvyestee?]
light (noun) свет [svyet]
(not heavy) лёгкий [lyoнkee]
do you have a light? (for
cigarette) нет ли у вас
огонька? [nyetlee oo vas
aganka?]
light green светло-зелёный
[svyetla-zelyoni]
light bulb лампочка
[lampachka]
I need a new light bulb мне
нужна новая лампочка
[mnyeh nooJna nova-ya
lampachka]
lighter (cigarette) зажигалка
[zaJigalka]
lightning молния [molnee-ya]
like: I like it мне это
нравится [mnyeh eta
nraveetsa]
I like going for walks я

люблю гулять [ya lyooblyoo
goolyat]
I like you вы мне
нравитесь [viy mnyeh
nraveetyes]
I don't like it мне это не
нравится [mnyeh eta nyeh
nraveetsa]
do you like ...? вам
нравится ...? [vam
nraveetsa ...?]
I'd like a beer (said by
man/woman) я бы выпил/
выпила кружку пива [ya
biy viypeel/viypeela krooshkoo
peeva]
I'd like to go swimming (said
by man/woman) я бы
хотел/хотела поплавать
[ya biy нatyel/нatyela paplavat]
would you like a drink? не
хотите что-нибудь
выпить? [nyeh нateetyeh
shto-neeboot viypeet?]
would you like to go for a
walk? не хотите
прогуляться? [nyeh нateetyeh
pragoolyatsa?]
what's it like? на что это
похоже? [na shto eta paнoJeh?]
I want one like this я такой
же хочу [ya takoyJeh нachoo]
lime лайм [lim]
line линия [leenee-ya]
lips губы [goobi]
lip salve гигиеническая
помада
[geegee-yeneechyeska-ya pamada]
lipstick губная помада

[goobna-ya pamada]

liqueur ликёр [leekyor]

listen слушать [slooshat]

litre литр [leetr]

a litre of milk литр молока [leetr malaka]

little маленький [malyenkee]

just a little, thanks чуть-чуть, спасибо [choot-choot, spaseeba]

a little milk немного молока [nyemnoga malaka]

a little bit more ещё немного [yesh-cho nyemnoga]

live (verb) жить [Jit]

we live together мы живём вместе [miy Jivyom vmyestyeh]

dialogue

where do you live? где вы живёте? [gdyeh viy Jivyotyeh?]

I live in London я живу в Лондоне [ya Jivoo vlondanyeh]

lively оживлённый [aJivlyon-ni]

liver (in body, food) печень **f** [pyechyen]

loaf буханка [booнanka]

lobby (in hotel) вестибюль **m** [vyesteebyool]

lobster омар [amar]

local местный [myesni]

can you recommend a local restaurant? вы можете порекомендовать местный ресторан? [viy moJetyeh paryekamyendavat myesni ryestaran?]

lock (noun) замок [zamok] (verb) запирать/запереть [zapeerat/zapyeryet]

it's locked это заперто [eta zapyerta]

lock in запирать/запереть [zapeerat/zapyeryet]

lock out: I've locked myself out (said by man/woman) я случайно захлопнул/захлопнула дверь [ya sloochına zaнlopnool/zaнlopnoola dvyer]

locker шкафчик [shkafcheek] (for luggage etc) автоматическая камера хранения [aftamateechyeska-ya kamyera нranyenee-ya]

lollipop леденец [lyedeenyets]

London Лондон [londan]

long длинный [dleen-ni]

how long will it take to fix it? сколько времени займёт починка? [skolka vryemeenee zimyot pacheenka?]

how long does it take? сколько времени это занимает? [skolka vryemeenee eta zaneema-yet?]

a long time долго [dolga]

one day/two days longer ещё один день/два дня [yesh-cho adeen dyen/dva dnya]

long-distance call междугородный разговор [myeJdoogarodni razgavor]

look: I'm just looking, thanks я
просто смотрю, спасибо
[ya prosta smatryoo, spaseeba]

you don't look well вы
неважно выглядите [viy
nyeh vaJna viyglyadeetyeh]

look out! осторожно!
[astaroJna!]

can I have a look? можно
мне взглянуть? [moJna
mnyeh vzglyanoot?]

look after ухаживать за
[ooHaJivat za]

look at смотреть/
посмотреть на [smatryet/
pasmatryet na]

look for искать/поискать
[eeskat/pa-eeskat]

I'm looking for ... я ищу ...
[ya eesh-choo ...]

look forward to с
нетерпением ждать
[snyetyerpyenee-yem Jdat]

I'm looking forward to it я с
нетерпением жду этого
[ya snyetyerpyenee-yem Jdoo
etava]

loose (handle etc)
расшатанный [rasshatan-ni]

lorry грузовик [groozaveek]

lose терять/потерять
[tyeryat/patyeryat]

I've lost my way (said by
man/woman) я
заблудился/заблудилась
[ya zabloodeelsya/zabloodeelas]

I'm lost, I want to get to ...
(said by man/woman) я

заблудился/заблудилась,
мне нужно добраться
до ... [ya
zabloodeelsa/zabloodeelas, mnyeh
nooJna dabratsa da ...]

I've lost my bag (said by
man/woman) я
потерял/потеряла сумку
[ya patyeryal/patyeryala soomkoo]

lost property (office) бюро
находок [byooro naHodak]

lot: a lot, lots много [mnoga]

not a lot немного [nyemnoga]

a lot of people много
народу [mnoga narodoo]

a lot bigger намного
больше [namnoga bolsheh]

I like it a lot мне очень
нравится [mnyeh ochyen
nraveetsa]

lotion лосьон [lasyon]

loud громкий [gromkee]

lounge (in house) гостиная
[gasteena-ya]
(in hotel) фойе [fay-yeh]
(in airport) зал ожидания [zal
aJidanee-ya]

love (noun) любовь f [lyoobof]
(verb) любить [lyoobeet]

lovely замечательный
[zamyechatyelni]

low низкий [neeskee]

luck удача [oodacha]

good luck! желаю успеха!
[Jila-yoo oospyeHa!]

luggage багаж [bagash]

luggage trolley тележка для
багажа [tyelyeshka dlya bagaJa]

lunch обед [abyet]

lungs лёгкие [**lyo**нkee-yeh]
luxurious (hotel, furnishings)
роскошный [rask**o**shni]
luxury роскошь f [**ro**skash]

M

machine машина [mash**i**yna]
mad (insane) сумасшедший
  [soomash**e**tshi]
  (angry) рассерженный
  [rass**ye**rJen-ni]
magazine журнал [**J**oornal]
maid (in hotel) горничная
  [**go**rneechna-ya]
maiden name девичья
  фамилия [**dye**veechya
  fam**ee**lee-ya]
mail (noun) почта [**po**chta]
  (verb) отправлять/
  отправить [atpravl**ya**t/
  atpr**a**veet]
  is there any mail for me?
  есть ли для меня почта?
  [**ye**stlee dlya myen**ya po**chta?]
  see **post office**
mailbox почтовый ящик
  [pachtovi **ya**sh-cheek]
main главный [**g**lavni]
main course основное
  блюдо [asnavn**o**-yeh bl**yoo**da]
main post office
  главпочтамт [glafpachtamt]
main road (in town) главная
  улица [**g**lavna-ya **oo**leetsa]
  (in country) главная дорога
  [**g**lavna-ya dar**o**ga]
make (brand name) марка
  [**m**arka]
  (verb) делать/сделать
  [**d**yelat/sd**ye**lat]
  I make it 130,000 roubles по
  моим расчётам, сто
  тридцать тысяч рублей
  [pa ma-**ee**m rash-ch**o**tam, sto
  tr**ee**tsat t**i**ysyach roobl**ya**y]
  what is it made of? из чего
  это сделано? [ees chy**e**vo **e**ta
  zd**ye**lana?]
make-up косметика
  [kasm**ye**teeka]
man мужчина [moosh-ch**ee**na]
manager (of hotel)
  администратор
  [admeeneestr**a**tar]
  (of company) менеджер
  [m**e**nedjer]
  can I see the manager?
  позовите
  администратора,
  пожалуйста [pazav**ee**tyeh
  admeeneestr**a**tara, paJ**a**lsta]
manageress (in shop etc)
  заведующая
  [zavy**e**doosh-cha-ya]
manual (with manual gears) с
  ручной коробкой
  передач [sroochn**oy** kar**o**pkı
  pyeryed**a**ch]
many многие [mn**o**gee-yeh]
  not many немногие
  [nyemn**o**gee-yeh]
map (city plan) план [plan]
  (road map, geographical) карта
  [**k**arta]
  network map схема [sн**ye**ma]
March март [mart]

margarine маргарин
[margar**een**]
market рынок [**riy**nak]

Any self-respecting town
has a market (r**iy**nak)
selling all kinds of fresh
produce, where shoppers can
sample morsels with no obligation
to buy and haggling is very much
the order of the day. Generally
speaking, opening hours are
8am–8pm.
The primitive form of capitalism
currently flourishing is best
illustrated by the ever-multiplying
number of street kiosks, selling
everything from alcohol to shoes.
Another product of Russia's
economic chaos is the appearance
of unofficial street vendors
(pyeryek**oo**psh-cheekee) and flea
markets (talk**oo**chkee), where the
newly poor dispose of family
possessions to make ends meet.
see bargaining

marmalade мармелад
[marmy**e**lat]
married: I'm married (said by a
man/woman) я женат/
замужем [ya Jen**a**t/zam**oo**Jem]
are you married? (to
man/woman) вы женаты/
замужем? [viy Jen**a**ti/
zam**oo**Jem?]
mascara тушь для ресниц
[toosh dlya ryesn**ee**ts]
match (football etc) матч

[match]
matches спички [sp**ee**chkee]
material (fabric) ткань f [tkan]
matter: it doesn't matter
неважно [nyev**a**Jna]
what's the matter? в чём
дело? [fchom dy**e**la?]
mattress матрас [m**a**tras]
May май m [mI]
may: may I have another one?
можно ещё один,
пожалуйста? [m**o**Jna yesh-cho
ad**ee**n, paJ**a**lsta]
may I come in? можно
войти? [m**o**Jna vIt**ee**?]
may I see it? можно мне
взглянуть? [m**o**Jna mnyeh
vzglyan**oo**t?]
may I sit here? здесь
свободно? [zdyes
svab**o**dna?]
maybe может быть [m**o**Jet
bIyt]
mayonnaise майонез
[mI-an**e**s]
me*: that's for me это для
меня [**e**ta dlya myen**ya**]
send it to me пошлите это
мне [pashl**ee**tyeh **e**ta mnyeh]
me too я тоже [ya t**o**Jeh]
meal еда [yed**a**]

dialogue

did you enjoy your meal?
понравилась ли вам
еда? [panrav**ee**laslee vam
yed**a**?]
it was excellent, thank you

было очень вкусно, спасибо [biyla ochyen fkoosna, spaseeba]

mean (verb) значить [znacheet]
what do you mean? что вы имеете в виду? [shto viy eemyeh-yetyeh v-veedoo?]

dialogue

what does this word mean? что значит это слово? [shto znacheet eta slova?]
it means ... это значит ... [eta znacheet ...]

measles корь f [kor]
German measles краснуха [krasnooна]
meat мясо [myasa]
mechanic механик [myeнaneek]
medicine медицина [myedeetsiyna]
medium (adj: size) средний [sryednee]
medium-dry полусухой [poloo-soohoy]
medium-rare немного недожаренный [nyemnoga nyedaJaryen-ni]
medium-sized среднего размера [sryednyeva razmyera]
meet встречаться/встретиться [fstryechatsa/fstryeteetsa]

nice to meet you приятно познакомиться [pree-yatna paznakomeetsa]
where shall I meet you? где мы встретимся? [gdyeh miy fstryeteemsa?]
meeting встреча [fstryecha]
(business, with more than one person) совещание [savyesh-chanee-yeh]
(gathering) собрание [sabranee-yeh]
meeting place место для встречи [myesta dlya fstryechee]
melon дыня [diynya]
men мужчины [moosh-cheeni]
mend чинить/починить [cheeneet/pacheeneet]
could you mend this for me? вы не могли бы это починить? [viy nyeh magleebi eta pacheeneet?]
mens' room мужской туалет [mooshskoy too-alyet]
menswear мужская одежда [mooshska-ya adyeJda]
mention (verb) упоминать/упомянуть [oopameenat/oopameenoot]
don't mention it не за что [nyeh-za-shta]
menu меню [myenyoo]
may I see the menu, please? можно меню, пожалуйста? [moJna myenyoo, paJalsta]
see menu reader page 252

message сообщение
[sa-apsh-chyenee-yeh]
are there any messages for
me? мне что-нибудь
передавали? [mnyeh
shto-neeboot pyeryedavalee?]
I want to leave a message
for ... вы не могли бы
передать ... [viy nyeh magleebi
pyeryedat ...?]
metal (noun) металл [myetal]
metre метр [myetr]
microwave oven
высокочастотная печь
[visoka-chastotna-ya pyech]
midday полдень m [poldyen]
at midday в полдень
[fpoldyen]
middle: in the middle в
середине [fsyereedeenyeh]
in the middle of the night
посреди ночи [pasreedee
nochee]
the middle one средний
[sryednee]
midnight полночь f [polnach]
at midnight в полночь
[fpolnach]
might: I might want to stay
another day возможно я
захочу остаться ещё на
один день [vazmoJna ya
zaHachoo astatsa yesh-cho na
adeen dyen]
migraine мигрень f
[meegryen]
mild (weather) тёплый [tyopli]
(taste) неострый [nyeh-ostri]
milk молоко [malako]

milkshake молочный
коктейль m [malochni
kaktyayl]
millimetre миллиметр
[meeleemyetr]
minced meat фарш [farsh]
mind: never mind не важно
[nyeh vaJna]
I've changed my mind (said by
man/woman) я
передумал/передумала
[ya pyeryedoomal/pyeryedoomala]

dialogue

do you mind if I open the
window? вы не
возражаете, если я
открою окно? [viy nyeh
vazraJa-yetyeh, yeslee ya
atkro-yoo akno?]
no, I don't mind нет, я не
возражаю [nyet, ya nyeh
vazraJa-yoo]

mine*: it's mine это моё [eta
ma-yo]
mineral water минеральная
вода [meenyeralna-ya vada]
mints мятные конфеты
[myatni-yeh kanfyeti]
minute минута [meenoota]
in a minute через минуту
[chyeryez meenootoo]
just a minute минуточку
[meenootachkoo]
mirror зеркало [zyerkala]
Miss девушка [dyevooshka]
miss: I missed the bus (said by

a man/woman) я опоздал/
опоздала на автобус [ya
apazd**a**l/apazd**a**la na aft**o**boos]

**missing: one of my ... is
missing** пропал один из
моих ... [prap**a**l ad**ee**n eez
ma-**ee**н ...]

there's a suitcase missing
одного чемодана не
хватает [adnav**o** chyemad**a**na
nyeh Hvat**a**-yet]

mist туман [too**ma**n]

mistake (noun) ошибка
[ash**i**ypka]

I think there's a mistake мне
кажется, здесь ошибка
[mnyeh k**a**Jetsa, zdyes ash**i**ypka]

sorry, I've made a mistake
(said by a man/woman)
извините, я ошибся/
ошиблась [eezveen**ee**tyeh, ya
ash**i**ypsya/ash**i**yblas]

**mix-up: sorry, there's been a
mix-up** извините,
произошла путаница
[eezveen**ee**tyeh, pra-eezashl**a**
p**oo**taneetsa]

mobile phone мобильный
телефон [mab**ee**lni tyelyef**o**n]

modern современный
[savryem**ye**n-ni]

modern art gallery галерея
современного искусства
[galyer**yeh**-ya savryem**ye**n-nava
eesk**oo**stva]

moisturizer увлажняющий
крем [oovlaJn**ya**-yoosh-chee
kryem]

moment: I won't be a moment

минутку [meen**oo**tkoo]

monastery монастырь **m**
[manast**i**yr]

Monday понедельник
[panyed**ye**lneek]

money деньги pl [d**ye**ngee]

 The dual economy has
become a permanent
fixture in Russia, dividing
the population into those with
access to hard currency (valy**oo**ta)
and therefore protection against
inflation, and those who are stuck
with roubles. As a foreigner, you will
routinely be charged many times
what the locals pay, either officially
(as at museums) or unofficially (by
street vendors).
There's a large variety of
denominations in circulation: 5, 10,
50 and 100 rouble coins and notes
to the value of 100, 200, 500, 1,000,
5,000, 10,000, 50,000, 100,000 and
500,000 roubles. Higher
denominations may be introduced in
the future. Counterfeiting is a major
problem and shops and bureaux de
change therefore err on the side of
caution, which makes it hard to
change foreign banknotes that are
worn or scribbled upon. All cash
transactions in Russia must be
carried out in roubles, and the use of
foreign money is banned. At the
many stores and agencies that still
price goods or services in dollars (or
Deutschmarks), you have to pay in
roubles at a rate of exchange set by

MO

125

the management, usually to the customers' disadvantage. If it's way out of line with the bank rate, and if they accept credit cards, you'll save money by paying by credit card instead. But as many places still don't take plastic, you must either go armed with large sums of roubles or be sure that you have access to an exchange point (not so easy after 6pm).

month месяц [**mye**syats]
monument памятник [**pa**myatneek]
moon луна [loon**a**]
more* больше [**bo**lsheh]
  can I have some more water, please? можно ещё воды, пожалуйста [**mo**лna yesh-ch**o** vod**iy**, paJalsta]
  more expensive/interesting более дорогой/интересный [**bo**lyeh-yeh darag**oy**/eentyer**ye**sni]
  more than 50 больше пятидесяти [**bo**lsheh pyat**ee**dyestee]
  more than that более того [**bo**lyeh-yeh tav**o**]
  a lot more гораздо больше [gar**a**zda **bo**lsheh]

dialogue

  would you like some more? вы хотите ещё? [viy нat**ee**tyeh yesh-ch**o**?]
  no, no more for me, thanks

нет, спасибо, мне больше не надо [nyet, spas**ee**ba, mnyeh b**o**lsheh nyeh n**a**da]
  how about you? а вы? [a viy?]
  I don't want any more, thanks спасибо, я больше не хочу [spas**ee**ba, ya b**o**lsheh nyeh наch**oo**]

morning утро [**oo**tra]
  this morning сегодня утром [syev**o**dnya **oo**tram]
  in the morning утром [**oo**tram]
Moscow Москва [maskv**a**]
mosquito комар [kam**ar**]
mosquito repellent средство от комаров [sr**ye**tstva at kamar**of**]
most: I like this one most of all мне больше всего нравится вот это [mnyeh b**o**lsheh fsyev**o** nr**a**veetsa vot **e**ta]
  most of the time большую часть времени [b**o**lshoo-yoo chast vr**ye**myenee]
  most tourists большинство туристов [balshinstv**o** toor**ee**staf]
mostly главным образом [gl**a**vnim **o**brazam]
mother мать [mat]
mother-in-law (wife's mother) тёща [**tyo**sh-cha] (husband's mother) свекровь [svyekr**of**]

motorbike мотоцикл
[matatsiykl]
motorboat моторная лодка
[matorna-ya lotka]
motorway автострада
[aftastrada]
mountain гора [gara]
  in the mountains в горах
  [vgaraн]
mountaineering альпинизм
[alpeeneezm]
mouse мышь f [miysh]
moustache усы pl [oosiy]
mouth рот [rot]
mouth ulcer язвочка во рту
[yazvachka vartoo]
move (verb) двигать/
подвинуть [dveegat/
padveenoot]
  he's moved to another room
  он перешёл в другую
  комнату [on pyeryeshol
  vdroogoo-yoo komnatoo]
  could you move up a little?
  вы не могли бы
  подвинуться? [viy nyeh
  magleebi padveenootsa?]
  where has it moved to? где
  это теперь находится?
  [gdyeh eta tyepyer naнodeetsa?]
movie кинофильм
[keenafeelm]
movie theater (US)
  кинотеатр [keenatyeh-atr]
Mr господин [gaspadeen]
Mrs/Ms госпожа [gaspaja]
much много [mnoga]
  much better/worse гораздо
  лучше/хуже [garazda

loochsheh/нooJeh]
  much hotter гораздо жарче
  [garazda Jarchyeh]
  not much немного
  [nyemnoga]
  not very much не очень
  много [nyeh ochyen mnoga]
  I don't want very much я не
  хочу много [ya nyeh нachoo
  mnoga]
mud грязь f [gryas]
mug (for drinking) кружка
  [krooshka]
  I've been mugged меня
  ограбили [menya
  agrabeelee]
mum мама [mama]
mumps свинка [sveenka]
museum музей m
  [moozyay]

 Opening hours for museums and galleries tend to be 9 or 10am to 5 or 6pm. You'll find that they are closed at least one day a week, which varies from place to place, and one further day in the month will be set aside as a санитарный день (cleaning day). Visitors are often required to put on 'тапачкее' (felt overshoes) to protect the parquet floors. It's quite common for museums, galleries, cafés, shops and government buildings to be closed 'for repair' (закрыто на ремонт) or 'for technical reasons' (по техническим

 Mu

причинам). Given this fact, it's a good idea to have alternative plans when visiting galleries and museums.

mushrooms грибы [greebiy]
music музыка [moozika]
musician (man/woman) музыкант/музыкантша [moozikant/moozikantsha]
Muslim (adj) мусульманский [moosoolmanskee]
mussels мидии [meedee-ee]
must*: I must (said by a man/woman) я должен/должна [ya dolJen/dalJna]
I mustn't drink alcohol мне не следует пить алкоголь [mnyeh nyeh slyedoo-yet peet alkagol]
mustard горчица [garcheetsa]
my* мой [moy] m, моя [ma-ya] f, моё [ma-yo] n, мои [ma-ee] pl
myself: I'll do it myself (said by a man/woman) я сам/сама это сделаю [ya sam/sama eta zdyela-yoo]
by myself (said by man/woman) один/одна [adeen/adna]

N

nail (finger) ноготь m [nogat] (metal) гвоздь m [gvost]
nailbrush щёточка для ногтей [sh-chotachka dlya naktyay]
nail varnish лак для ногтей [lak dlya naktyay]
name имя n [eemya]
my name's ... меня зовут ... [menya zavoot ...]
what's your name? как вас зовут? [kak vas zavoot?]
what is the name of this street? как называется эта улица [kak naziva-yetsa eta ooleetsa?]

Besides their first name and surname, every Russian has a patronymic derived from their father's name (such as Konstanteenovich, son of Konstanteen, or Ivanovna, daughter of Ivan), which is used in conjunction with their first name as a polite form of address. This is the norm among older Russians, who find American informality – 'Hi, I'm Bob' – rather crass.

napkin салфетка [salfyetka]
nappy пелёнка [pyelyonka]
narrow узкий [ooskee]
nasty (weather, person) скверный [skvyerni] (accident) тяжёлый [tyaJoli]
national национальный [natsi-analni]
nationality национальность [natsi-analnast]
natural натуральный [natooralni]
nausea тошнота [tashnata]

navy (blue) тёмно-синий
[**tyo**mna-s**ee**neei]

near рядом [**rya**dam]

is it near the city centre? это
недалеко от центра
города? [**e**ta nyedalyek**o** at
ts**e**ntra gor**o**da?]

do you go near the Winter
Palace? вы не проезжаете
Зимний дворец? [viy nyeh
pra-ye**JJ**a-yetyeh z**ee**mnee
dvar**ye**ts?]

where is the nearest ...? где
ближайший ...? [gdyeh
blee**J**Ishi ...?]

nearby поблизости
[pabl**ee**zastee]

nearly почти [pacht**ee**]

necessary необходимый
[nyeh-apHad**ee**mi]

neck шея [sh**eh**-ya]

necklace ожерелье
[aJer**yeh**-lyeh]

necktie галстук [**ga**lstook]

need: I need ... мне надо ...
[mnyeh n**a**da ...]

do I need to pay? нужно ли
мне заплатить? [n**oo**Jnalee
mnyeh zaplat**ee**t]

needle иголка [eeg**o**lka]

negative (film) негатив
[nyegat**ee**f]

neither: neither (one) of them
ни один из них [nee ad**ee**n
eez neeH]

neither ... nor ... ни ... ни ...
[nee ... nee ...]

nephew племянник
[plyem**ya**n-neek]

net (in tennis) сетка [**sye**tka]
(in football) ворота [var**o**ta]

Netherlands Нидерланды
[n**ee**derlandi]

never никогда [neekagd**a**]

dialogue

have you ever been to
Pskov? вы когда-
нибудь были в Пскове?
[viy kagd**a**-neebot b**i**ylee
fpsk**o**vyeh?]

no, never, I've never been
there (said by man/woman)
нет, я там никогда не
был/не была [nyet, ya tam
neekagd**a** ny**e**bil/nyeh bil**a**]

new новый [n**o**vi]

news (radio, TV etc) новости pl
[n**o**vastee]

newsagent's (kiosk) газетный
киоск [gaz**ye**tni kee-**o**sk]

newspaper газета [gaz**ye**ta]

newspaper kiosk газетный
киоск [gaz**ye**tni kee-**o**sk]

New Year Новый год [n**o**vi
got]

Happy New Year! с Новым
годом! [sn**o**vim g**o**dam!]

New Year's Eve новогодняя
ночь f [navag**o**dnya-ya noch]

New Zealand Новая
Зеландия [n**o**va-ya
zyel**a**ndee-ya]

New Zealander: I'm a New
Zealander (man/woman) я
новозеландец/новозелан

дка [ya novazyelandyets/novazyelantka]

next следующий [slyedoosh-chee]

the next turning on the left следующий поворот налево [slyedoosh-chee pavarot nalyeva]

at the next stop на следующей остановке [na slyedoosh-chyay astanofkyeh]

next week на следующей неделе [na slyedoosh-chyay nyedyelyeh]

next to рядом с [ryadam s]

nice (food) вкусный [fkoosni] (looks, view etc) красивый [kraseevi] (person) приятный [pree-yatni]

niece племянница [plyemyan-neetsa]

night ночь f [noch]

at night ночью [nochyoo]

good night спокойной ночи [spakoyni nochee]

dialogue

do you have a single room for one night? у вас есть одноместный номер на одни сутки? [oo vas yest adnamyestni nomyer na adnee sootkee?]

yes, madam да, есть [da, yest]

how much is it per night? сколько это стоит в сутки? [skolka eta sto-eet fsootkee?]

it's 300,000 roubles for one night триста тысяч рублей в сутки [treesta tiysyach rooblyay fsootkee]

OK, I'll take it хорошо, это меня устраивает [Harasho, eta myenya oostra-eeva-yet]

nightclub ночной клуб [nachnoy kloop]

nightdress ночная рубашка [nachna-ya roobashka]

night porter ночной портье m [nachnoy partyeh]

no нет [nyet]

I've no change у меня нет мелочи [oo myenya nyet myelachee]

there's no ... left ... больше нет [bolsheh nyet]

no way! ни за что! [nee-za-shto!]

nobody никто [neekto]

there's nobody there там никого нет [tam neekavo nyet]

noise шум [shoom]

noisy: it's too noisy слишком шумно [sleeshkam shoomna]

non-alcoholic безалкогольный [byezalkagolni]

none ничего [neechyevo]

nonsmoking compartment купе для некурящих [koopeh dlya nyekooryash-cheen]

noon полдень m [poldyen]

at noon в полдень [fp**o**ldyen]

no-one никто [neekt**o**]

nor: nor do I я тоже нет [ya t**o**Jeh nyet]

normal нормальный [narm**a**lni]

north север [s**ye**vyer]

  in the north на севере [na s**ye**vyeryeh]

  to the north на север [na s**ye**vyer]

  north of Moscow к северу от Москвы [ks**ye**vyeroo at maskv**iy**]

northeast северо-восточный [s**ye**vyera-vast**o**chni]

northern северный [s**ye**vyerni]

Northern Ireland Северная Ирландия [s**ye**vyerna-ya eerl**a**ndee-ya]

northwest северо-западный [s**ye**vyera-z**a**padni]

Norway Норвегия [narv**ye**gee-ya]

Norwegian (adj) норвежский [narv**ye**shskee]

nose нос [nos]

not* не [nyeh]

  I'm not hungry (said by man/woman) я не голоден/голодна [ya nyeh g**o**ladyen/galadn**a**]

  I don't want any, thank you я не хочу, спасибо [ya nyeh Hach**oo**, spas**ee**ba]

  it's not necessary в этом нет необходимости [**v**etam nyet nyeh-арнаd**ee**mastee]

I didn't know that (said by man/woman) я этого не знал/знала [ya **e**tava nyeh znal/zn**a**la]

not that one, this one не тот, а этот [nyeh tot, a **e**tat]

note (banknote) банкнота [bankn**o**ta]

notebook блокнот [blakn**o**t]

notepaper (for letters) почтовая бумага [pacht**o**va-ya boom**a**ga]

nothing ничего [neechev**o**]

  nothing for me, thanks мне ничего, спасибо [mnyeh neechev**o**, spas**ee**ba]

  nothing else больше ничего [b**o**lsheh neechev**o**]

novel роман [ram**a**n]

November ноябрь **m** [na-**ya**br]

now сейчас [seech**a**s]

number (room, telephone etc) номер [n**o**myer]

  (figure) число [cheesl**o**]

  I've got the wrong number (said by man/woman) я не туда попал/попала [ya nyeh tood**a** pap**a**l/pap**a**la]

  what is your phone number? какой ваш номер телефона? [kak**oy** vash n**o**myer tyelyef**o**na?]

number plate номерной знак [namyern**oy** znak]

nurse (man/woman) медбрат/медсестра [myedbr**a**t/myetsyestr**a**]

nut (for bolt) гайка [g**i**ka]

nuts орехи [ar**ye**Hee]

O

occupied (toilet/telephone)
занято [zanyata]
o'clock*: it's 3 o'clock три
часа [tree chasa]
October октябрь **m** [aktyabr]
odd (strange) странный
[stran-ni]
of*
off (lights) выключено
[viyklyoochyena]
it's just off Pushkin Square
это рядом с Пушкинской
площадью [eta ryadam
spooshkeenski plosh-chadyoo]
we're off tomorrow мы
уезжаем завтра [miy
oo-yeJ-Ja-yem zaftra]
offensive (language, behaviour)
оскорбительный
[askarbeetyelni]
office (place of work) офис
[ofees]
often часто [chasta]
not often нечасто [nyechasta]
how often are the buses?
как часто ходят
автобусы? [kak chasta Hodyat
aftoboosi?]
oil масло [masla]
ointment мазь **f** [maz]
OK хорошо [Harasho]
are you OK? с вами всё в
порядке? [svamee fsyo
fparyatkyeh?]
is that OK with you? вы не
возражаете? [viy nyeh

vazraJa-yetyeh?]
is it OK to ...? можно ...?
[moJna...?]
that's OK thanks ничего,
спасибо [neechyevo, spaseeba]
I'm OK мне ничего,
спасибо [mnyeh neechyevo,
spaseeba]
(I feel OK) со мной всё в
порядке [sa mnoy fsyo
fparyatkyeh]
is this train OK for ...? этот
поезд идёт до ...? [etat
po-yest eedyot da ...?]
I said I'm sorry, OK? (said by
man/woman) я же уже
извинился/извинилась!
[ya Jeh ooJeh
eezveeneelsya/eezveeneelas]
old старый [stari]

dialogue

how old are you? сколько
вам лет? [skolka vam lyet?]
I'm 25 мне двадцать
пять [mnyeh dvatsat pyat]
and you? а вам? [a vam?]

old-fashioned старомодный
[staramodni]
old town (old part of town)
старая часть города
[stara-ya chast gorada]
in the old town в старой
части города [fstari chastee
gorada]
omelette омлет [amlyet]
on* на [na]

on the street/beach на улице/пляже [na **oo**leetseh/pl**ya**Jeh]

is it on this road? это на этой дороге? [eta na eti dar**o**gyeh?]

on the plane на самолёте [na samal**yo**tyeh]

on Saturday в субботу [fsoob**o**too]

on television по телевизору [pa tyelyev**ee**zaroo]

I haven't got it on me у меня его нет с собой [oo men**ya** yevo nyet s-sab**oy**]

this one's on me (drink) этот за мой счёт [etat za moy sh-chot]

the light wasn't on свет не горел [svyet nyeh gar**yel**]

what's on tonight? что идёт сегодня? [shto eed**yot** syev**o**dnya?]

once (one time) один раз [ad**een** ras]

at once (immediately) сразу же [sr**a**zooJeh]

one* один [ad**een**]

the white one белый [b**ye**li]

one-way ticket билет в один конец [beel**yet** vad**een** kan**ye**ts]

onion лук [look]

only только [t**o**lka]

only one только один [t**o**lka ad**een**]

it's only 6 o'clock сейчас только шесть часов [syech**a**s t**o**lka shest chas**of**]

I've only just got here (said by

man/woman) я только что пришёл/пришла [ya t**o**lka shto preesh**o**l/preeshl**a**]

on/off switch выключатель m [viklyooch**a**tyel]

open (adj) открытый [atkr**i**ti]

(verb: door) открывать/ открыть [atkriv**a**t/atkr**i**yt]

when do you open? когда вы открываетесь? [kagd**a** viy atkriv**a**-yetyes?]

I can't get it open я не могу это открыть [ya nyeh mag**oo** eta atkr**i**yt]

in the open air на открытом воздухе [na atkr**i**ytam v**o**zdoonyeh]

opening times время открытия [vr**ye**mya atkr**i**ytee-ya]

open ticket билет с открытой датой [beel**yet** satkr**i**ytı d**a**ti]

opera опера [**o**pyera]

operation (medical) операция [apyer**a**tsi-ya]

operator (telephone: man/woman) телефонист/телефонистк а [tyelyefan**ee**st/tyelyefan**ee**stka]

opposite: in the opposite direction в противоположном направлении [fprateevapal**o**Jnam naprav**lye**nee-ee]

the bar opposite бар напротив [bar napr**o**teef]

opposite my hotel

Op

напротив моей гостиницы [naproteef ma-**yay** gasteeneetsi]

optician оптика [**o**pteeka]

or или [**ee**lee]

orange (fruit) апельсин [apyelseen]

(colour) оранжевый [aranJevi]

fizzy orange газированный апельсиновый напиток [gazeerovan-ni apyelseenavi napeetak]

orange juice апельсиновый сок [apyelseenavi sok]

orchestra оркестр [arkyestr]

order: can we order now? (in restaurant) можно заказать сейчас? [moJna zakazat syechas?]

I've already ordered, thanks (said by man/woman) я уже заказал/заказала, спасибо [ya ooJeh zakazal/zakazala, spaseeba]

I didn't order this (said by man/woman) я этого не заказывал/заказывала [ya etava nyeh zakazival/zakazivala]

out of order не работает [nyeh rabota-yet]

ordinary обычный [abiychni]

Orthodox православный [pravaslavni]

other другой [droogoy]

the other one другой [droogoy]

the other day на днях [na dnyaн]

I'm waiting for the others я жду остальных [ya Jdoo astalniyн]

do you have any others? у вас нет других? [oo vas nyet droogeeн?]

otherwise иначе [eenachyeh]

our*/ours* наш [nash] m, наша [nasha] f, наше [nasheh] n, наши [nashi] pl

out: he's out его нет [yevo nyet]

three kilometres out of town в трёх километрах от города [ftryoн keelamyetraн at gorada]

outdoors на открытом воздухе [na atkriytam vozdooнyeh]

outside снаружи [snarooJi]

can we sit outside? можно сесть снаружи? [moJna syest snarooJi?]

oven духовка [dooнofka]

over: over here вот здесь [vot zdyes]

over there вон там [von tam]

over 500 свыше пятисот [sviysheh pyateesot]

our holidays are over наш отпуск кончился [nash otpoosk koncheelsa]

overcharge: you've overcharged me вы с меня слишком много взяли [viy smenya sleeshkam mnoga vzyalee]

overcoat пальто [palto]

overlooking: I'd like a room overlooking the courtyard

(said by man/woman) я хотел/
хотела бы номер с
окнами во двор [ya
Hatyel/Hatyela biy nomyer
soknamee va dvor]

overnight (travel) ночной
[nachnoy]

overtake обгонять/
обогнать [abganyat/abagnat]

owe: how much do I owe you?
(said by man/woman) сколько я
вам должен/должна?
[skolka ya vam dolJen/dalJna?]

own: my own ... мой
собственный ... [moy
sopstvyen-ni ...]

are you on your own? (to
man/woman) вы один/одна?
[viy adeen/adna?]

I'm on my own (said by
man/woman) я один/одна [ya
adeen/adna]

owner (man/woman)
владелец/владелица
[vladyelyets/vladyeleetsa]

P

pack (verb) складывать/
сложить вещи
[skladivat/slaJiyt vyesh-chee]

a pack of ... пачка ...
[pachka]

package (parcel) посылка
[pasiylka]

package holiday
организованный отдых
[arganeezovan-ni oddiн]

packet: a packet of cigarettes
пачка сигарет [pachka
seegaryet]

padlock висячий замок
[veesyachee zamok]

page (of book) страница
[straneetsa]

could you page Mr ...?
вызовите, пожалуйста,
господина ... [viyzaveetyeh,
paJalsta gaspadeena ...]

pain боль [bol]

I have a pain here у меня
здесь болит [oo myenya zdyes
baleet]

painful болезненный
[balyeznyen-ni]

painkillers болеутоляющие
[bolyeh-ootalya-yoosh-chee-yeh]

paint (noun) краска [kraska]

painting (occupation)
живопись **f** [Jivapees]
(picture) картина [karteena]

pair: a pair of ... пара ...
[para ...]

Pakistani (adj)
пакистанский
[pakeestanskee]

palace дворец [dvaryets]

pale бледный [blyedni]

pale blue светло-голубой
[svyetla-galooboy]

pan кастрюля [kastryoolya]

pancakes блины [bleeniy]

panties (women's) трусики
[trooseekee]

pants (underwear: men's) трусы
[troosiy]
(women's) трусики

135

[**troo**seekee]
(US: trousers) брюки
[br**yoo**kee]
pantyhose колготки pl
[kalg**o**tkee]
paper бумага [boom**a**ga]
(newspaper) газета [gaz**ye**ta]
a piece of paper листок
бумаги [leest**o**k boom**a**gee]
paper handkerchiefs
бумажные носовые
платки
[boom**a**Jni-yeh nasa**vi**y-yeh
platk**ee**]
parcel посылка [pas**i**ylka]
pardon (me)? (didn't understand/
hear) простите? [prast**ee**tyeh?]
parents родители
[rad**ee**telee]
park (noun) парк [park]
(verb) парковаться/
припарковаться
[parkav**a**tsa/preeparkav**a**tsa]
can I park here? можно
здесь припарковаться?
[m**o**Jna zdyes preeparkav**a**tsa?]
parking lot стоянка
[sta-**ya**nka]
part часть f [chast]
partner (boyfriend, girlfriend)
друг/подруга
[drook/padr**oo**ga]
party (group) группа
[gr**oo**p-pa]
(celebration) вечеринка
[vyechyer**ee**nka]
pass (in mountains) перевал
[pyeryev**a**l]
passenger (man/woman)

пассажир/пассажирка
[pasaJ**i**yr/pasaJ**i**yrka]
passport паспорт [**pa**spart]
past*: in the past в
прошлом [fpr**o**shlam]
just past the post office
сразу за почтой [sr**a**zoo za
p**o**chti]
path тропинка [trap**ee**nka]
patronymic отчество
[**o**chyestva]
pattern узор [ooz**o**r]
pavement тротуар [tratoo-**a**r]
on the pavement на
тротуаре [na tratoo-**a**ryeh]
pay (verb) платить/
заплатить [plat**ee**t/zaplat**ee**t]
can I pay, please? можно
заплатить? [m**o**Jna zaplat**ee**t?]
it's already paid for это уже
оплачено [**e**ta oo**J**eh
apl**a**chyena]

dialogue

who's paying? кто
платит? [kto pl**a**teet?]
I'll pay я заплачу [ya
zaplach**oo**]
no, you paid last time, it's
my turn now нет, вы
платили в прошлый
раз, теперь моя
очередь [nyet, viy plat**ee**lee
fpr**o**shli ras, tyep**ye**r ma-**ya
o**chyeryet]

payphone телефон-
автомат [tyelyef**o**n-aftam**a**t]

peaceful мирный [**meer**ni]

peach персик [**pyer**seek]

peanuts арахис [a**ra**Hees]

pear груша [**groo**sha]

peas горох [ga**ro**H]

peculiar странный [**stran**-ni]

pedestrian crossing
пешеходный переход
[pyeshe**Ho**dni pyerye**Ho**t]

peg (for washing) прищепка
[preesh-ch**yep**ka]
(for tent) колышек [**ko**lishek]

pen ручка [**rooch**ka]

pencil карандаш [karan**dash**]

penfriend (man/woman)
знакомый/знакомая по
переписке [zna**ko**mi/
zna**ko**ma-ya pa pyerye**pee**skyeh]

penicillin пенициллин
[pyeneetsil**een**]

penknife перочинный
ножик [pyera**chee**n-ni **no**Jik]

pensioner (man/woman)
пенсионер/пенсионерка
[pyensee-an**yer**/pyensee-an**yer**ka]

people люди [**lyoo**dee]

the other people in the hotel
другие люди в гостинице
[droog**ee**-yeh **lyoo**dee
vgast**ee**neetse]

too many people слишком
много народу [**slee**shkam
mnoga na**ro**doo]

pepper (spice, vegetable) перец
[**pye**rets]

peppermint (sweet) мятная
конфета [**mya**tna-ya kan**fye**ta]

per: per night за ночь
[**za**nach]

how much per day? сколько
стоит в сутки? [**sko**lka
sto-eet f**soo**tkee?]

per cent процент
[prat**sent**]

perfect идеальный
[eedee-**al**ni]

perfume духи pl [doo**Hee**]

perhaps может быть [**mo**Jet
biyt]

perhaps not может быть,
нет [**mo**Jet biyt, nyet]

period (of time) период
[pyer**ee**-ot]
(menstruation) месячные pl
[**mye**syachni-yeh]

perm перманент
[pyerman**yent**]

permit (noun) разрешение
[razryeshenee-yeh]

person человек [chyela**vyek**]

personal stereo плейер
[**play**-yer]

petrol бензин [byen**zeen**]

petrol can канистра для
бензина [kan**ee**stra dlya
byen**zee**na]

petrol station бензоколонка
[byenzaka**lon**ka]

pharmacy аптека [ap**tye**ka]

 For minor medical
complaints, it's easiest to
go to a pharmacy
аптека (ap**tye**ka), many of which
now have a reasonable selection of
Western drugs. Choice is more
limited in provincial towns and
cities, so if you are on any

137

prescribed medication, bring enough supplies for your stay. This is particularly true for diabetics.

phone (noun) телефон
[tyelyefon]
(verb) звонить/позвонить
[zvaneet/pazvaneet]

 Virtually all public phones (taksafoni) now take brown plastic tokens (jetoni) – though you might still find the occasional old-style phone, taking 1-rouble coins (no longer legal tender, but still valid for making calls). The 'jetoni', which you can buy at most metro stations, must be placed in the slot before dialling; when your call connects, it will drop. A series of beeps indicates that the money is about to run out. Ordinary public phones can only be used for local calls, and the few inter-city payphones (myeJdoogarodni tyelyefon) in existence usually require special tokens that are impossible to find. There are various ways of making long-distance or international calls. If you are lucky enough to have access to a private phone, it is now possible to call just about anywhere direct, from the main cities, and considerably cheaper than booking calls through the international operator. The cost varies, depending on the time of day: it's cheapest to call between 10pm and 8am or at weekends.

Another way of making international calls is to go to a communications centre (pyeryegavorni poonkt) – there's one in every district of large cities. You pay in advance at the касса (kas-sa) and are given the number of booth from which you can dial direct; it might take several attempts to get through. If you don't succeed you'll have to stand in line again at the same counter to reclaim your money.

In Moscow it is also possible to use Comstar phones in the lobbies of major hotels, which take prepaid cards (sold on the spot) or Amex, Visa or JCB credit cards. These phones enable you to dial direct (but not call collect) at even steeper rates, but still works out cheaper than calling through a hotel switchboard or business centre.

phone book телефонный
справочник [tyelyefon-ni
spravachneek]
phone box телефонная
будка [tyelyefon-na-ya bootka]
phone call звонок [zvanok]
phonecard карточка для
телефона-автомата
[kartachka dlya
tyelyefona-aftamata]
phone number номер
телефона [nomyer tyelyefona]
photo фотография
[fatagrafee-ya]
excuse me, could you take a

photo of us? извините, пожалуйста, вы не могли бы нас сфотографировать? [eezveen**ee**tyeh, pa**J**alsta, viy nyeh mag**lee**bi nas sfatagraf**ee**ravat?]

phrasebook разговорник [razgav**o**rneek]

piano пианино [pee-an**ee**na]

pickpocket (man/woman) вор/воровка-карманник [vor/var**o**fka-karm**a**n-neek]

pick up: will you pick me up? вы заедете за мной? [viy za-**ye**deetyeh za mnoy?]

picnic пикник [peek**n**eek]

picture (painting) картина [kart**ee**na]
(photo) фотография [fatagrafee-ya]

pie пирог [peer**o**k]

piece кусок [koos**o**k]
a piece of ... кусок ... [koos**o**k ...]

pill таблетка [tabl**ye**tka]
I'm on the pill я принимаю противозачаточные таблетки [ya preeneema-yoo proteeva-zachatachni-yeh tabl**ye**tkee]

pillow подушка [pad**oo**shka]

pillow case наволочка [**n**avalachka]

pin булавка [bool**a**fka]

pineapple ананас [anan**a**s]

pineapple juice ананасовый сок [anan**a**savi sok]

pink розовый [**r**ozavi]

pipe (for smoking) трубка [tr**oo**pka]
(for water) трубопровод [troobaprav**o**t]

pity: it's a pity жаль [Jal]

place (noun) место [m**ye**sta]
at your place у вас [oo vas]
at his place у него [oo nyev**o**]

plain (not patterned) однотонный [adnat**o**n-ni]

plane самолёт [samal**yo**t]
by plane самолётом [samal**yo**tam]

plant растение [rast**ye**nee-yeh]

plasters пластыри [pl**a**stiree]

plastic пластмассовый [plasm**a**s-savi]

plastic bag пластиковый пакет [pl**a**steekavi pak**ye**t]

plate тарелка [tar**ye**lka]

platform платформа [platf**o**rma]
which platform is it for Sergiev Posad? с какой платформы идут поезда до сергиева посада? [skak**oy** platf**o**rmi eed**oo**t po-yezda da s**ye**rgee-yeva pas**a**da?]

play (verb) играть/сыграть [eegr**a**t/sigr**a**t]
(noun: in theatre) пьеса [p**ye**sa]

playground детская площадка [d**ye**tska-ya plash-ch**a**tka]

pleasant приятный [pree-**ya**tni]

please пожалуйста [pa**J**alsta]

yes please да, спасибо [da, spaseeba]

could you please ...? вы не могли бы ...? [viy nyeh magleebi ...?]

please don't пожалуйста, не надо [paJalsta, nyeh nada]

pleased: pleased to meet you очень приятно [ochyen pree-yatna]

pleasure: my pleasure пожалуйста [paJalsta]

plenty: plenty of ... много ... [mnoga ...]

we have plenty of time у нас много времени [oo nas mnoga vryemyenee]

that's plenty, thanks достаточно, спасибо [dastatachna, spaseeba]

pliers плоскогубцы [plaskagooptsi]

plug (electrical) штепсельная вилка [shtepsyelna-ya veelka] (for car) свеча [svyecha] (in sink) пробка [propka]

plumber сантехник [santyeHneek]

pm*: 2pm два часа дня [dva chasa dnya]

10pm десять часов вечера [dyesyat chasof vyechyera]

poached egg яйцо-пашот [yitso-pashot]

pocket карман [karman]

point: two point five две целых пять десятых [dvyeh tseliH pyat dyesyatiH]

there's no point нет смысла [nyet smiysla]

poisonous ядовитый [yadaveeti]

Poland Польша [polsha]

police милиция [meeleetsi-ya]

call the police! вызовите милицию! [viyzaveetyeh meeleetsi-yoo!]

 The police (meeleetsi-ya) are easily recognised by their blue-grey uniforms with red lapels and cap bands. Some of them now drive Western cars or police jeeps and, like the traffic police, they may well be armed.
In theory, you're supposed to carry some form of identification at all times, and the police can stop you in the street and demand it. In practice, they're rarely bothered if you're clearly a foreigner and tend to confine themselves to activities such as traffic control and harassing gypsies.
In an emergency dial 02 for the police.

policeman милиционер [meeleetsi-anyer]

police station отделение милиции [addyelyenee-yeh meeleetsee-ee]

policewoman женщина-милиционер [Jensh-cheena-meeleetsi-anyer]

Polish польский [polskee]

polish (for shoes) крем для обуви [kryem dlya aboovee]

polite вежливый [**vye**Jleevi]

polluted загрязнённый [zagryazn**yon**-ni]

pool (for swimming) бассейн [bas**yayn**]

poor (not rich) бедный [b**ye**dni] (quality) низкокачественный [n**ee**ska-ka**ch**yestvyen-ni]

pop music поп-музыка [pop m**oo**zika]

pop singer (man/woman) поп-певец/певица [pop pyev**yet**s/pyev**ee**tsa]

popular популярный [papool**ya**rni]

pork свинина [sveen**ee**na]

port (for boats) порт [port] (drink) портвейн [partv**yayn**]

porter (in hotel) швейцар [shvyayts**ar**]

portrait портрет [partr**yet**]

posh шикарный [shik**a**rni]

possible возможный [vazm**o**Jni]

is it possible to ...? возможно ли ...? [vazm**o**Jnalee]

as soon as possible как можно быстрее [kak m**o**Jna bistr**yeh**-yeh]

post (noun: mail) почта [p**o**chta] (verb) отправлять/отправить [atpravl**yat**/atpr**a**veet]

could you post this for me? вы не могли бы отправить это? [viy nyeh magl**ee**bi atpr**a**veet **e**ta]

postbox почтовый ящик [p**a**chtovi **ya**sh-cheek]

postcard открытка [atkr**iy**tka]

postcode почтовый индекс [p**a**chtovi **ee**ndeks]

poster плакат [plak**at**]

poste restante до востребования [da vastr**ye**bavanee-ya]

post office почта [p**o**chta]

The Russian postal system is notoriously inefficient, with outbound international mail taking on average a couple of weeks to reach its destination and incoming mail up to three weeks to arrive.

Most main post offices have post restante **до востребования** (da vastr**ye**bavanee-ya) sections, while American Express offices in Moscow and St. Petersburg will hold mail for Amex card or traveller's cheque holders for up to a month. Main post offices are open Mon–Fri 8am–8pm; Sat 8am–7pm; Sun 9am–7pm.)

Parcels must be taken to a main or international post office unwrapped; there they'll be inspected and wrapped for you, whereupon you can send them from any post office, or by a courier (a very expensive option). If you only want stamps, it's easier to go to the postal couriers in hotels, rather than queue in a post office, though there's a mark-up on the price.

potato картофель **m** [kartofyel]

pots and pans кухонная посуда [kooHan-na-ya pasooda]

pottery керамика [kyerameeka]

pound (money) фунт стерлингов [foont styerleengaf]

power cut отключение электричества [atklyoochyenee-yeh elyektreechyestva]

power point розетка [razyetka]

practise: I want to practise my Russian я хочу поупражняться в русском языке [ya Hachoo pa-oopraJnyatsa vrooskam yazikyeh]

prawns креветки [kreevyetkee]

prefer: I prefer ... я предпочитаю ... [ya pryetpacheeta-yoo ...]

pregnant беременная [byeryemyen-na-ya]

prescription (for medicine) рецепт [ryetsept]
see doctor and pharmacy

present (gift) подарок [padarak]

president (of country) президент [pryezeedyent]

pretty симпатичный [seempateechni]
it's pretty expensive это довольно дорого [eta davolna doraga]

price цена [tsena]

priest священник [svyash-chyen-neek]

prime minister премьер-министр [pryemyer meeneestr]

printed matter печатный материал [pechatni matyeryal]

prison тюрьма [tyoorma]

private частный [chasni]

private bathroom отдельная ванная [addyelna-ya van-na-ya]

probably вероятно [vyera-yatna]

problem проблема [prablyema]
no problem! нет проблем! [nyet prablyem]

program(me) программа [pragram-ma]

promise: I promise я обещаю [ya abyesh-cha-yoo]

pronounce: how is this pronounced? как это произносится? [kak eta pra-eeznoseetsa?]

properly (repaired, locked etc) как следует [kak slyedoo-yet]

protection factor (of suntan lotion) защитный фактор [zash-cheetni faktar]

Protestant протестантский [pratyestantskee]

public holiday официальный праздник [afeetsalni prazneek]

Public holidays are:
1 January (New Year's Day)

7 January (Orthodox Christmas)
23 February (Defender of the
Motherland Day)
8 March (International Women's Day)
Orthodox Easter
1 & 2 May (International Labour Day/
Spring Festival)
9 May (Victory Day)
12 June (Russian Independence Day)
21 August (anniversary of the 1991
putsch)
7 November (formerly the
anniversary of the Great October
Socialist Revolution)
12 December (Russian Constitution
Day)

public toilet туалет [too-al**yet**]
pudding (dessert) десерт
  [dyes**yert**]
pull тянуть/потянуть
  [tyan**oot**/patyan**oot**]
pullover свитер [sv**ee**ter]
puncture (noun) прокол
  [prak**ol**]
purple фиолетовый
  [fee-al**ye**tavi]
purse (for money) кошелёк
  [kashel**yok**]
  (US: handbag) сумочка
  [s**oo**machka]
push толкать/толкнуть
  [talk**at**/talkn**oot**]
pushchair детская коляска
  [d**ye**tska-ya kal**ya**ska]
put класть/положить
  [klast/palaj**iyt**]
  where can I put ...? куда
  мне положить ...? [kood**a**

mnyeh palaj**iyt** ...?]
  **could you put us up for the
  night?** нельзя ли нам
  переночевать у вас?
  [nyelz**ya**lee nam
  pyeryenacheev**at** oo vas?]
pyjamas пижама [peej**a**ma]

Q

quality качество [k**a**chyestva]
quarantine карантин
  [karant**een**]
quarter четверть f
  [ch**ye**tvyert]
question вопрос [vapr**os**]
queue (noun) очередь f
  [**o**chyeryet]
quick быстрый [b**iy**stri]
  **what's the quickest way
  there?** как туда побыстрее
  добраться? [kak tood**a**
  pabistr**yeh**-yeh dabr**a**tsa?]
  fancy a quick drink? не
  хотите пропустить
  стаканчик? [nyeh нат**ee**tyeh
  prapoost**eet** stakancheek?]
quickly быстро [b**iy**stra]
quiet (place, hotel) тихий
  [t**ee**нee]
  quiet! тише! [t**ee**sheh!]
quite: that's quite right
  совершенно верно
  [savyershen-na v**ye**rna]
  quite a lot довольно много
  [dav**o**lna mn**o**ga]

R

rabbit кролик [kroleek]
race (for cars) гонки pl [gonkee]
  (for runners) забег [zabyek]
  (for horses) скачки pl [skachkee]
racket (tennis, squash) ракетка [rakyetka]
radiator (in room) батарея [bataryeh-ya]
  (in car) радиатор [radee-atar]
radio радио [radee-o]
  on the radio по радио [pa radee-o]
rail: by rail поездом [po-yezdam]
railway железная дорога [Jelyezna-ya daroga]
rain (noun) дождь m [dosht]
  in the rain под дождём [pad daJdyom]
  it's raining идёт дождь [eedyot dosht]
raincoat плащ [plash-ch]
rape (noun) изнасилование [eeznaseelavanee-yeh]
rare (uncommon) редкий [ryetkee]
  (steak) с кровью [skrovyoo]
rash (on skin) сыпь f [siyp]
raspberry малина [maleena]
rat крыса [kriysa]
rate (for changing money) курс [koors]
rather: it's rather good очень неплохо [ochyen nyeploнa]

I'd rather ... (said by man/woman) я предпочёл/предпочла бы ... [ya pryetpachol/pryetpachla biy ...]
razor бритва [breetva]
razor blades лезвия бритвы [lyezvee-ya breetvi]
read читать/прочесть [cheetat/prachyest]
ready готовый [gatovi]
  are you ready? вы готовы? [viy gatovi?]
  I'm not ready yet (said by man/woman) я ещё не готов/готова [ya yesh-cho nyeh gatof/gatova]

dialogue

when will it be ready?
когда это будет готово?
[kagda eta boodyet gatova?]
it should be ready in a couple of days это будет готово через пару дней
[eta boodyet gatova chyeryes paroo dnyay]

real настоящий [nasta-yash-chee]
really действительно [dyestveetyelna]
  I'm really sorry я очень сожалею [ya ochyen saJalyeh-yoo]
  that's really great! это замечательно! [eta zamyechatyelna!]

really? (doubt) серьёзно? [syer**yo**zna?]
(polite interest) да? [da?]

rear lights задние фары [**za**dnee-ee **fa**ri]

rearview mirror зеркало заднего вида [**zy**erkala **za**dnyeva v**ee**da]

reasonable (prices etc) умеренный [oom**ye**ryen-ni]

receipt квитанция [kvee**ta**ntsi-ya]

recently недавно [nyed**a**vna]

reception (in hotel) служба размещения [sl**oo**Jba razmyesh-ch**ye**nee-ya]
at reception в службе размещения [fsl**oo**Jbyeh razmyesh-ch**ye**nee-ya]

reception desk конторка дежурного администратора [kant**o**rka dyeJ**oo**rnava admeeneestr**a**tara]

receptionist дежурный администратор [dyeJ**oo**rni admeeneestr**a**tar]

recognize узнать [ooz**na**t]

recommend: could you recommend ...? вы можете порекомендовать ...? [viy m**o**Jetyeh paryekamyendav**a**t ...?]

record (music) пластинка [plast**ee**nka]

red красный [kr**a**sni]

red wine красное вино [kr**a**sna-yeh veen**o**]

refund возмещение [vazmyesh-ch**ye**nee-yeh]
can I have a refund? могу я

получить обратно деньги? [mag**oo** ya palooch**ee**t abr**a**tna d**ye**ngee?]

region область f [**o**blast]

registered: by registered mail заказной почтой [zakazn**oy** p**o**cht]

registration number номер машины [n**o**myer mash**i**ni]

relative (man/woman) родственник/родственница [r**o**tstvyen-neek/ r**o**tstvyen-neetsa]

religion религия [ryel**ee**gee-ya]

remember: I don't remember я не помню [ya nyeh p**o**mnyoo]
I remember я помню [ya p**o**mnyoo]
do you remember? вы помните? [viy p**o**mneetyeh?]

rent (noun: for apartment) квартирная плата [kvart**ee**rna-ya pl**a**ta]
(verb: car etc) брать/взять напрокат [brat/vzyat naprak**a**t]

dialogue

I'd like to rent a car (said by a man/woman) я хотел/хотела бы взять напрокат машину [ya Hat**yel**/Hat**ye**la biy vzyat naprak**a**t mash**i**noo]
for how long? на какой срок? [na kak**oy** srok?]
two days два дня [dva dnya]
this is our range вот

перечень наших
машин [vot p**ye**ryechyen
n**a**shiн mash**i**yn]
I'll take the ... я возьму ...
[ya vazm**oo** ...]
is that with unlimited
mileage? это с
неограниченным
километражем? [**e**ta
snyeh-agran**ee**chyen-nim
keelamyetr**a**gem?]
it is да [da]
can I see your licence
please? ваши
водительские права,
пожалуйста [**v**ashi
vad**ee**tyelskee-yeh pr**a**va,
p**a**лalsta]
and your passport и ваш
паспорт [ee vash p**a**spart]
is insurance included?
включена ли страховка?
[fklyoochy**e**nalee straн**o**fka?]
yes, but you pay the first
1,000,000 roubles да, но
вы выплачиваете
первый миллион
рублей [da, no viy
vipl**a**cheeva-yetyeh p**ye**rvi
meelee-**o**n roobl**ya**y]
you have to leave a
deposit of 170,000 roubles
вы должны оставить
задаток в размере ста
семидесяти тысяч
рублей [viy dalжn**i**y ast**a**veet
zad**a**tak vrazm**ye**ryeh sta
syem**ee**dyestee t**i**ysyach
roobl**ya**y]

rented car взятая напрокат
машина [vz**ya**ta-ya naprak**a**t
mash**i**yna]
repair (verb) чинить/
починить [cheen**ee**t/
pacheen**ee**t]
can you repair it? вы
можете это починить? [viy
m**o**жetyeh **e**ta pacheen**ee**t?]
repeat повторять/
повторить [paftar**ya**t/
paftar**ee**t]
could you repeat that?
повторите, пожалуйста
[paftar**ee**tyeh, p**a**лalsta]
reservation
предварительный заказ
[pryedvar**ee**tyelni zak**a**s]
I'd like to make a reservation
(at hotel/theatre: said by a
man/woman) я хотел/хотела
бы заказать номер/билет
[ya на**tyel**/на**tyela** biy zakaz**a**t
n**o**myer/beel**ye**t]

dialogue

I have a reservation (at
hotel/theatre) у меня
заказан номер/билет
[oo myen**ya** zak**a**zan
n**o**myer/beel**ye**t]
what name please? ваше
имя, пожалуйста [v**a**sheh
eemya, p**a**лalsta]

reserve (verb) заказывать/
заказать заранее
[zak**a**zivat/zakaz**a**t zar**a**nyeh-yeh]

146

dialogue

can I reserve a table for tonight? могу я заказать столик на сегодня вечером? [mag**oo** ya zakaz**a**t st**o**leek na syev**o**dnya v**ye**chyeram]

yes madam, for how many people? да, пожалуйста, на сколько человек? [da, paJ**a**lsta, na sk**o**lka chyelav**ye**k?]

for two на двоих [na dva-**ee**н]

and for what time? на какое время? [na kak**o**-yeh vr**ye**mya?]

for eight o'clock на восемь часов [na v**o**syem chas**o**f]

and could I have your name please? ваше имя, пожалуйста [v**a**sheh **ee**mya, paJ**a**lsta]

see **alphabet** for spelling

rest: I need a rest мне нужно отдохнуть [mnyeh n**oo**Jna ad-daнn**oo**t]

the rest of the group остальные члены группы [astaln**iy**-yeh chl**ye**ni gr**oo**p-pi]

restaurant ресторан [ryestar**a**n]

Moscow and St Petersburg now abound with private cafés and restaurants offering everything from pizza to Indian, French and Chinese food. Prices are frequently astronomical. Although more and more privately owned eating places are opening up in the outlying towns and cities too, these are still relatively few and far between. In the regional centres, hotel restaurants generally offer a reasonable variety and standard of dishes and are relatively inexpensive.

For a full meal, you can go anywhere from the most basic self-service canteen **столовая** (stalova-ya) to a proper restaurant **ресторан** (ryestaran). In general restaurants open from mid-morning to about 11pm or midnight, usually with a break of a couple of hours in the afternoon. Russians like to unwind of an evening, so loud bands and energetic dancing are very much the order of the day in traditional Russian restaurants. Good affordable restaurants are usually full in the evenings, so advance booking is strongly advised.

restaurant car вагон-ресторан [vag**o**n-ryestar**a**n]

rest room туалет [too-al**ye**t]

retired: I'm retired я на пенсии [ya na p**ye**nsee-ee]

return: a return to ... туда и обратно до ... [tood**a** ee abr**a**tna da ...]

return ticket обратный билет [abratni beelyet]
see ticket

reverse charge call разговор, оплачиваемый вызываемым лицом [razgavor, aplacheeva-yemi viziva-yemim leetsom]

reverse gear задний ход [zadnee нot]

revolting отвратительный [atvrateetyelni]

rib ребро [ryebro]

rice рис [rees]

rich (person) богатый [bagati]
(food) жирный [jiyrni]

ridiculous нелепый [nyelyepi]

right (correct) правильный [praveelni]
(not left) правый [pravi]
you were right вы были правы [viy biylee pravi]
that's right правильно [praveelna]
this can't be right не может такого быть [nyeh moʌet takova biyt]
right! хорошо [нarasho]
is this the right road for ...? я доеду по этой дороге до ...? [ya da-yedoo pa eti darogyeh da ...?]
on the right справа [sprava]
to the right направо [naprava]
turn right поверните направо [pavyerneetyeh naprava]

right-hand drive вождение

по правой стороне [vaʌdyenee-yeh pa pravi staranyeh]

ring (on finger) кольцо [kaltso]
I'll ring you я вам позвоню [ya vam pazvanyoo]

ring back перезвонить [pyeryezvaneet]

ripe (fruit) зрелый [zryeli]

rip-off: it's a rip-off это обдираловка [eta abdeeralofka]

rip-off prices грабительские цены [grabeetyelskee-yeh tseni]

risky рискованный [reeskovan-ni]

river река [ryeka]

road дорога [daroga]
is this the road for ...? это дорога до ... [eta daroga da ...?]
it's just down the road это совсем близко отсюда [eta safsyem bleeska atsyooda]

road accident дорожная катастрофа [daroʌna-ya katastrofa]

road map дорожная карта [daroʌna-ya karta]

roadsign дорожный знак [daroʌni znak]

rob: I've been robbed меня ограбили [menya agrabeelee]

rock скала [skala]
(music) рок [rok]
on the rocks (with ice) со льдом [saldom]

roll (bread) булочка

[**boo**lachka]

Romania Румыния
[room**i**ynee-ya]

roof крыша [kr**i**ysha]

room (in hotel) номер [n**o**myer]
(in house) комната [k**o**mnata]
in my room в моём номере
[vma-**yom** n**o**myeryeh]

dialogue

do you have any rooms?
есть ли у вас
свободные номера?
[**yes**tlee oo vas svab**o**dni-yeh
namyer**a**?]

for how many people? для
скольких человек? [dlya
sk**o**lkeeн chyelav**yek**?]

for one/for two для
одного/двух [dlya
adnav**o**/dvooн]

yes, we have rooms free
да, у нас есть
свободные номера [da,
oo nas yest svab**o**dni-yeh
namyer**a**]

for how many nights will it
be? на сколько ночей?
[na sk**o**lka nach**yay**?]

just for one night только
на одну ночь [t**o**lka na
adn**oo** noch]

how much is it? сколько
это стоит? [sk**o**lka **e**ta
st**o**-eet?]

... with bathroom and ...
without bathroom ... с
ванной и ... без ванной

[... sv**a**n-nı ee ... byez v**a**n-nı]

can I see a room with
bathroom? можно
посмотреть номер с
ванной? [m**o**jna pasmatr**yet**
n**o**myer sv**a**n-nı?]

OK, I'll take it хорошо,
это подойдёт [нar**a**sho, eta
padidy**ot**]

room service обслуживание
в номере [apsl**oo**jivanee-yeh
vn**o**myeryeh]

rope канат [k**a**nat]

rosé (wine) розовое вино
[r**o**zava-yeh veen**o**]

roughly (approximately)
приблизительно
[preebleez**ee**tyelna]

round: it's my round моя
очередь [m**a**-ya **o**chyeryet]

roundabout (for traffic)
круговое движение
[kroogav**o**-yeh dveeж**e**nee-yeh]

route маршрут
[marshr**oot**]

what's the best route to ...?
как лучше добраться
до ...? [kak l**oo**chsheh dabr**a**tsa
da ...?]

rubber (material) резина
[ryez**ee**na]
(eraser) ластик [l**a**steek]

rubber band резинка
[ryez**ee**nka]

rubbish (waste) мусор
[m**oo**sar]
(poor quality goods) барахло
[baraнl**o**]

rubbish! (nonsense) чепуха!
[chyeрооna!]
rucksack рюкзак [ryookzak]
rude грубый [groobi]
ruins развалины [razvaleeni]
rum ром [rom]
  rum and Coke® кока-кола с
  ромом [koka-kola sromam]
run (verb: person) бежать/
  побежать [byeжat/pabyeжat]
  how often do the buses run?
  как часто ходят
  автобусы? [kak chasta нodyat
  aftoboosi?]
  I've run out of money у меня
  кончились деньги [oo
  menya koncheelees dyengee]
Russia Россия [rassee-ya]
Russian (adj, man) русский
  [rooskee]
  (woman) русская [rooska-ya]
  (language) русский язык
  [rooskee yaziyk]
  the Russians русские
  [rooskee-yeh]

S

sad грустный [groosni]
saddle (for bike, horse) седло
  [syedlo]
safe (not in danger) в
  безопасности
  [vbyezapasnastee]
  (not dangerous) безопасный
  [byezapasni]
safety pin английская
  булавка [angleeska-ya boolafka]

sail (verb) плавать/плыть
  [plavat/pliyt]
sailing (sport) парусный
  спорт [paroosni sport]
salad салат [salat]
salad dressing заправка к
  салату [zaprafka ksalatoo]
salami салями f [salyamee]
sale: for sale продаётся
  [prada-yotsa]
salmon лосось m [lasos]
salt соль f [sol]
same: the same то же самое
  [toжeh sama-yeh]
  the same as this такой же
  как этот [takoyжeh kak etat]
  the same again, please то
  же самое, пожалуйста
  [toжeh sama-yeh, paжalsta]
  it's all the same to me мне
  всё равно [mnyeh fsyo ravno]
sand песок [pyesok]
sandals сандали [sandalee]
sandwich бутерброд
  [booterbrot]
sanitary napkins/towels
  гигиенические
  прокладки [geegee-
  yeneechyeskee-yeh praklatkee]
Saturday суббота [soobota]
sauce соус [so-oos]
saucepan кастрюля
  [kastryoolya]
saucer блюдце [blyootseh]
sauna сауна [sa-oona]
sausage (salami) колбаса
  [kalbasa]
  (frankfurter) сосиска
  [saseeska]

say говорить/сказать
[gavar**eet**/sk**a**zat]

  **how do you say ... in
Russian?** как по-русски ...?
[kak pa-r**oo**skee ...?]

  what did he say? что он
сказал? [shto on skaz**a**l?]

  she said ... она сказала ...
[an**a** skaz**a**la ...]

  could you say that again?
повторите, пожалуйста
[paftar**ee**tyeh, paJ**a**lsta]

scarf (for neck) шарф [sharf]
  (for head) платок [plat**ok**]

scenery пейзаж [pyayz**a**sh]

schedule (US: timetable)
расписание [raspees**a**nee-yeh]

scheduled flight рейсовый
полёт [r**ya**ysavi pal**yo**t]

school школа [shk**o**la]

scissors: a pair of scissors
ножницы pl [n**o**Jneetsi]

scooter мотороллер
[matar**o**l-lyer]

scotch виски **n** [v**ee**skee]

Scotch tape® клейкая
лента [kl**ya**yka-ya l**ye**nta]

Scotland Шотландия
[shatl**a**ndee-ya]

Scottish шотландский
[shatl**a**ntskee]

  I'm Scottish (man/woman) я
шотландец/шотландка
[ya shatl**a**ndyets/shatl**a**ntka]

scrambled eggs яичница-
болтунья [ya-**ee**shneetsa-
balt**oo**nya]

scratch (noun) царапина
[tsar**a**peena]

screw (noun) винт [veent]

screwdriver отвёртка
[atv**yo**rtka]

sea море [m**o**ryeh]
  by the sea у моря [oo
m**o**rya]

seafood морские
продукты [marsk**ee**-yeh
prad**oo**kti]

search (verb) искать [eesk**a**t]

seasick: I feel seasick меня
укачало [men**ya** ookach**a**la]

  I get seasick меня
укачивает [men**ya**
ook**a**cheeva-yet]

seaside: by the seaside на
море [na m**o**ryeh]

seat место [m**ye**sta]

  is this seat taken? это
место свободно? [eta
m**ye**sta svab**o**dna?]

seat belt ремень **m** [ry**e**myen]

secluded уединённый
[oo-yedeen**yo**n-ni]

second (adj) второй [ftar**oy**]
  (in time) секунда [syek**oo**nda]

  just a second! секундочку!
[syek**oo**ndachkoo!]

second class (travel etc)
второй класс [ftar**oy** klas]

second floor третий этаж
[tr**ye**tee et**a**sh]
  (US) второй этаж [ftar**oy**
et**a**sh]

second-hand подержанный
[pad**ye**rJan-ni]

second-hand bookshop
букинистический
магазин

[bookeeneest**ee**chyeskee
magaz**ee**n]
see видеть/увидеть
[v**ee**dyet/oov**ee**dyet]
can I see? можно
посмотреть? [**mo**Jna
pasmatr**ye**t?]
have you seen ...? вы не
видели ...? [viy nyeh
v**ee**dyelee ...?]
I saw him this morning (said by
man/woman) я видел/видела
его сегодня утром [ya
v**ee**dyel/v**ee**dyela yevo syev**o**dnya
ootram]
see you! пока! [paka!]
I see (I understand) понятно
[pan**ya**tna]
self-service
самообслуживание
[sama-aps**loo**Jivanee-yeh]
sell продавать/продать
[pradav**a**t/prad**a**t]
do you sell ...? у вас
продаётся ...? [oo vas
prada-**yo**tsa ...?]
Sellotape® клейкая лента
[kl**ya**yka-ya l**ye**nta]
send посылать/послать
[pasil**a**t/pasl**a**t]
I want to send this to England
я хочу послать это в
Англию [ya Hach**oo** pasl**a**t eta
v**a**nglee-yoo]
senior citizen (man/woman)
пожилой человек/
пожилая женщина [paJil**oy**
chyelav**yek**/paJila-ya Jensh-cheena]
separate (adj) отдельный

[ad-d**ye**lni]
separated: we're separated
мы разошлись [miy
razashl**ee**s]
separately (pay, travel)
отдельно [ad-d**ye**lna]
September сентябрь m
[syent**ya**br]
septic септический
[syept**ee**chyeskee]
serious серьёзный [syer**yo**zni]
(illness) опасный [ap**a**sni]
service charge плата за
обслуживание [pl**a**ta za
aps**loo**Jivanee-yeh]
service station (for repairs)
станция
техобслуживания
[st**a**ntsi-ya
tyeHaps**loo**Jivanee-ya]
(for petrol) бензоколонка
[byenzakal**o**nka]
serviette салфетка [salf**ye**tka]
set menu комплексный
обед [k**o**mplyeksni ab**ye**t]
several несколько [n**ye**skolka]
sew шить/сшить
[shiyt/s-shiyt]
could you sew this back on?
вы не могли бы пришить
это [viy nyeh magl**ee**bi preesh**iy**t
eta]
sex секс [seks]
sexy привлекательный
[preevlyek**a**tyelni]
shade: in the shade в тени
[ftyenee]
shake: to shake hands
пожимать/пожать руку

[paJimat/paJat rookoo]

shallow мелкий [**my**elkee]

shame: what a shame! как жаль! [kak Jal!]

shampoo шампунь **m** [shamp**oo**n]

shampoo and set мытьё и укладка волос [mit**yo** ee ookl**a**tka val**o**s]

share: to share a room жить в одной комнате [Jiyt vadn**oy** k**o**mnatyeh]

to share a table сидеть за одним столом [seed**yet** za adn**ee**m stal**o**m]

sharp острый [**o**stri]

shattered: I'm shattered я совершенно без сил [ya savyersh**en**-na byes seel]

shaver бритва [br**ee**tva]

shaving foam пена для бритья [p**ye**na dlya breet**ya**]

shaving point розетка для электробритвы [raz**ye**tka dlya elyektrabr**ee**tvi]

shawl шаль **f** [shal]

she* она [an**a**]

is she here? она здесь? [an**a** zdyes?]

sheet (for bed) простыня [prastin**ya**]

shelf полка [**po**lka]

shellfish моллюск [mal**yoo**sk]

sherry херес [**H**y**e**ryes]

ship корабль **m** [kar**a**bl]

by ship на корабле [na karabl**yeh**]

shirt рубашка [roob**a**shka]

shit! чёрт! [chort!]

shock шок [shok]

I got an electric shock меня ударило током [men**ya** ood**a**reela t**o**kam]

shocking ужасный [oo**J**asni]

shoe (man's/woman's) ботинок/туфля [bat**ee**nak/t**oo**flya]

a pair of shoes ботинки/туфли [bat**ee**nkee/t**oo**flee]

shoelaces шнурки [shnoork**ee**]

shoe polish крем для обуви [kryem dlya **o**boovee]

shoe repairer's мастерская по ремонту обуви [mastyersk**a**-ya pa ryem**o**ntoo **o**boovee]

shop магазин [magaz**ee**n]

 The older-style, state-run stores tend to stock a fairly limited range of goods, although choice is improving all the time. At the other end of the scale, there are boutiques and supermarkets which cater for the new rich and where everything is imported and even foreigners reel at the prices (sometimes up to six times what you'd pay back home). In between are the countless private shops and street kiosks, given to cut-throat trading and selling goods past their sell-by dates.

In general, food stores are open Mon–Sat 8am–8pm with a break for lunch 1–2 pm. Other shops generally open 9, 10 or 11am to 7 or 8pm, usually with a 2–3pm or 3–4pm lunch break. Sunday opening hours are less predictable, although an increasing number of shops open on Sundays, as do most bars and restaurants. Many street kiosks are open 24 hours every day.

In most state-owned shops you order and get the price at the counter before paying at the cash desk касса (kas-sa) and taking the receipt back to claim your goods – a system that entails queuing at least twice. Stores quite often have only one 'kas-sa' serving a number of counters, in which case you will need to specify which one the receipt is for. Look out for a number above the counter and refer to it when you go to pay at the cash desk (e.g. 'pyat tiysyach rooblyay, pyerva-ya syektsi-ya' – five thousand roubles, 1st Section).

Fortunately, shopping in the private sector is much easier as most places operate on a self-service, pay-as-you-leave basis. Here, however, the pitfall is pricing. Items are often priced in US dollars or Deutschmarks, which the cashier converts into roubles at a rate (koors) set by the store (which should be posted). You may end up paying five to ten per cent more in real terms, unless you pay by credit card. Credit cards are fairly widely accepted in private shops, but haven't yet penetrated the state sector.

shopping: I'm going shopping я иду за покупками [ya eedoo za pakoopkamee]
shopping centre торговый центр [targovi tsentr]
shop window витрина [veetreena]
shore берег [byeryek]
short (person) невысокий [nyevisokee]
(time, journey) короткий [karotkee]
shortcut кратчайший путь [kratchishi poot]
shorts шорты [shorti]
should: what should I do? что мне делать? [shto mnyeh dyelat?]
you should ... вам следует ... [vam slyedoo-yet ...]
you shouldn't ... вам не следует ... [vam nyeh slyedoo-yet ...]
he should be back soon он должен скоро вернутся [on dolJen skora vyernootsa]
shoulder плечо [plyecho]
shout (verb) кричать/крикнуть [kreechat/kreeknoot]
show (in theatre) представление [pryetstavlyenee-yeh]
could you show me? покажите, пожалуйста [pakaJIytyeh, paJalsta]
shower (of rain) ливень m [leevyen]
(in bathroom) душ [doosh]
with shower с душем

154

[sd**oo**shem]

shower gel гель для душа **m**
[gyel dlya d**oo**sha]

shut (verb) закрывать/
закрыть [zakriv**a**t/zakr**iy**t]

  when do you shut? когда
  вы закрываетесь? [kagd**a** viy
  zakriv**a**-yetyes?]

  they're shut они закрыты
  [an**ee** zakr**iy**ti]

  I've shut myself out я не
  могу попасть внутрь [ya
  nyeh mag**oo** pap**a**st vnootr]

  shut up! замолчите!
  [zamalch**ee**tyeh!]

shutter (on camera) затвор
[zatv**o**r]

  (on window) ставень **m**
  [st**a**vyen]

shy застенчивый
[zast**ye**ncheevi]

sick (ill) больной [baln**oy**]

  I'm going to be sick (vomit)
  меня сейчас стошнит
  [myen**ya** syech**a**s stashn**ee**t]

  I feel sick меня тошнит
  [men**ya** tashn**ee**t]

side сторона [staran**a**]

  on the other side of the street
  на другой стороне улицы
  [na droog**oy** staran**yeh oo**leetsi]

side lights подфарники
[patf**a**rneekee]

side street переулок
[pyeryeh-**oo**lak]

sidewalk тротуар [tratoo-**a**r]

  on the sidewalk на
  тротуаре [na tratoo-**a**ryeh]

sight: the sights of ...

достопримечательности
... [dastapreemech**a**tyelnastee ...]

**sightseeing: we're going
sightseeing** мы идём
осматривать
достопримечательности
[miy eed**yo**m asmatreev**a**t
dastapreemech**a**tyelnastee]

sightseeing tour экскурсия
[eksk**oo**rsee-ya]

sign (roadsign etc) знак [znak]

signature подпись **f** [p**o**tpees]

signpost указатель **m**
[ookaz**a**tyel]

silence тишина [teesh**i**na]

silk шёлк [sholk]

silly глупый [gl**oo**pi]

silver серебро [syeryebr**o**]

similar похожий [pax**o**Ji]

simple (easy) простой
[prast**oy**]

since: since last week с
прошлой недели [spr**o**shli
nyed**ye**lee]

  since I got here (said by
  man/woman) с тех пор, как я
  приехал/приехала [styeн
  por, kak ya pree-**ye**нal/pree-**ye**нala]

sing петь/спеть [pyet/spyet]

singer (man/woman) певец/
певица [pyev**ye**ts/pyev**ee**tsa]

single: a single to ... билет в
один конец до ... [beel**ye**t
vad**ee**n kan**ye**ts da ...]

  I'm single (said by man/woman)
  я не женат/замужем [ya
  nyeh ɟen**a**t/z**a**mooɟem]

single bed односпальная
кровать [adnasp**a**lna-ya krav**a**t]

single room одноместный
номер [adnam**ye**sni **no**myer]

single ticket билет в один
конец [beel**yet** vad**ee**n kan**ye**ts]

sink (in kitchen) раковина
[**ra**kaveena]

sister сестра [syest**ra**]

sister-in-law (wife's sister)
свояченица
[sva-**ya**chyeneetsa]
(husband's sister) золовка
[zal**o**fka]

sit: can I sit here? можно
здесь сесть? [m**o**Jna zdyes
syest?]

is anyone sitting here? здесь
кто-нибудь сидит? [zdyes
kt**o**-neeboot seed**ee**t?]

sit down садится/сесть
[sad**ee**tsa/syest]

please, sit down садитесь,
пожалуйста [sad**ee**tyes,
pa**J**alsta]

size размер [razm**ye**r]

skate (verb) кататься на
коньках [kat**a**tsa na kank**a**н]

skates коньки [kank**ee**]

skating rink каток [kat**o**k]

ski (verb) кататься на
лыжах [kat**a**tsa na l**iy**Jaн]

skin кожа [k**o**Ja]

skinny тощий [t**o**sh-chee]

skirt юбка [**yoo**pka]

skis лыжи [l**iy**Ji]

sky небо [n**ye**ba]

sleep (verb) спать/поспать
[spat/pasp**a**t]

did you sleep well? вам
хорошо спалось? [vam

Harash**o** spal**o**s?]

sleeper (on train) спальный
вагон [sp**a**lni vag**o**n]

sleeping bag спальный
мешок [sp**a**lni myesh**o**k]

sleeping car спальный
вагон [sp**a**lni vag**o**n]

sleeping pills снотворные
таблетки [snatv**o**rni-yeh
tabl**ye**tkee]

sleepy: I'm feeling sleepy
меня клонит ко сну
[myen**ya** kl**o**neet ka snoo]

sleeve рукав [rook**a**f]

slide (photographic) слайд [slid]

slippers тапочки [t**a**pachkee]

slippery скользкий [sk**o**lskee]

Slovakia Словакия
[slav**a**kee-ya]

slow медленный
[m**ye**dlyen-ni]

slow down! помедленнее,
пожалуйста
[pam**ye**dleen-nyeh-yeh, pa**J**alsta]

slowly медленно
[m**ye**dlyen-na]

very slowly очень
медленно [**o**chyen
m**ye**dlyen-na]

**could you speak more
slowly?** вы не могли бы
говорить помедленнее?
[viy nyeh mag**lee**bi gavar**ee**t
pam**ye**dleenyeh-yeh?]

small маленький [m**a**lyenkee]

smell: it smells (smells bad)
плохо пахнет [pl**o**нa p**a**нnyet]

smile (verb) улыбаться/
улыбнуться

[oolibatsa/oolibnootsa]

smoke (noun) дым [diym]

  do you mind if I smoke? вы не возражаете, если я закурю? [viy nyeh vazraJa-yetyeh, **ye**slee ya zakoor**yoo**?]

  I don't smoke я не курю [ya nyeh koor**yoo**]

  do you smoke? вы курите? [viy **koo**reetyeh?]

snack: I'd just like a snack (said by man/woman) я хотел/хотела бы слегка перекусить [ya Hat**yel**/Hat**ye**la biy sl**ye**Hka pyeryekoos**eet**]

sneeze (verb) чихать/чихнуть [cheeнat/cheeнnoot]

snorkel дыхательная трубка [diнatyelna-ya tr**oo**pka]

snow снег [snyek]

  it's snowing снег идёт [snyek eed**yot**]

snowstorm метель **f** [myet**yel**]

so так [tak]

  this wine is so good очень хорошее вино [**o**chyen нar**o**sheh-yeh veen**o**]

  it's so expensive это так дорого [**e**ta tak d**o**raga]

  not so much не так много [nyeh tak mn**o**ga]

  not so bad не так уж плохо [nyeh tak oosh pl**o**нa]

  so am I, so do I я тоже [ya t**o**Jeh]

  so-so так себе [tak seeb**yeh**]

soaking solution (for contact lenses) раствор для линз

[rastv**or** dlya leenz]

soap мыло [**mi**yla]

soap powder стиральный порошок [steer**a**lni parash**ok**]

sober трезвый [**tr**yezvi]

sock носок [nas**ok**]

socket (electrical) розетка [raz**ye**tka]

soda (water) газированная вода [gazeer**o**van-na-ya vad**a**]

sofa диван [deev**an**]

soft (material etc) мягкий [**mya**нkee]

soft-boiled egg яйцо всмятку [yits**o** fsm**ya**tkoo]

soft drink безалкогольный напиток [byezalkag**o**lni nap**ee**tak]

soft lenses мягкие линзы [**mya**нkee-yeh l**ee**nzi]

soldier солдат [sald**at**]

sole (of foot) ступня [stoopn**ya**] (of shoe) подошва [pad**o**shva]

  could you put new soles on these? вы не могли бы поставить сюда новые подмётки? [viy nyeh magl**ee**bi past**a**veet sy**oo**da n**o**vi-yeh padm**yo**tkee?]

some: can I have some? дайте мне, пожалуйста [d**i**tyeh mnyeh, paJ**a**lsta]

  can I have some water/bread? дайте мне, пожалуйста воды/хлеба [d**i**tyeh mnyeh, paJ**a**lsta, vad**iy**/Hl**ye**ba]

somebody, someone кто-то [kt**o**-ta]

something что-нибудь
[shto-neeboot]
something to eat что-
нибудь поесть [shto-neeboot
pa-yest]
sometimes иногда [eenagda]
somewhere где-нибудь
[gdyeh-neeboot]
son сын [siyn]
song песня [pyesnya]
son-in-law зять [zyat]
soon скоро [skora]
I'll be back soon я скоро
вернусь [ya skora vyernoos]
as soon as possible как
можно скорее [kak mojna
skaryeh-yeh]
sore: it's sore болит [baleet]
sore throat: I've got a sore
throat у меня болит горло
[oo myenya baleet gorla]
sorry: I'm sorry прошу
прощения [prashoo
prash-chyenee-ya]
sorry! извините!
[eezveeneetyeh!]
sorry? (didn't understand)
простите? [prasteet-yeh?]
sort: what sort of ...?
какой ...? [kakoy ...?]
this sort такой [takoy]
soup суп [soop]
sour (taste) кислый [keesli]
soured cream сметана
[smyetana]
south юг [yook]
in the south на юге [na
yoogyeh]
South Africa Южная

Африка [yoojna-ya afreeka]
South African (adj)
южно-африканский
[yoojna-afreekanskee]
I'm South African я из
Южной Африки [ya eez
yoojni afreekee]
southeast юго-восточный
[yooga-vastochni]
southern южный [yoojni]
southwest юго-западный
[yooga-zapadni]
souvenir сувенир [soovyeneer]
Soviet советский [savyetskee]
Soviet Union Советский
Союз [savyetskee sa-yoos]
spade лопата [lapata]
Spain Испания [eespanee-ya]
Spanish (adj) испанский
[eespanskee]
spanner гаечный ключ
[ga-yechni klyooch]
spare part запчасть f
[zapchast]
spares запчасти [zapchastee]
spare tyre запасная шина
[zapasna-ya shiyna]
speak: do you speak English?
вы говорите
по-английски? [viy
gavareetyeh pa-angleeskee?]
I don't speak Russian я не
говорю по-русски [ya nyeh
gavaryoo pa-rooskee]

dialogue

can I speak to Nikolai?
можно Николая,

пожалуйста? [**mo**Jna neekal**a**-ya, paJ**a**lsta?]
who's calling? кто говорит? [kto gavar**eet**?]
it's Patricia это Патриша [**e**ta patr**ee**sha]
I'm sorry, he's not in, can I take a message? извините, его нет, вы хотите что-нибудь передать? [eezveen**ee**tyeh, yev**o** nyet, viy н**a**t**ee**tyeh sht**o**-neeboot pyeryed**a**t?]
no thanks, I'll call back later нет, спасибо, я перезвоню попозже [nyet, spas**ee**ba, ya pyeryezvan**yoo** pap**o**J-Jeh]
please tell him I called пожалуйста, передайте ему, что я звонила [paJ**a**lsta, pyeryed**ay**tyeh yem**oo**, shto ya zvan**ee**la]

spectacles очки [achk**ee**]
speed (noun) скорость f [sk**o**rast]
speed limit максимальная скорость [makseem**a**lna-ya sk**o**rast]
spell: how do you spell it? как это пишется по буквам? [kak **e**ta p**ee**shetsa pa b**oo**kvam?]
see **alphabet**
spend тратить/потратить [tr**a**teet/patr**a**teet]
spider паук [pa-**oo**k]
spin-dryer центробежная сушилка [tsentrab**ye**Jna-ya sooshi**y**lka]

spirits
Russia produces cognac (kan**ya**k) as well as vodka. It can be pretty rough compared with the genuine article. The best cognac hails from Armenia and Moldova, for instance белый аист (b**ye**li a-eest), 'white stork'.
see **vodka**

spoon ложка [l**o**shka]
sport спорт [sport]
sprain: I've sprained my ... (said by man/woman) я растянул/растянула ... [ya rastyan**oo**l/rastyan**oo**la ...]
spring (of car, seat) рессора [ryes-s**o**ra]
  (season) весна [vyesn**a**]
  in the spring весной [vyesn**oy**]
square (in town) площадь f [pl**o**sh-chat]
stairs лестница [l**ye**sneetsa]
stale несвежий [nyesv**ye**Ji]
stalls партер [part**er**]
stamp (noun) марка [m**a**rka]

dialogue

how much is a stamp for England? сколько стоит марка для Англии? [sk**o**lka st**o**-eet m**a**rka dlya angl**ee**-ee?]
what are you sending? что вы посылаете [shto

viy pasila-yeteyeh?]
this postcard эту
открытку [**e**too atkr**iy**tkoo]

star звезда [zvyezd**a**]
start (noun) начало [nach**a**la]
(verb) начинать/начать
[nacheen**a**t/nach**a**t]
when does it start? когда
начало? [kagd**a** nach**a**la?]
my car won't start моя
машина не заводится
[ma-**ya** mash**iy**na nyeh
zav**o**deetsa]
starter (food) закуска
[zak**oo**ska]
starving: I'm starving я
умираю от голода [ya
oomeer**a**-yoo at g**o**lada]
state (country) государство
[gasood**a**rstva]
(adj) государственный
[gasood**a**rstvyen-ni]
the States штаты [sht**a**ti]
station (rail) вокзал [vakz**a**l]
(underground, bus) станция
[st**a**ntsi-ya]
stationery канцелярские
принадлежности
[kantsel**ya**rskee-yeh
preenadl**ye**Jnastee]
statue статуя [st**a**too-ya]
stay: where are you staying?
где вы остановились?
[gdyeh viy astanav**ee**lees?]
I'm staying at ... (said by
man/woman) я остановился/
остановилась в ... [ya
astanav**ee**lsa/astanav**ee**las v ...]

**I'd like to stay another two
nights** (said by man/woman) я
бы хотел/хотела остаться
ещё на пару суток [**ya**bi
Hat**yel**/Hat**ye**la ast**a**tsa yesh-ch**o** na
par**oo** s**oo**tak]
steak бифштекс [beefsht**e**ks]
steal красть/украсть
[krast/ookr**a**st]
my bag has been stolen у
меня украли сумку [oo
men**ya** ookr**a**lee s**oo**mkoo]
steep (hill) крутой [kroot**oy**]
step: on the steps на
ступеньках [na stoop**ye**nkaH]
stereo стерео [st**ye**ryeh-o]
sterling фунт стерлингов
[foont st**ye**rleengaf]
steward (on plane) стюард
[st**yoo**-art]
stewardess стюардесса
[styoo-ard**e**s-sa]
still: I'm still here я ещё здесь
[ya yesh-ch**o** zdyes]
is he still there? он ещё
здесь? [on yesh-ch**o** zdyes?]
keep still! не двигайтесь!
[nyeh dv**ee**gityes!]
**sting: I've been stung by a
wasp** меня укусила оса
[men**ya** ook**oo**s**ee**la as**a**]
stockings чулки [ch**oo**lkee]
stomach желудок [Jel**oo**dak]
**stomach ache: I have stomach
ache** у меня болит живот
[oo men**ya** bal**ee**t Jiv**o**t]
stone (rock) камень **m**
[k**a**myen]
stop (verb)

останавливать/остановить [astanavleevat/astanaveet]
stop here, please (to taxi driver etc) пожалуйста, остановитесь здесь [paJalsta, astanaveetyes zdyes]
do you stop near ...? вы останавливаетесь у ...? [viy astanavleeva-yetyes oo ...?]
stop it! прекратите! [pryekrateetyeh!]
stopover остановка (в пути) [astanofka (fpootee)]
storm буря [boorya]
St Petersburg Санкт-Петербург [sankt-peetyerboork]
straight прямой [pryamoy]
(whisky etc) неразбавленный [nyerazbavlyen-ni]
it's straight ahead это прямо [eta pryama]
straightaway немедленно [nyemyedlyen-na]
strange (odd) странный [stran-ni]
stranger (man/woman) незнакомец/незнакомка [nyeznakomyets/nyeznakomka]
I'm a stranger here (said by man/woman) я здесь чужой/чужая [ya zdyes chooJoy/chooJa-ya]
strap (on watch, suitcase) ремешок [ryemyeshok]
(on dress) бретелька [bryetelka]
strawberry клубника

[kloobneeka]
stream ручей m [roochay]
street улица [ooleetsa]
on the street на улице [na ooleetseh]
streetmap план города [plan gorada]
string верёвка [vyeryofka]
strong (person, material, taste) сильный [seelni]
(drink) крепкий [kryepkee]
stuck: it's stuck застряло [zastryala]
student (male/female) студент/студентка [stoodyent/stoodyentka]
stupid глупый [gloopi]
suburb пригород [preegarat]
subway подземный переход [padzyemni pyeryeuenot]
(US: underground) метро [myetro]
suede замша [zamsha]
sugar сахар [saHar]
suit (noun) костюм [kastyoom]
it doesn't suit me (jacket etc) мне это не идёт [mnyeh eta nyeh eedyot]
it suits you вам это идёт [vam eta eedyot]
suitcase чемодан [chyemadan]
summer лето [lyeta]
in the summer летом [lyetam]
sun солнце [sontseh]
in the sun на солнце [na sontseh]
out of the sun в тени [vtyenee]

161

sunbathe загорать [zagar**a**t]
sunblock средство против
загара [sr**ye**tstva pr**o**teef zag**a**ra]
sunburn солнечный ожог
[s**o**lnyechni aJ**o**k]
sunburnt (burnt) обгорелый
[abgar**ye**li]
Sunday воскресенье
[vaskryes**ye**nyeh]
sunglasses очки от солнца
[ach**kee** at s**o**ntsa]
sunny: it's sunny солнечно
[s**o**lnyechna]
sunset закат [zak**a**t]
sunshade зонтик от солнца
[z**o**nteek at s**o**ntsa]
sunshine солнечный свет
[s**o**lnyechni svyet]
sunstroke солнечный удар
[s**o**lnyechni ood**a**r]
suntan загар [zag**a**r]
suntan lotion лосьон для
загара [las**yo**n dlya zag**a**ra]
suntanned загорелый
[zagar**ye**li]
suntan oil масло для загара
[m**a**sla dlya zag**a**ra]
super замечательный
[zamech**a**telni]
supermarket универсам
[ooneev**ye**rsam], супермаркет
[soopyerm**a**rkyet]

superstitions
Russians consider it bad
luck to kiss or shake
hands across a threshold or to go
back home for something that's
been forgotten. When offering

flowers, make sure there's an odd
number of blooms, as even-
numbered bouquets are for funerals.
Before going on a long journey,
Russians gather all their luggage by
the door and sit on it for a minute or
two to bring themselves good luck.

supper ужин [**oo**Jin]
supplement (extra charge)
доплата [dapl**a**ta]
sure: are you sure? вы
уверены? [viy oov**ye**ryeni?]
I'm sure (said by man/woman) я
уверен/уверена [ya
oov**ye**ryen/oov**ye**ryena]
sure! конечно! [kan**ye**shna!]
surname фамилия
[fam**ee**lee-ya]
sweater свитер [sv**ee**ter]
sweatshirt спортивная
майка [spart**ee**vna-ya m**i**ka]
Sweden Швеция [shv**ye**tsi-ya]
Swedish (adj) шведский
[shv**ye**tskee]
sweet (taste) сладкий
[sl**a**tkee]
(noun: dessert) десерт
[dyes**ye**rt]
sweets конфеты [kanf**ye**ti]
swelling опухоль f [**o**poohal]
swim (verb) плавать/
поплавать [pl**a**vat/papl**a**vat]
I'm going for a swim я иду
плавать [ya eed**oo** pl**a**vat]
let's go for a swim пойдём
поплаваем [p**i**d**yo**m
papl**a**va-yem]
swimming costume

su

купальник [koo**pa**lneek]

swimming pool бассейн [bas**ya**yn]

swimming trunks плавки [**pla**fkee]

Swiss швейцарский [shvyet**sa**rskee]

switch (noun) выключатель **m** [viklyoo**cha**tyel]

switch off выключать/ выключить [viklyoo**cha**t/ **viy**klyoocheet]

switch on включать/ включить [fklyoo**cha**t/ fklyoo**chee**t]

Switzerland Швейцария [shvyet**sa**ree-ya]

swollen распухший [ras**poo**Hshi]

T

table стол [stol]
  a table for two столик на двоих [**sto**leek na dva-**ee**H]
tablecloth скатерть **f** [**ska**tyert]
table tennis настольный теннис [nas**to**lni **te**nees]
table wine столовое вино [sta**lo**va-yeh vee**no**]
tailor портной [part**noy**]
take (verb: lead) брать/взять [brat/vzyat]
  (accept) принимать/ принять [preenee**ma**t/ pree**nya**t]
  can you take me to the ...?

вы можете отвезти меня в ...? [viy **mo**Jetyeh atvyes**tee** men**ya** v ...?]

do you take credit cards? вы принимаете кредитные карточки? [viy preeneema-yetyeh kryed**ee**tni-yeh kar**ta**chkee?]

fine, I'll take it хорошо, я возьму это [Hara**sho**, ya vaz**moo** eta]

can I take this? (leaflet etc) можно это взять? [**mo**Jna eta vzyat?]

how long does it take? сколько времени это займёт? [s**ko**lka v**rye**myenee eta zim**yo**t?]

it takes three hours это займёт три часа [eta zim**yo**t tree cha**sa**]

is this seat taken? это место свободно? [eta **mye**sta svabo**dna**?]

hamburger to take away гамбургер на вынос [**ga**mboorgyer na **viy**nas]

can you take a little off here? (to hairdresser) вы можете немного подстричь здесь? [viy **mo**Jetyeh nyem**no**ga patst**ree**ch zdyes?]

talcum powder тальк [tallk]

talk (verb) говорить/ поговорить [gava**ree**t/ pagava**ree**t]

tall высокий [vi**so**kee]

tampons тампоны [tam**po**ni]

tan загар [za**ga**r]

163

to get a tan загореть
[zagar**yet**]
tap кран [kran]
tape measure рулетка
[rool**ye**tka]
tape recorder магнитофон
[magneetaf**on**]
taste (noun) вкус [fkoos]
can I taste it? можно
попробовать? [**mo**Jna
pap**ro**bavat?]
taxi такси n [tak**see**]
will you get me a taxi?
вызовите для меня такси,
пожалуйста [**viy**zaveetyeh dlya
myen**ya** tak**see**, pa**J**alsta]
where can I find a taxi? где
можно поймать такси?
[gdyeh mo**J**na p**i**mat tak**see**?]

dialogue

to the airport/to the ...
Hotel, please в аэропорт/
в гостиницу ...,
пожалуйста [va-erap**o**rt/
vgast**ee**neetsoo ..., pa**J**alsta]
how much will it be?
сколько это будет
стоить? [sk**o**lka **e**ta b**oo**dyet
st**o**-eet?]
60,000 roubles
шестьдесят тысяч
рублей [shezdyes**ya**t t**iy**syach
roobl**yay**]
that's fine right here thanks
я выйду здесь, спасибо
[ya v**iy**doo zdyes, spas**ee**ba]

Taxis come in all shapes
and sizes. The official
ones are pale blue or
yellow Volgas or Moskveeches, with
a chequered logo on the door and a
dome light on the roof or green light
in the window. In practice, though,
you're more likely to find yourself
using an unmetered, unmarked
private taxi. Most Russians simply
flag down any vehicle, even
ambulances and trucks, and
negotiate the destination and fare.
Try to estimate the length of taxi ride
beforehand and offer what you think
is an appropriate fare. You should
pay about $5 for short journeys
around the town centre and $10 or
more (depending on the distance) to
go across town. Taxi fares are
considerably cheaper in the regions,
compared with Moscow and St
Petersburg. Rates are especially
high at airports where business is
monopolised by a 'taxi Mafia'.
see bus

taxi driver таксист [tak**see**st]
taxi rank стоянка такси
[sta-**ya**nka tak**see**]
tea (drink) чай m [chl]
one tea/two teas, please
один чай/два чая,
пожалуйста [ad**ee**n chl/dva
cha-ya, pa**J**alsta]
tea with milk чай с
молоком [chl smalak**o**m]
tea with lemon чай с
лимоном [chl sleem**o**nam]

Russians traditionally prepare a strong leaf brew (zavarka), topping it up with boiling water, from a samovar (a traditional ornate tea-urn). Note that tea is usually served with sugar already added, so you should make it clear when you order if you don't want sugar (byes saнara, paлalsta). If you're offered tea in someone's home, it may well be 'travyanoy', a tisane made of herbs and leaves.

Russians drink tea without milk; if you ask for milk it is likely to be condensed.

teabags чайные пакетики [chıni-yeh pak**ye**teekee]

teach: could you teach me? вы могли бы меня научить ...? [viy mag**lee**bi men**ya** na-ooch**ee**t ...?]

teacher (man/woman) учитель/учительница [ooch**ee**tyel/ooch**ee**tyelneetsa]

team команда [kam**a**nda]

teaspoon чайная ложка [ch**ı**na-ya l**o**shka]

tea towel чайное полотенце [ch**ı**na-yeh palat**ye**ntseh]

teenager подросток [padr**o**stak]

telegram телеграмма [tyelyegr**a**m-ma]

telephone телефон [tyelyef**o**n] see **phone**

television (set) телевизор [tyelyev**ee**zar]

(medium) телевидение [tyelyev**ee**dyenyeh]

tell: could you tell him ...? скажите ему, пожалуйста ... [ska**ı**tyeh yemoo, pa**л**alsta ...]

could you tell me where ...? вы не скажете, где ...? [viy nyeh ska**ı**tyeh, gdyeh ...?]

temperature (weather) температура [tyempyerat**oo**ra]

tennis теннис [t**e**n-nees]

tent палатка [pal**a**tka]

term (at university, school) семестр [syem**ye**str]

terminus (rail, underground) конечная станция [kan**ye**chna-ya st**a**ntsi-ya]

(bus, tram) конечная остановка [kan**ye**chna-ya astan**o**fka]

terrible ужасный [oo**ı**asni]

terrific замечательный [zamyech**a**tyelni]

than* чем [chyem]

smaller than ... меньше, чем ... [m**ye**nsheh, chyem ...]

thank: thank you/thanks спасибо [spas**ee**ba]

thank you very much большое спасибо [balsh**o**-yeh spas**ee**ba]

thanks for the lift спасибо, что подвезли [spas**ee**ba, shto padvyezl**ee**]

no, thanks нет, спасибо [nyet, spas**ee**ba]

165

dialogue

thanks спасибо [spaseeba]
that's OK, don't mention it
не за что [nyezashto]

that* тот m [tot], та f [ta], то n
[to]
that boy тот мальчик [tot
malcheek]
that girl та девочка [ta
dyevachka]
that one тот m [tot], та f [ta],
то n [to]
I hope that ... я надеюсь,
что ... [ya nadyeh-yoos, shto ...]
that's great отлично
[atleechna]
is that ...? это ...? [eta ...?]
that's it (that's right) точно
[tochna]
thaw (noun) оттепель f
[ot-tyepyel]
the*
theatre театр [tyeh-atr]
their*/theirs* их [eeн]
them*: I'll tell them я им
скажу [ya eem skaзoo]
I know them я их знаю [ya
eeн zna-yoo]
for them для них [dlya neeн]
with them с ними [sneemee]
to them им [eem]
who? -- them кто? – они
[kto? - anee]
then (at that time) тогда [tagda]
(after that) потом [patom]
there там [tam]
over there вон там [von tam]

up there там, наверху [tam,
navyerнoo]
is there/are there ...? есть
ли ...? [yestlee ...?]
there you are (giving something)
вот, пожалуйста [vot,
paзalsta]
thermometer термометр
[tyermomyetr]
Thermos® flask термос
[termas]
these* эти [etee]
I'd like these (said by
man/woman) я бы
хотел/хотела вот эти [yabi
Hatyel/Hatyela vot etee]
they* они [anee]
thick густой [goostoy]
(stupid) тупой [toopoy]
thief (man/woman)
вор/воровка [vor/varofka]
thigh бедро [byedro]
thin (person) худой [Hoodoy]
(thing) тонкий [tonkee]
thing вещь f [vyesh-ch]
my things мои вещи [ma-ee
vyesh-chee]
think думать/подумать
[doomat/padoomat]
I think so думаю, да
[dooma-yoo, da]
I don't think so я так не
думаю [ya tak nyeh
dooma-yoo]
I'll think about it я подумаю
об этом [ya padooma-yoo ab
etam]
third третий [tryetee]
thirsty: I'm thirsty мне

хочется пить [mnyeh Hochyetsa peet]

this* этот m [etat], эта f [eta], это n [eto]

this boy этот мальчик [etat malcheek]

this girl эта девочка [eta dyevachka]

this one этот m [etat], эта f [eta], это n [eto]

this is my wife это моя жена [eta ma-ya Jena]

is this ...? это ...? [eta ...?]

those* те [tyeh]

which ones? – those какие? – те [kakee-yeh? – tyeh]

thread (noun) нитка [neetka]

throat горло [gorla]

throat pastilles пастилки для горла [pasteelkee dlya gorla]

through через [chyeryes]

does it go through ...? (train, bus) он проезжает через ...? [on pra-yeJ-Ja-yet chyeryes ...?]

throw бросать/бросить [brasat/broseet]

throw away выбрасывать/выбросить [vibrasivat/viybraseet]

thumb большой палец [balshoy palyets]

thunderstorm гроза [graza]

Thursday четверг [chyetvyerk]

ticket билет [beelyet] (for bus) талон [talon]

dialogue

a return to Sergiev Posad обратный билет до сергиева посада [abratni beelyet da syergee-yeva pasada]

coming back when? когда обратно? [kagda abratna?]

today/next Tuesday сегодня/в следующий вторник [syevodnya/fslyedoosh-chee ftorneek]

that will be 10,000 roubles (это будет) десять тысяч рублей [(eta boodyet) dyesyat tiysyach rooblyay]

ticket office билетная касса [beelyetna-ya kas-sa]

ticket punch компостер [kampostyer]

tie (necktie) галстук [galstook]

tight (clothes etc) тесный [tyesni]

it's too tight тесновато [tyesnavata]

tights колготки [kalgotkee]

till касса [kas-sa]

time* время [vryemya]

what's the time? который час? [katori chas?]

this time в этот раз [vetat ras]

last time в прошлый раз [fproshli ras]

next time в следующий

раз [fsl**ye**doosh-chee ras]
three times три раза [tree r**a**za]
timetable расписание [raspees**a**nee-yeh]
tin (can) консервная банка [kans**e**rvna-ya b**a**nka]
tinfoil оловянная фольга [alav**ya**n-na-ya fal**ga**]
tin-opener консервный нож [kans**e**rvni nosh]
tiny крошечный [kr**o**shechni]
tip (to waiter etc) чаевые pl [cha-yev**iy**-yeh]

In taxis the fare will be agreed in advance, so there's no need to tip. In restaurants it's considered proper to leave an extra ten per cent or so, but it's not compulsory; check that it hasn't already been included in the bill. It's also customary to give a small tip to the cloakroom attendant if he helps you on with your coat.

tired усталый [**oo**stali]
I'm tired (said by man/woman) я устал/устала [ya oost**a**l/oost**a**la]
tissues бумажные носовые платки [boom**a**Jni-yeh nasav**iy**-yeh platkee]
to: to Moscow/London в Москву/в Лондон [vmaskv**oo**/vl**o**ndan]
to Russia/England в Россию/Англию [vrass**ee**-yoo/v**a**nglee-yoo]

to the post office на почту [na p**o**chtoo]
toast (bread) гренок [gryen**ok**]
tobacco табак [tab**ak**]
today сегодня [syev**o**dnya]
toe палец ноги [**pa**lyets nag**ee**]
together вместе [vm**ye**styeh]
we're together (in shop etc) мы вместе [miy vm**ye**styeh]
toilet туалет [too-al**ye**t]
where is the toilet? где туалет? [gdyeh too-al**ye**t?]
I have to go to the toilet мне нужно в туалет [mnyeh n**oo**Jna ftoo-al**ye**t]

Public toilets are few and far between; toilet paper is unlikely to be provided and standards of hygiene are often low. Assuming you can get past the bouncers, the toilets in restaurants or hotels are preferable.

toilet paper туалетная бумага [too-al**ye**tna-ya boom**a**ga]
token жетон [Jet**on**]
tomato помидор [pameed**or**]
tomato juice томатный сок [tam**a**tni sok]
tomato ketchup кетчуп [k**ye**tchoop]
tomorrow завтра [z**a**ftra]
tomorrow morning завтра утром [z**a**ftra **oo**tram]
the day after tomorrow послезавтра [poslyez**a**ftra]

toner (cosmetic)
тонизирующий лосьон
[taneezeeroo-yoosh-chee lasyon]
tongue язык [yazik]
tonic (water) тоник [toneek]
tonight сегодня вечером
[syevodnya vyechyeram]
tonsillitis тонзиллит
[tanzeeleet]
too (excessively) слишком
[sleeshkam]
(also) тоже [tojeh]
too hot слишком жарко
[sleeshkam jarka]
too much слишком много
[sleeshkam mnoga]
me too я тоже [ya tojeh]
tooth зуб [zoop]
toothache зубная боль **f**
[zoobna-ya bol]
toothbrush зубная щётка
[zoobna-ya sh-chotka]
toothpaste зубная паста
[zoobna-ya pasta]
top: on top of ... на ... [na ...]
at the top наверху
[navyerHoo]
top floor верхний этаж
[vyerHnee etash]
topless с обнажённой
грудью [sabnaJon-nI groodyoo]
torch фонарик [fanareek]
total (noun) итог [eetog]
tour (noun) экскурсия
[ekskoorsee-ya]
is there a tour of ...? есть ли
экскурсия по ...? [yestlee
ekskoorsee-ya pa ...?]
tour guide (man/woman)

экскурсовод [ekskoorsavot]
tourist (man/woman) турист/
туристка [tooreest/tooreestka]

 tourist information
Moscow and St Petersburg
have no centralized tourist
information centre where you can
walk in and get a map or an answer
to any question. The main Intourist
office can help with car rental,
currency exchange, theatre bookings
and other services. Most travellers
use the information/service desks at
major hotels which are usually
willing to help out for a fee even if
you're not staying there.
Useful sources for details of what's
on in Moscow are the local English-
language free newspapers, the
Moscow Times and the Moscow
Tribune. In St Petersburg, you might
want to consult the St Petersburg
Times (the St Petersburg equivalent
of the Moscow Times) or the St
Petersburg Yellow Pages.

tour operator бюро
путешествий [byooro
pootyeshestvee]
towards к [k]
towel полотенце
[palatyentseh]
town город [gorat]
in town в городе [vgoradyeh]
just out of town за городом
[zagaradam]
town centre центр города
[tsentr gorada]

169

town hall мэрия [**me**ree-ya]
toy игрушка [eeg**roo**shka]
track (US: platform)
  платформа [plat**for**ma]
tracksuit тренировочный
  костюм [tryenee**ro**vachni
  kas**tyoom**]
traditional традиционный
  [tradeetsi-**on**-ni]
traffic движение
  [dveeJe**nee**-yeh]
traffic jam пробка [**prop**ka]
traffic lights светофор
  [svyeta**for**]
train поезд [**po**-yest]
  by train поездом [**po**-yezdam]

 Buying tickets for long-distance or international trains is rarely easy. Aside from being unsure which outlet currently handles bookings for their destination, foreigners are also subject to constantly changing rules and charged twice as much for tickets as Russians are. If you're in Moscow you'll find it extremely tempting to use the Travellers' Guest House booking facility which frequently offers discounts on train tickets to Russian destinations, China or Europe, and charges only a modest fee.

When travelling by overnight train it's advisable to try and get a place in a two-berth 'soft class' compartment (es-veh). Although more expensive, these carriages are more comfortable and generally have a higher degree of security. Alternatively, there are the less expensive four-berth soft 'koop**eh**' in which the majority of Russians try to travel. Shortly after departure, the sleeping-car attendant will come around dispensing sheets (for a surcharge) and offering tea. A train journey is a good opportunity to socialize with your Russian fellow passengers – don't be surprised if they invite you to share a bottle of vodka and some 'kalbas**a**' (sausage) even before you leave the station. Sleeping arrangements on Russian trains are 'mixed' – if you feel uncomfortable with this, ask to change places with someone else (viy nyeh magle**e**bi pamyeny**a**tsa sa mnoy myesta**mee**?).

Tourist attractions outside the major towns and cities are generally accessible by suburban train (pree**g**aradni-yeh pa-yezda, or elyektr**ee**chka). Most mainline stations have a separate ticket office пригородная касса (pree**g**aradna-ya k**a**s-sa) for suburban trains, which may depart from an annexe to the main building. To make it easier to buy tickets and check timetables, get someone to write out the name of your destination in Cyrillic. Fares on these trains are extremely cheap, as foreigners pay the same price as Russians do.

see **underground**

dialogue

is this the train for Ufa?
это поезд до Уфы? [eta
po-yest da oofy?]
sure да [da]
**no, you want that platform
there** нет, вам нужна та
платформа [nyet, vam
nooJna ta platforma]

trainers (shoes) кроссовки
[krasofkee]
train station
железнодорожная
станция [Jelyeznadarojna-ya
stantsi-ya]
tram трамвай m [tramvI]
translate переводить/
перевести [pyeryevadeet/
pyeryeh-vyestee]
would you translate that?
переведите это,
пожалуйста
[pyeryeh-vyedeetyeh eta, paJalsta]
translator (man/woman)
переводчик/переводчица
[pyeryevotcheek/pyeryevotcheetsa]
trash мусор [moosar]
trash can мусорное ведро
[moosarna-yeh vyedro]
travel путешествовать
[pootyeshestvavat]
we're travelling around мы
путешествуем [miy
pootyeshestvoo-yem]
travel agent's бюро
путешествий [byooro
pootyeshestvee]

traveller's cheque
дорожный чек [daroJni
chyek]

Traveller's cheques
represent the safest form
of money available. US
dollar cheques are quite widely
accepted now in Moscow and St
Petersburg, and you should
encounter few problems with
Deutschmarks or sterling. Outside
big cities, however, it's more of a
problem finding somewhere to
change traveller's cheques, so you
may have to take a good proportion
of your money in dollar bills (low
denominations are best). With
opportunistic street crime generally
on the increase, a well concealed
money-belt is a must for the
traveller in Russia. It should also be
noted that the only brand of
traveller's cheque that can be easily
replaced if lost or stolen in Moscow
is American Express.
Amex will cash traveller's cheques
into dollars, Deutschmarks or
sterling, but it's better to change
them into roubles somewhere else.
In the two big cities traveller's
cheques are accepted by most
hotels but few bureaux de change
accept them.

tray поднос [padnos]
tree дерево [dyeryeva]
tremendous (large)
огромный [agromni]

171

(splendid) замечательный [zamyech**a**tyelni]

trendy модный [m**o**dni]

trim: just a trim please (to hairdresser) немного подровняйте, пожалуйста [nyemn**o**ga padravn**y**ltyeh, pa**J**alsta]

trip (excursion) экскурсия [eksk**oo**rsee-ya]

I'd like to go on a trip to ... я хочу съездить в ...[ya нach**oo** sy**e**zdeet v ...]

trolley тележка [tyel**ye**shka]

trolley bus троллейбус [tral**yay**boos]

trouble неприятность [nyepree-**ya**tnast]

I'm having trouble with ... у меня проблемы с ... [oo men**ya** prabl**ye**mi s ...]

trousers брюки [br**yoo**kee]

true верно [v**ye**rna]

that's not true это неправда [**e**ta nyepr**a**vda]

trunk (US: of car) багажник [bag**a**Jneek]

trunks (swimming) плавки [pl**a**fkee]

try (verb) пробовать/ попробовать [pr**o**bavat/ papr**o**bavat]

can I try it? можно я попробую [m**o**Jna ya papr**o**boo-yoo]

try on мерить/померить [m**ye**reet/pam**ye**reet]

can I try it on? можно померить? [m**o**Jna pam**ye**reet?]

T-shirt футболка [footb**o**lka]

Tuesday вторник [ft**o**rneek]

tuna тунец [toon**ye**ts]

tunnel m туннель m [t**oo**nel]

turn: turn left/right повернуть налево/ направо [pavyern**oot** nal**ye**va/ napr**a**va]

turn off: where do I turn off? где мне надо свернуть? [gdyeh mnyeh n**a**da svyern**oot**?]

can you turn the heating off? вы можете выключить отопление? [viy m**o**Jetyeh v**iy**klyoocheet atapl**ye**nee-yeh?]

turn on: can you turn the heating on? вы можете включить отопление? [viy m**o**Jetyeh fklyoocheet atapl**ye**nee-yeh?]

turning (in road) поворот [pavar**o**t]

TV (set) телевизор [tyelyev**ee**zar]

(medium) телевидение [tyelyev**ee**dyenyeh]

tweezers пинцет [peents**e**t]

twice дважды [dv**a**Jdi]

twice as much в два раза больше [vdva r**a**za b**o**lsheh]

twin beds две односпальные кровати [dvyeh adnasp**a**lni-yeh krav**a**tee]

twin room номер с двумя кроватями [n**o**myer sdvoom**ya** kpav**a**tyemee]

twist: I've twisted my ankle (said by man/woman) я

подвернул/подвернула ногу [ya padvyern**oo**l/ padvyern**oo**la n**o**goo]

type (noun) тип [teep]
 another type of ... ... другого типа [... droog**o**va t**ee**pa]

typical типичный [teep**ee**chni]

tyre шина [sh**i**yna]

U

ugly некрасивый [nyekras**ee**vi]

UK Соединённое Королевство [sa-yedeen**yon**-na-yeh karal**ye**fstva]

Ukraine Украина [ookra-**ee**na]

Ukrainian (adj) украинский [ookra-**ee**nskee]

ulcer язва [**ya**zva]

umbrella зонтик [**zo**nteek]

uncle дядя [d**ya**dya]

uncomfortable неудобный [nyeh-ood**o**bni]

unconscious без сознания [byes sazn**a**nee-ya]

under (in position) под [pot]
 (less than) меньше [m**ye**nsheh]

underdone (meat) недожаренный [nyedaJ**a**ryen-ni]

underground (railway) метро [myetr**o**]

Currently only Moscow and St Petersburg have major underground

systems, although Novosibirsk and Ekaterinburg now also offer limited services. In Moscow the underground runs daily 5.30am–1am. In St Petersburg trains run from 5.30am to midnight. On major holidays like New Year and the Russian Orthodox Christmas and Easter, trains run until 2am. Stations are marked with a large 'M' and have separate doors for incoming and outgoing passengers. Many have two or three exits, located 500-700 metres apart at street level, which can be disorienting if you pick the wrong one. Each exit is signposted with the appropriate street names (and even bus routes) at platform level. All signs and maps are in Russian only, so you'll have to learn to recognize the Cyrillic form of the words for 'entrance' **вход** (fHot), 'exit' **выход** (v**iy**Hat) and 'passage to another line' **переход** (pyereH**o**t).

Since the platforms carry few signs indicating which station you're at, it's advisable to pay attention to tannoy announcements in the carriages. As the train pulls into each station, you'll hear its name, immediately followed by the words 'sl**ye**doosh-cha-ya st**a**ntsi-ya' – and then the name of the next station. Most importantly, be sure to heed the words 'astar**o**Jna, dv**ye**ree zakriva-yootsa' – 'caution, doors closing'. For the metro, passengers buy plastic tokens (Jet**o**ni) to slip into the seemingly barrier-less turnstiles. If you don't insert a token, or try to walk through before the light turns green, automatic barriers slam shut, with painful force. Providing you don't leave the metro you can travel any distance and change lines as many times as you like using a single token. In Moscow, magnetic cards have also now been introduced on a trial basis.

If you're using a lot of public transport, you can save money by buying a monthly pass (yedeeni beelyet), which goes on sale in metro stations and kiosks towards the end of the month, for a few days only. This covers all forms of transport, but it's also possible to buy a pass just for the metro or for surface transport. To use the pass on the metro, flash it as you walk by the barrier at the end of the line of turnstiles.

underpants трусы [troosiy]
understand: I understand я понимаю [ya paneema-yoo]
I don't understand я не понимаю [ya nyeh paneema-yoo]
do you understand? вы понимаете? [viy paneema-yetyeh?]
unemployed безработный [byezrabotni]
unfashionable немодный [nyemodni]
United States Соединённые Штаты [sa-yedeenyon-ni-yeh shtati]
university университет [ooneevyerseetyet]
unleaded petrol неэтилированный бензин [nyeh-eteeleeravan-ni byenzeen]
unlimited mileage неограниченный километраж [nyeh-agraneechyen-ni keelamyetrash]
unlock открывать/открыть [atkrivat/atrkriyt]
unpack распаковывать/ распаковать [raspakovivat/ raspakavat]
until до [do]
unusual необыкновенный [nyeh-abiknavyen-ni]
up вверх [v-vyerн]
up there там наверху [tam navyerнoo]
he's not up yet он ещё не встал [on yesh-cho nyeh fstal]
what's up? в чём дело? [fchom dyela?]
upmarket элитарный [eleetarni]
upset stomach расстройство желудка [rastroystva Jelootka]
upside-down вверх дном [v-vyerн dnom]
upstairs наверху [navyerнoo]
up-to-date современный [savryemyen-ni]
urgent срочный [srochni]
us* мы [miy]

with us с нами [snamee]

for us для нас [dlya nas]

USA США [seh-sheh-a]

use (verb) пользоваться/воспользоваться [polzavatsa/vaspolzavatsa]

may I use your pen? можно воспользоваться вашей ручкой? [moJna vaspolzavatsa vashay roochki?]

useful полезный [palyezni]

usual обыкновенный [abiknavyen-ni]

the usual (drink etc) то, что обычно [to, shto abiychna]

usually обычно [abiychna]

V

vacancy: do you have any vacancies? у вас есть свободные номера? [oo vas yest svabodni-yeh namyera?]

see room

vacation отпуск [otpoosk]

on vacation в отпуске [votpooskyeh]

see holiday

vaccination прививка [preeveefka]

vacuum cleaner пылесос [pilyesos]

valid (ticket etc) действительный [dyaystveetyelni]

how long is it valid for? на сколько времени он действителен? [na skolka

vryemyenye on dyaystveetyelyen?]

valley долина [daleena]

valuable (adj) ценный [tsen-ni]

can I leave my valuables here? можно оставить здесь ценные вещи? [moJna astaveet zdyes tsen-ni-yeh vyesh-chee?]

value ценность f [tsen-nast]

van фургон [foorgon]

vanilla ваниль f [vaneel]

a vanilla ice cream ванильное мороженое [vaneelna-yeh maroJena-yeh]

vase ваза [vasa]

veal телятина [tyelyateena]

vegetables овощи [ovash-chee]

vegetarian (noun: man/woman) вегетарианец/вегетарианка [vyegeetaree-anyets/vyegeetaree-anka]

Russia is no place for vegetarians: meat takes pride of place in the country's cuisine. Pancakes блины (bleeniy) are a good option (ask for them with sour cream), but the best dishes to look out for are mushrooms cooked with onions and sour cream known as жульен (Joolyen), and окрошка (akroshka), the cold summer soup. In general the ethnic restaurants (Georgian, Armenian, Indian or Chinese) are better for vegetarians.

vending machine
(торговый) автомат
[(targ**o**vi) aftam**a**t]
very очень [**o**chyen]
very little for me совсем
чуть-чуть для меня
[safs**ye**m choot-ch**oo**t dlya
myen**ya**]
I like it very much мне
очень нравится [mnyeh
ochyen nr**a**veetsa]
vest (under shirt) майка [m**ı**ka]
via через [ch**ye**ryes]
video (noun: film) видео
[**vee**dee-o]
video recorder
видеомагнитофон
[**vee**dee-omagneet**a**fon]
view вид [veet]
village деревня [dyer**ye**vnya]
vinegar уксус [**oo**ksoos]
visa виза [**vee**za]

All foreign nationals
visiting Russia require a
passport and a visa,
which must be obtained in advance
from a Russian embassy or
consulate. Each embassy sets its
own visa prices according on how
quickly you need it. It's worth
spending the extra money to have
the entire business done through a
visa agency or tour operator.
There are several types of visa: the
most common one is a straight
tourist visa, valid for a precise
number of days up to a maximum of
thirty. To get this, you must have

proof of pre-booked accommodation.
If you're going on a package tour, all
the formalities can be sorted out for
you by the travel agency, though they
may charge extra for this.
A business visa is more flexible in
that it is valid for up to sixty days
(occasionally longer), and doesn't
require you to book accommodation
in advance. The procedure for
obtaining a business visa is now
quite bureaucratic. The host
company in Russia has to apply to
the Ministry of Foreign Affairs and it
may take 2–3 weeks for you to
receive an official invitation. Only
then can you apply for a visa.
If you wish to stay with Russian
friends, you'll need a private
individual visa, which is the most
difficult kind to obtain. This requires
a personal invitation from your
Russian host – cleared through OVIR
(Visa and Foreign Citizen's
Registration Department)
guaranteeing to look after you for
the duration of your stay. The whole
process can take up to three or four
months to complete.
If you are only planning to pass
through Russia en route to another
country, you must apply for a transit
visa, which is valid for up to 48
hours, for air transit. Note that if you
intend to leave Russia and enter any
other republic of the former Soviet
Union, you not only need a separate
visa for each independent state, but
also a multiple-entry visa to get

back into Russia.

By law, all foreigners are supposed to register with the OVIR within three days of arrival and obtain a stamp on their exit visa to that effect. In practice, registration isn't as bad as it sounds, since anyone coming on a tour or staying at a hotel will have this done for them automatically, so it only applies to those staying in some kind of 'unofficial' accommodation. Visitors who do not get a registration stamp may be fined on leaving Russia. OVIR is also responsible for issuing visa extensions, residence permits, and passports for Russian citizens. Its bureaucrats are notoriously unhelpful – so bring along a Russian to help out if possible.

visit (verb) посещать/
посетить [pasyesh-ch**at**/
pasyet**eet**]
I'd like to visit ... (said by man/woman) я хотел/хотела
бы посетить ... [ya
нat**yel**/нat**ye**la biy pasyet**eet** ...]
vital: it's vital that ...
абсолютно необходимо,
чтобы ... [apsal**yoo**tna
nyeh-apнad**ee**ma, sht**o**bi ...]
vodka водка [v**o**tka]

Vodka is the Russian national drink – its name means something like 'a little drop of water'. Normally served chilled, it is drunk neat in one gulp, preceded by a toast and followed by a mouthful of food. Unlike most drinks, taste isn't a prime consideration; what counts is that the vodka is pure (ch**ee**sta-ya), since many well known brands like **Столичная**® (stal**ee**chna-ya) are now counterfeited by bootleggers.

In shops and bars, you will also see flavoured vodkas such as **Перцовка** (pyerts**o**vka) – hot pepper vodka; **Лимонная**® (leem**o**n-na-ya) – lemon vodka; **Охотничья**® (aн**o**tneechya) – hunter's vodka, with juniper berries, ginger and cloves; **Старка**® (st**a**rka) – apple and pear-leaf vodka; and **Зубровка**® (zoobr**o**fka) – bison-grass vodka.

voice голос [g**o**las]
voltage напряжение
[napreeж**ye**nee-yeh]

Voltage is a standard continental 220 volts AC; most European appliances should work as long as you have an adapter for European-style two-pin round plugs. North Americans will need this plus a transformer. When using a computer in Russia, be wary of the fluctuations in the electricity current.

vomit тошнить/стошнить
[tashn**eet**/stashn**eet**]

177

waist талия [talee-ya]
waistcoat жилет [Jilyet]
wait ждать/подождать
[Jdat/padaJdat]
wait for me подождите
меня [padaJdeetyeh menya]
don't wait for me не ждите
меня [nyeh Jdeetyeh myenya]
can I wait until my wife/my
friend gets here? я могу
подождать до прихода
моей жены/моего друга?
[ya magoo padaJdat da preeноda
ma-yay Jeniy/ma-yevo drooga?]
can you do it while I wait?
вы можете это сделать
при мне? [viy moJetyeh eta
zdyelat pree mnyeh?]
could you wait here for me?
вы можете меня здесь
подождать? [viy moJetyeh
myenya zdyes padaJdat?]
waiter официант [afeetsi-ant]
waiter! официант!
[afeetsi-ant!]
waiting room (doctor's etc)
приёмная [pree-yomna-ya]
(station) зал ожидания [zal
aJidanee-ya]
waitress официантка
[afeetsi-antka]
waitress! девушка!
[dyevooshka!]
wake: can you wake me up at
5.30? пожалуйста,
разбудите меня в

половине шестого
[paJalsta, razboodeetyeh menya
fpalaveenyeh shestova]
wake-up call телефонный
будильник [tyelyefon-ni
boodeelneek]
Wales Уэльс [oo-els]
walk: is it a long walk? это
далеко пешком? [eta dalyeko
pyeshkom?]
it's only a short walk это в
нескольких шагах отсюда
[eta vnyeskalkeeн shagaн
atsyooda]
I'll walk я пойду пешком
[ya pidoo pyeshkom]
I'm going for a walk я иду
прогуляться [ya eedoo
pragoolyatsa]
Walkman® плейер [play-yer]
wall стена [styena]
wallet бумажник
[boomaJneek]
wander: I like just wandering
around я люблю бродить
[ya lyooblyoo bradeet]
want: I want ... я хочу ... [ya
Haчoo ...]
I don't want any ... я не
хочу ... [ya nyeh Haчoo ...]
I want to go home я хочу
пойти домой [ya Haчoo pitee
damoy]
I don't want to я не хочу [ya
nyeh Haчoo]
he wants to ... он хочет ...
[on Hoчyet ...]
what do you want? что вы
хотите? [shto viy Hateetyeh?]

ward (in hospital) палата
[pa**la**ta]

warm тёплый [**tyo**pli]
  I'm so warm мне жарко
  [mnyeh **ja**rka]

was*: **he was** он был ... [on
biyl ...]
  she was она была ... [on**a**
  bil**a** ...]
  it was это было ... [**e**ta
  biyla ...]

wash (verb: hands etc)
мыть/помыть [miyt/pam**iy**t]
(clothes) стирать/постирать
[steer**a**t/pasteer**a**t]
  can you wash these? вы
  можете это постирать?
  [viy **mo**jetyeh **e**ta pasteer**a**t?]

washhand basin раковина
[**ra**kaveena]

washing (clothes) бельё
[byel**yo**]

washing machine
стиральная машина
[steer**a**lna-ya mash**iy**na]

washing powder
стиральный порошок
[steer**a**lni parash**o**k]

**washing-up: to do the
washing-up** мыть/помыть
посуду [miyt/pam**iy**t
pas**oo**doo]

washing-up liquid жидкость
для мытья посуды **f**
[**Ji**ytkast dlya mit**ya** pas**oo**di]

wasp оса [as**a**]

watch (wristwatch) часы pl
[chas**iy**]
  will you watch my things for

me? присмотрите,
пожалуйста, за моими
вещами [preesmatr**ee**tyeh,
pa**Ja**lsta, za ma-**ee**mee
vyesh-ch**a**mee]

watch strap ремешок для
часов [ryemyesh**o**k dlya chas**o**f]

water вода [va**da**]
  may I have some water?
  можно мне воды,
  пожалуйста? [**mo**Jna mnyeh
  vad**iy**, pa**Ja**lsta?]

 Tap water is suspect in
some Russian cities and
should very definitely be
avoided in St Petersburg. You must
either use bottled water, or ensure
that the water has been boiled for
fifteen minutes.

Local fizzy mineral water is all right,
if a bit too salty and sulphurous for
most Westerners; Нарзан
(narz**a**n) and Боржоми (bar-
J**o**mee) from the Caucasus are the
best-known brands. Imported
mineral waters are also widely
available, as is local bottled spring
water such as 'Saint Springs', which
is produced by a Russian-American
joint venture.

waterproof (adj)
непромокаемый
[nyepramak**a**-yemi]

water-skiing воднолыжный
спорт [vadna-l**iy**Jni sport]

way: it's this way в эту
сторону [**ve**too st**o**ranoo]

it's that way в ту сторону [ftoo storanoo]
is it a long way to ...? далеко ли до ... [dalyekolee da ...?]
no way! ни в коем случае! [nee fko-yem sloocha-yeh!]

dialogue

could you tell me the way to ...? скажите, пожалуйста, как дойти до ...? [skaJiytyeh, paJalsta, kak ditee da ...?]
go straight on until you reach the traffic lights идите прямо, до светофора [eedeetyeh pryama, da svyetafora]
turn left сверните налево [svyerneetyeh nalyeva]
take the first turn on the right первый поворот направа [pyervi pavarot naprava]
see where

we* мы [miy]
weak слабый [slabi]
weather погода [pagoda]

dialogue

what's the weather forecast? какой прогноз погоды? [kakoy pragnos pagodi?]
it's going to be fine будет

хорошая погода [boodyet Harosha-ya pagoda]
it's going to rain будет дождливо [boodyet daJdleeva]
it'll brighten up later обещают просветление позже [abyesh-cha-yoot prasvyetlyenee-yeh poJ-Jeh]

wedding свадьба [svadba]
wedding ring обручальное кольцо [abroochalna-yeh kaltso]
Wednesday среда [sryeda]
week неделя [nyedyelya]
a week (from) today ровно через неделю [rovna chyeryes nyedyelyoo]
a week (from) tomorrow через неделю, считая с завтрашнего дня [chyeryes nyedyelyoo, sh-cheeta-ya z-zaftrashnyeva dnya]
weekend конец недели [kanyets nyedyelee]
at the weekend в субботу-воскресенье [vsoob-botoo-vaskryesyenyeh]
weight вес [vyes]
weird странный [stran-ni]
welcome: welcome to ... добро пожаловать [dabro paJalavat]
you're welcome (don't mention it) не за что [nyezashta]
well: I don't feel well мне нехорошо [mnyeh nyeHarasho]
she's not well ей нехорошо [yay nyeHarasho]

you speak English very well
вы очень хорошо
говорите по-английски
[viy **o**chyen Harash**o** gavar**ee**tyeh
pa-angl**ee**skee]

well done! молодец!
[malad**ye**ts]

this one as well этот тоже
[**e**tat t**o**Jeh]

well well! ну и ну! [noo ee
noo!]

dialogue

how are you? как вы
поживаете? [kak viy
paJiva-**ye**tyeh?]
very well, thanks, and you?
спасибо, хорошо, а вы?
[spas**ee**ba, Harash**o**, a viy?]

well-done (meat) хорошо
прожаренный [Harash**o**
praJ**a**ryen-ni]

Welsh уэльский [oo-**e**lskee]

I'm Welsh я из Уэльса [ya
eez oo-**e**lsa]

were*: we were мы были ...
[miy b**i**ylee ...]

you were вы были ... [viy
b**i**ylee ...]

they were они были ...
[an**ee** b**i**ylee ...]

West: the West Запад [**za**pat]

west запад [**za**pat]

in the west на западе [na
zapadyeh]

western западный [**za**padni]

West Indian (adj)

вест-индский
[vyest-**ee**ntskee]

wet мокрый [**mo**kri]

what? что? [shto?]

what's that? что это?
[shto-**e**ta?]

what should I do? что мне
делать? [shto mnyeh d**ye**lat?]

what a view! вот это вид!
[vot**e**ta veet!]

what bus do I take? на
какой автобус мне надо
сесть? [na kak**oy** aft**o**boos mnyeh
n**a**da syest?]

wheel колесо [kalyes**o**]

wheelchair инвалидная
коляска [eenval**ee**dna-ya
kal**ya**ska]

when? когда? [kagd**a**?]

when we get back когда мы
вернёмся [kagd**a** miy
vyern**yo**msya]

when's the train? когда
поезд? [kagd**a** p**o**-yest?]

where? где? [gdyeh?]

I don't know where it is я не
знаю, где это [ya nyeh
zn**a**-yoo, gd**ye**h-eta]

dialogue

where is the cathedral?
где собор? [gdyeh sab**o**r?]
it's over there вон там
[von tam]
**could you show me where
it is on the map?** вы
можете показать это
на карте? [viy m**o**Jetyeh

pakaz**a**t **e**ta na k**a**rtyeh?]
it's just here вот здесь
[vot zdyes]
see way

which: which bus? какой
автобус? [kak**oy** aft**o**boos?]

dialogue

which one? какой из
них? [kak**oy** eez neeн?]
that one тот [tot]
this one? этот? [etat?]
no, that one нет, тот [nyet,
tot]

while: while I'm here пока я
здесь [pak**a** ya zdyes]
whisky виски **n** [v**ee**skee]
white белый [b**ye**li]
white wine белое вино
[b**ye**la-yeh veen**o**]
who? кто? [kto?]
who is it? кто там? [kto tam?]
the man who ... человек,
который ... [chyelav**ye**k,
kat**o**ri ...]
whole: the whole week всю
неделю [vsyoo nyed**ye**lyoo]
the whole lot всё [fsyo]
whose: whose is this? чьё
это? [chyo **e**ta?]
why? почему? [pacheem**oo**?]
why not? почему бы нет?
[pacheem**oo**bi nyet?]
wide широкий [shir**o**kee]
wife жена [лen**a**]
will*: will you do it for me? вы

это сделаете для меня?
[viy **e**ta sdy**e**la-yetyeh dlya
myen**ya**?]
wind (noun) ветер [v**ye**tyer]
window окно [akn**o**]
near the window у окна [oo
akn**a**]
in the window (of shop) в
витрине [v-veetr**ee**nyeh]
window seat место у окна
[m**ye**sta oo akn**a**]
windscreen ветровое
стекло [vyetrav**o**-yeh styekl**o**]
windscreen wipers
стеклоочистители
[styekla-acheest**ee**tyelee],
дворники [dv**o**rneekee]
windsurfing виндсёрфинг
[veents**yo**rfeenk]
windy ветреный [v**ye**tryen-ni]
wine вино [veen**o**]
can we have some more
wine? можно ещё вина,
пожалуйста [m**o**лna yesh-ch**o**
veen**a**, paл**a**lsta]

The wine on sale in
Russia comes mostly
from Moldova, Georgia
and the Crimea, though some of the
Georgian wine has been subject to
counterfeiting. The ones to look out
for are the Georgian reds
Мукузани (mookoozanee) and
Саперави (sapyeravee), which
are both dry and drinkable, or the
sweeter Киндзмараули
(keendzmara-**oo**lee) and Акашени (akashenee). Georgia also

produces some of the best white wines, like the dry **Гурджани** (goordJanee) and **Цинандали** (tsinandalee) (traditionally served at room temperature). The best fortified wines, such as **Массандра** (massandra), come from the Crimea. Avoid what the Russians call 'baramat**oo**на' or 'babbling juice'.

wine list карта вин [**k**arta veen]
winter зима [**z**eema]
  in the winter зимой [zeem**oy**]
winter holiday зимний отпуск [**z**eemnee **o**tpoosk]
wire проволока [**pr**ovalaka] (electric) провод [**pr**ovat]
wish: best wishes с наилучшими пожеланиями [sna-eel**oo**chshimee paJilanee-yamee]
with с [s]
  I'm staying with ... я живу у ... [ya Jiv**oo** oo ...]
without без [byes]
witness (man/woman) свидетель/свидетельница [sveed**ye**tyel/sveed**ye**tyelneetsa]
  will you be a witness for me? (to man/woman) вы можете быть моим свидетелем/ моей свидетельницей? [viy moJetyeh biyt ma-**ee**m sveed**ye**tyel-yem/ma-**yay** sveed**ye**tyelneetsay?]
woman женщина [J**e**nsh-cheena]

women
As a visitor to Moscow, you will find that Russian men veer between extreme gallantry and crude chauvinism. Attitudes in Moscow and St Petersburg are much more liberal than in the countryside, where women travelling alone can still expect to encounter stares and comments. Single women should avoid going to certain nightclubs and bars, where their presence may be misconstrued by the local pimps and prostitutes. Although you'll see plenty of Russian women flagging down cars as potential taxis, unaccompanied foreign women would be ill-advised to do likewise.

Most hotels and nightclubs have their quota of prostitutes, run by whichever Mafia gang has struck a deal with the management. This causes problems for Russian women not involved in prostitution, who fear to enter such places alone lest they be mistaken for a freelance prostitute. If you should arrange to meet a Russian woman, respect any doubts she might express about the venue, and rendezvous outside so that you can go in together.

wonderful замечательный [zamyech**a**tyelni]
won't*: it won't start не заводится [nyeh zav**o**deetsa]
wood (material) дерево [d**ye**ryeva]

(forest) лес [lyes]

wool шерсть f [sherst]

word слово [slova]

work (noun) работа [rabota]

(verb) работать [rabotat]

it's not working это не
работает [eta nyeh rabota-yet]

I work in ... я работаю в ...
[ya rabota-yoo v ...]

world мир [meer]

worry: I'm worried я
беспокоюсь [ya
byespako-yoos]

worse: it's worse это хуже
[eta HooJeh]

worst самый плохой [sami
plaHoy]

worth: is it worth a visit?
стоит ли туда ехать?
[sto-eetlee tooda yeHat?]

would: would you give this
to ...? передайте это,
пожалуйста ... [pyeryedItyeh
eta, paJalsta ...]

wrap: could you wrap it up?
заверните, пожалуйста
[zavyerneetyeh, paJalsta]

wrapping paper обёрточная
бумага [abyortachna-ya
boomaga]

wrist запястье [zapyastyeh]

write писать/написать
[peesat/napeesat]

could you write it down?
запишите, пожалуйста
[zapeeshIytyeh, paJalsta]

how do you write it? как это
пишется? [kak eta peeshetsa?]

writing paper почтовая

бумага [pachtova-ya boomaga]

wrong неправильно
[nyepraveelna]

it's the wrong key это не
тот ключ [eta nyeh tot klyooch]

this is the wrong train вы не
на том поезде [viy nyeh na
tom po-yezdyeh]

the bill's wrong счёт
ошибочный [sh-chot
ashIybachni]

sorry, wrong number (said by
man/woman) извините, я не
туда попал/попала
[eezveeneetyeh, ya nyeh tooda
papal/papala]

sorry, wrong room (said by
man/woman) извините, я
ошибся/ошиблась
номером [eezveeneetyeh, ya
ashIypsya/ashIyblas nomyeram]

there's something wrong
with ... что-то не так с ...
[shto-ta nyeh tak s ...]

what's wrong? в чём дело?
[fchom dyela?]

X

X-ray рентгеновский
снимок [ryentgyenafskee
sneemak]

Y

yacht яхта [yaHta]

yard двор [dvor]

year год [got]
yellow жёлтый [Jolti]
yes да [da]
yesterday вчера [fchyera]
 yesterday morning вчера утром [fchyera ootram]
 the day before yesterday позавчера [pazafchyera]
yet ещё [yesh-cho]

dialogue

 is it here yet? оно ещё не пришло? [ano yesh-cho nyeh preeshlo?]
 no, not yet нет ещё [nyet yesh-cho]
 you'll have to wait a little longer yet вам придётся ещё немного подождать [vam preedyotsa yesh-cho nyemnoga padaJdat]

yoghurt йогурт [yogoort]
you* (sing pol or pl) вы [viy]
 (sing, fam) ты [tiy]
 this is for you это для вас [eta dlya vas]
 with you с вами [svamee]

Russian has two words for 'you': вы (viy) and ты (tiy). Вы (viy) is the polite form used when you are addressing someone you do not know at all or do not know well enough to consider a friend; it's also used as a sign of respect to an older person. It is also the plural form,

used for addressing more than one person. Ты is the singular, familiar form used when addressing a child or a friend. If you feel it is appropriate to start addressing someone in the ты form, but are unsure, just ask 'moJna pyeryaytee na tiy?'.

young молодой [maladoy]
your*/yours* (sing pol or pl) ваш m [vash], ваша f [vasha], ваше n [vasheh], ваши pl [vashee]
 (sing, fam) твой m [tvoy], твоя f [tva-ya], твоё n [tva-yo], твои pl [tva-ee]
 is this yours? это ваше? [eta vasheh?]
youth hostel молодёжная гостиница [maladyoJna-ya gasteeneetsa]

Z

zero нуль m [nool]
 below zero ниже нуля [neeJeh noolya]
zip молния [molnee-ya]
 could you put a new zip on? вставьте, пожалуйста, новую молнию [fstaftyeh, paJalsta, novoo-yoo molnee-yoo]
zip code почтовый индекс [pachtovi eendeks]
zoo зоопарк [zo-opark]

English → Russian

185

Russian

→

English

Colloquialisms

The following are words you may well hear. You shouldn't be tempted to use any of the stronger ones unless you are sure of your audience.

алкаш [**alkash**] wino, boozer
баксы [**baksi**] dollars
безобразие! [byezabra**zee-yeh!**] it's disgraceful!
блин! [bleen!] damn!
выпивка [**viy**peefka] bevvy, drink
деревянные [dyeryev**yan**-ni-yeh] roubles
дура/дурак [**doo**ra/doo**rak**] idiot, thickhead
ёлки-палки! [**yo**lkee-pal**kee!**] bloody hell!
ерунда! [eroon**da!**] nonsense!
здорово! [**zdo**rava!] great!
иди к чёрту! [ee**dee** k**chor**too!] go to hell!
козёл! [ka**zyol!**] idiot!
какого чёрта ...? [ka**ko**va **chor**ta ...?] what the hell ...?
какой ужас! [ka**koy oo**Jas!] that's awful!
класс! [klass!] great!, brilliant!
клёвый! [**klyo**vi!] knockout!, brill!, fantastic!
кретин [kryet**ee**n] twit
к черту! [k**chor**too!] to hell with it!
лимон [lee**mon**] a million
молодец! [mala**dyets!**] well done!
ничего себе! [neechye**vo** sye**byeh!**] not bad!
отвяжись! [atvya**Jiys!**] get lost!
парень [**pa**ryen] bloke
пошёл ты! [pa**shol** tiy!] get lost!
псих [pseeн] nutter
ребята [rye**bya**ta] (the) lads, (the) guys
сволочь [**svo**lach] bastard
с приветом [spree**vye**tam] crackers, nuts
хреновый [нrye**no**vi] rotten, lousy
хрен с ним! [нryen sneem!] to hell with it!
чёрт! [chort!] damn!, shit!
чёрт знает что [chort zna-yet shto] God only knows
чёрт с тобой! [chort sta**boy!**] to hell with you!
чокнутый [**cho**knooti] barmy
ужасно! [oo**Jas**na!] it's awful!, it's ghastly!
штука [sht**oo**ka] a thousand
это обдираловка [**e**ta abdeer**a**lafka] it's a rip-off

A

A bus stop

авария [ava**ree**-ya] accident; breakdown

август [**av**goost] August

авиакомпания [avee-a-kamp**a**nee-ya] airline

авиапочта [avee-a-p**o**chta] airmail

авиапочтой [**a**vee-a-p**o**chti] by airmail

Австралия [afstr**a**lee-ya] Australia

Австрия [**a**fstree-ya] Austria

автобус [aft**o**boos] bus

автовокзал [aftavakz**a**l] bus station

автоматический [aftamat**ee**chyeskee] automatic

автомобилист [aftamabeel**ee**st] car driver

автомобиль m [aftamab**ee**l] car

автоответчик [afta-atv**ye**tcheek] answering machine

автостоянка [aftasta-**ya**nka] car park, parking lot

автострада [aftastr**a**da] motorway, freeway, highway

агентство [ag**ye**nstva] agency

адвокат [advak**a**t] lawyer

администратор [admeeneestr**a**tar] manager

адрес [**a**dryes] address

адресат [adryes**a**t] addressee

адресная книга [**a**dryesna-ya kn**ee**ga] address book

Азербайджан [azyerbidj**a**n] Azerbaijan

аккумулятор [ak-koomool**ya**tar] battery (for car)

акселератор [aksyelyer**a**tar] accelerator

акцент [akts**e**nt] accent

алкоголь m [alkag**o**l] alcohol

аллергия [al-lyerg**ee**-ya] allergy

алмаз [alm**a**s] diamond

Америка [am**ye**reeka] America

американский [amyereek**a**nskee] American

амперный: 13-и амперный [amp**ye**rni] 13-amp

английская булавка [angl**ee**ska-ya bool**a**fka] safety pin

английский [angl**ee**skee] English

английский язык [angl**ee**skee yaz**i**yk] English (language)

англичане [angleech**a**nyeh] the English

англичанин [angleech**a**neen] Englishman

англичанка [angleech**a**nka] English woman

Англия [**a**nglee-ya] England

антигистамин [anteegeestam**ee**n] antihistamine

антикварная вещь [anteekv**a**rna-ya vyesh-ch] antique

антикварный [anteekv**a**rni] antiquarian; antique

антикварный магазин
[anteekvarni magazeen] antique
shop

аппендицит [ap-pyendeetsiyt]
appendicitis

аппетит [ap-pyeteet] appetite

апрель m [apryel] April

аптека [aptyeka] chemist,
pharmacy

арестовать [aryestavat] to
arrest

Армения [armyenee-ya]
Armenia

аромат [aramat] flavour

Архангельск [arнangyelsk]
Archangel

аспирин [aspeereen] aspirin

Афганистан [afganeestan]
Afghanistan

афиша [afeesha] poster

аэропорт [a-eraport] airport

Аэрофлот [a-eraflot] Aeroflot

Б

бабушка [babooshka]
grandmother

багаж [bagash] luggage,
baggage

багажник [bagaлneek] boot (of
car), (US) trunk

бак [bak] tank

бакалея [bakalyeh-ya]
groceries

балалайка [balalIka] balalaika

балкон [balkon] balcony

Балтийское море [balteeska-
yeh moryeh] Baltic Sea

бальзам для волос [balzam
dlya valos] conditioner

бампер [bampyer] bumper,
(US) fender

банк [bank] bank

банкнота [banknota]
banknote, (US) bill

банкомат [bankamat] cash
dispenser, ATM

баня [banya] bathhouse

бар [bar] bar

бармен [barmyen] barman

бассейн [basyayn] swimming
pool

батарейка [bataryayka]
battery

батарея [bataryeh-ya] radiator

башня [bashnya] tower

бегать/бежать [byegat/byeлat]
to run

бегать/бежать трусцой
[byegat/byeлat troostsoy] to jog

беда [byeda] trouble;
misfortune

бедный [byedni] poor

бедро [byedro] thigh; hip

бежать [byeлat] to run

бежевый [byeлevi] beige

без [byez] without

без двадцати два [byez
dvatsatee dva] twenty to two

безопасность [byezapasnast]
safety

в безопасности
[fbyezapasnastee] safe

безработный [byezrabotni]
unemployed

белокурый [byelakoori] blond

Белорусь [byelaroos] Belarus

белый [byeli] white

Бельгия [byelgee-ya] Belgium

бельё [byelyo] washing; underwear

бензин [byenzeen] petrol, gasoline

берег [byeryek] coast; shore
на берегу моря [na byeryegoo morya] at the seaside

берегись ... [byeryegees ...] beware of ...

беременная [byeryemyen-na-ya] pregnant

бесплатный [byesplatni] free of charge

беспокоиться [byespako-eetsa] to worry about

бесполезный [byespalyezni] useless

беспорядок [byesparyadak] mess

беспошлинный [byesposhleen-ni] duty-free

библиотека [beeblee-atyeka] library

бизнес [beeznes] business

билет [beelyet] ticket

билет в один конец [beelyet vadeen kanyets] single ticket, one-way ticket

билетная касса [beelyetna-ya kas-sa] ticket office

билеты [beelyeti] tickets

бить/побить [beet/pabeet] to hit, to beat

благодарить/поблагодарить [blagadareet/pablagadareet] to thank

благодарный [blagadarni] grateful

бланк [blank] form

ближайший [bleeJIshi] nearest

ближе [bleeJeh] nearer

близкий [bleeskee] near, close

близнецы [bleeznyetsiy] twins

близорукий [bleezarookee] shortsighted

блокнот [blaknot] notebook

блоха [blaha] flea

блузка [blooska] blouse

блюдо [blyooda] dish

блюдце [blyoodtseh] saucer

бог [boh] God

богатый [bagati] rich

Болгария [balgaree-ya] Bulgaria

более [bolyeh-yeh] more

болезнь f [balyezn] disease; illness

болеть/заболеть [balyet/zabalyet] to be ill; to fall ill; to be sore, to ache, to hurt

болеутоляющее средство [bolyeh-ootalyayoosh-chyeh sryetstva] painkiller

боль f [bol] ache; pain

боль в желудке [bol vJelootkyeh] stomach ache

больница [balneetsa] hospital

больной [balnoy] ill, (US) sick; sore; patient

больше [bolsheh] more

большинство [balshinstvo] most (of); majority

большой [balshoy] big, large

бомж [bomJ] homeless person

борода [bara**da**] beard
борт-проводник
 [bort-pra**vad**neek] steward
боюсь: я боюсь [ya ba**yoos**]
 I'm afraid
бояться [ba-**ya**tsa] to be
 afraid (of)
браслет [bras**lyet**] bracelet
брат [brat] brother
бриллиант [breel-lee-**ant**]
 diamond
британский [bree**tan**skee]
 British
бритва [**breet**va] razor
бритвенное лезвие
 [**breet**vyen-na-yeh l**yez**vee-yeh]
 razor blade
бриться/побриться [**breet**sa/
 pa**breet**sa] to shave
бровь f [brof] eyebrow
бросать/бросить
 [bra**sat**/**bro**seet] to throw
брошь f [brosh] brooch
брошюра [bra**shoo**ra]
 brochure; leaflet
брюки [bry**oo**kee] trousers,
 (US) pants
будет [**boo**dyet] he will; she
 will; it will; he will be; she
 will be; it will be
будете [**boo**dyetyeh] you will;
 you will be
будешь [**boo**dyesh] you will;
 you will be
будильник [boodeel**neek**]
 alarm clock
будить/разбудить [boo**deet**/
 razboo**deet**] to wake
буду [**boo**doo] I will; I will be

будут [**boo**doot] they will;
 they will be
будущее [**boo**doosh-chyeh-yeh]
 future
будьте здоровы! [**boo**dtyeh
 zda**rov**i!] bless you!
буква [**book**va] letter (of
 alphabet)
букинист [bookee**neest**]
 secondhand bookseller
букинистический магазин
 [bookeeneest**ee**chyeskee
 maga**zeen**] secondhand
 bookshop/bookstore
булавка [boo**laf**ka] pin
булочная [**boo**lachna-ya]
 bakery
бульвар [bool**var**] boulevard
бумага [boo**ma**ga] paper
бумажник [booma**J**neek]
 wallet
бумажные носовые платки
 [boo**maJ**ni-yeh nasa**viy**-yeh
 plat**kee**] tissues, Kleenex®
буря [**boo**rya] storm
бутылка [boo**tiyl**ka] bottle
буфет [boo**fyet**] snack bar,
 café
бы: я хотел бы ... [ya hat**yel**
 biy ...] I would like ...
бывать/побывать [**biv**at/
 pabi**vat**] to be; to frequent
бывший [**biy**fshi] former
был [biyl], была [biy**la**] was;
 were
были [**biy**lee] were
было [**biy**la] was
быстрее! [bist**ryeh**-yeh!] hurry
 up!

быстро [**biy**stra] quickly, fast
быстрый [**biy**stri] quick, fast
бытовая химия [**bi**tava-ya
 неe**mee**-ya] household
cleaning materials
быть [biyt] to be
бюро [byoo**ro**] office
бюро находок [byoo**ro** наanadak]
lost property office
бюро обслуживания [byoo**ro**
apsl**oo**Jivanee-ya] service
bureau
бюро путешествий [byoo**ro**
pootyesh**es**tvee] travel agent's
бюстгальтер [byoost**gal**tyer]
bra

В

в [v] in
вагон [vag**on**] carriage
вагон-ресторан [vag**on**-
ryestar**an**] dining car
важный [**va**Jni] important
ваза [**va**za] vase
валюта [val**yoo**ta] foreign
currency
вам [vam] (to) you
вами [**va**mee] (by) you
ванна [**van**-na] bath
ванная [**van**-na-ya] bath;
bathroom
вас [vas] you; of you
вата [**va**ta] cotton wool,
absorbent cotton
ваш [vash], ваша [**va**sha],
ваше [**va**sheh] your; yours
вашего [**va**sheva] (of) your;

(of) yours
ваше здоровье! [**va**sheh
zda**ro**vyeh!] cheers!
вашей [**va**shay] your; yours;
of your; of yours; to your;
to yours; by your; by yours
вашем [**va**shem] your; yours
вашему [**va**shemoo] (to) your;
(to) yours
ваши [**va**shi] your; yours
вашим [**va**shim] your; yours;
by your; by yours; to your;
to yours
вашими [**va**shimee] (by) your;
(by) yours
ваших [**va**shiн] (of) your; (of)
yours
вашу [**va**shoo] your; yours
в воскресенья и
праздничные дни [v-
vaskryes**ye**nya ee pr**a**zneechni-yeh
dnee] Sundays and public
holidays
вдова [vda**va**] widow
вдовец [vdav**yets**] widower
вдруг [vdrook] suddenly
вегетарианец
[vyegyetaree-**a**nyets] vegetarian
ведро [vyed**ro**] bucket
вежливый [**vye**Jleevi] polite
везде [vyezd**yeh**] everywhere
век [vyek] century
вёл [vyol], вела [vy**ela**] led; was
leading
вели [vyel**ee**] led; were
leading
Великобритания
[vyeleekabreetanee-ya] Britain
великолепный [vyeleeka**lyep**ni]

terrific, magnificent, splendid

велосипед [vyelaseep**yet**] bicycle

велосипедная трасса [vyelaseep**ye**dna-ya tras-sa] cycle path

Венгрия [**vye**ngree-ya] Hungary

веник [**vye**neek] bunch of birch twigs; broom

вентилятор [vyenteel**ya**tar] fan

верёвка [vyer**yo**fka] string; rope

верить/поверить [**vye**reet/pav**ye**reet] to believe

вернуть [vyern**oot**] to give back, to return

вернуться [vyern**oot**sa] to get back, to come back, to return

верный [**vye**rni] true

вероятно [vyera-**ya**tna] probably

верхний этаж [**vye**rнnee et**ash**] upper floor

верховая езда [vyerнava-ya yezd**a**] horse riding

вес [vyes] weight

веселиться: веселитесь! [vyesyel**ee**tyes!] have fun!

весёлый [vyes**yo**li] cheerful

весна [vyesn**a**] spring
весной [vyesn**oy**] in spring

вести [vyest**ee**] to drive; to lead

весь [vyes] all; the whole
весь день [vyes dyen] all day

ветер [**vye**tyer] wind

вечер [**vye**chyer] evening
добрый вечер [**do**bri v**ye**chyer] good evening
11 часов вечера [chas**of** v**ye**chyera] 11 pm

вешалка [**vye**shalka] peg; rack; stand; coathanger

вещи [**vye**sh-chee] things, belongings

вещь f [vyesh-ch] thing

взбешённый [vzbyesh**on**-ni] furious

вздор [vzdor] rubbish, nonsense

взлёт [vzlyot] take-off

взрослые [vz**ro**sli-yeh] adults

взрослый [vz**ro**sli] adult

взять [vzyat] to take

взять напрокат [vzyat naprak**at**] to rent

вид [veet] view; appearance; form

видео [**vee**dyeh-o] video

видеомагнитофон [**vee**dyeh-omagneeta**fon**] video recorder

видеть/увидеть [**vee**dyet/oo**vee**dyet] to see

видоискатель m [**vee**da-eesk**a**tyel] viewfinder

виза [**vee**za] visa

визит [veez**eet**] visit

визитка [veez**ee**tka], визитная карточка [veez**ee**tna-ya k**a**rtachka] business card

вилка [**vee**lka] fork

Вильнюс [**vee**lnyoos] Vilnius

винный магазин [**vee**n-ni magaz**een**] wine and spirits

shop

вираж [veer**ash**] bend

витамины [veetam**ee**ni] vitamins

витрина [veetr**ee**na] shop window

включать/включить [fklyooch**at**/fklyooch**eet**] to switch on

включён [fklyooch**on**] on, switched on; included

включено в цену [fklyoochyen**o** fts**eno**o] included in the price

включить [fklyooch**eet**] to switch on

вкус [fkoos] taste

вкусный [fk**oo**sni] nice; delicious, tasty

владелец [vlad**ye**lyets] owner

Владивосток [vladeevast**ok**] Vladivostok

вместе [vm**ye**styeh] together

вместо [vm**ye**sta] instead of

внешний [vn**ye**shnee] outward; external; foreign

вниз [vnees] down, downwards

внизу [vneez**oo**] downstairs

внимание [vneem**a**nee-yeh] attention

внутренние рейсы [vn**oo**tryen-nee-yeh r**yay**si] domestic flights

внутренний [vn**oo**tryen-nee] inner; inside; internal; domestic; inland

внутри [vnootr**ee**] inside

во время [va vr**ye**mya] during

вовремя [v**o**vryemya] on time

вода [vad**a**] water

водитель [vad**ee**tyel] driver

водительские права [vad**ee**tyelskee-yeh prav**a**] driving licence

водить/вести [vad**ee**t/vyest**ee**] to drive; to lead

водопад [vadap**at**] waterfall

возвращать/вернуть [vazvrash-ch**at**/vyern**oot**] to give back, to return

возвращаться/вернуться [vazvrash-ch**a**tsa/vyern**oo**tsa] to get back, to come back, to return

воздух [v**o**zdooH] air

воздушный шар [vazd**oo**shni shar] balloon

возместить [vazmyest**eet**] to refund

возможно [vazm**o**Jna] possible; perhaps

возражать: вы не возражаете если я …? [viy nyeh vazraJ**a**-yetyeh **ye**slee ya …?] do you mind if I …?

возраст [v**o**zrast] age

возьмите тележку/корзину [vazm**ee**tyeh tyel**ye**shkoo/ karz**ee**noo] please take a trolley/basket

войдите! [vid**ee**tyeh!] come in!

война [vɪn**a**] war

войти [vɪt**ee**] to enter, to go in

вокзал [vakz**al**] station (main-line railway)

Волгоград [valgagr**at**]

Volgograd
волосы [volasi] hair
вон: вон! [von!] get out!
  вон там [von tam] over there
вонь [von] stink
вообще [va-apsh-chyeh] at all;
  on the whole, generally
вопрос [vapros] question
вор [vor] thief
вор-карманник [var-karman-
  neek] pickpocket
ворота [varota] gate
воротник [varatneek] collar
восемнадцатый
  [vasyemnatsati] eighteenth
восемнадцать [vasyemnatsat]
  eighteen
восемь [vosyem] eight
восемьдесят [vosyemdyesyat]
  eighty
восемьсот [vasyemsot] eight
  hundred
воскресенье [vaskryesyenyeh]
  Sunday
восток [vastok] east
  к востоку от [k vastokoo ot]
  east of
восьмой [vasmoy] eighth
вот [vot] here is; that's
  вот и всё [vot ee fsyo] that's
  all
  вот, пожалуйста [vot,
  paJalsta] here is, here are;
  here you are
вот эти [vot etee] these
вот этот [vot etat] this one
вперёд [vpyeryot] forwards; in
  future; in advance
впереди [fpyeryedee] in front,

ahead; in front of; before; in
  future
врач [vrach] doctor
вредить/повредить [vryedeet/
  pavryedeet] to damage
время [vryemya] time
время года [vryemya goda]
  season
время отправления [vryemya
  atpravlyenee-ya] departure
  time
все [fsyeh] everyone; all
всё [fsyo] everything; all
всё вместе [fsyo vmyestyeh]
  altogether
всегда [fsyegda] always
всего [fsyevo] in all, only
всё-таки [vsyo-takee] anyway
вспомнить [fspomneet] to
  remember, to recall
вспышка [fspiyshka] flash
вставать/встать [fstavat/fstat]
  to get up
встретить [fstryeteet] to meet
встреча [fstryecha]
  appointment; meeting
встречать/встретить
  [fstryechat/fstryeteet] to meet
всякий [fsyakee] any
вторник [ftorneek] Tuesday
второй [ftaroy] second
второй этаж [ftaroy etash] first
  floor, (US) second floor
вход [fHot] entrance, way in
вход бесплатный [fHot
  byesplatni] admission free
вход воспрещён [fHot
  vaspryesh-chon] no
  admittance

вход свободный [fHot svab**o**dni] admission free

входите [fHad**ee**tyeh] come in

входить/войти [fHadeet/vIt**ee**] to enter, to go in

вчера [fchyer**a**] yesterday

вчера вечером [fchyer**a** vy**e**chyeram] last night (before midnight)

вчера днём [fchyer**a** dnyom] yesterday afternoon

вчера ночью [fchyer**a** n**o**chyoo] last night (after midnight)

вы [vIy] you

выбирать/выбрать [vIbeer**a**t/ v**Iy**brat] to choose

выбросить [v**Iy**braseet] to throw away

выглядеть [v**Iy**glyadyet] to look; to seem

выдача багажа [v**Iy**dacha bagaJ**a**] baggage claim

выдача покупок [v**Iy**dacha pak**oo**pak] purchase collection point

выиграть [v**Iy**-eegrat] to win

выйти [v**Iy**tee] to go out; to get off

выключатель m [vIklyooch**a**tyel] switch

выключать/выключить [vIklyooch**a**t/v**Iy**klyoocheet] to switch off

выключен [v**Iy**klyoochyen] off, switched off

выключить [v**Iy**klyoocheet] to switch off

вылет [v**Iy**lyet] departure

вылетать/вылететь

[vIlyet**a**t/v**Iy**lyetyet] to take off

выпить [v**Iy**peet] to drink

высокий [vIs**o**kee] tall; high

высота [vIsat**a**] height, altitude

выставка [v**Iy**stafka] exhibition

выставочный зал [v**Iy**stavachni zal] exhibition hall

высший [v**Iy**s-shee] higher; highest

выхлопная труба [vIHlapn**a**-ya troob**a**] exhaust pipe

выход [v**Iy**Hat] way out, exit; gate (at airport)

выход в город [v**Iy**Hat vg**o**rat] exit

выходить/выйти [vIHad**ee**t/ v**Iy**tee] to go out; to get off

выход на посадку [v**Iy**Hat na pas**a**tkoo] gate

выходной день ... [vIHadn**o**y dyen ...] closed on ...

выходные [vIHadn**iy**-yeh] weekend

выше [v**Iy**sheh] higher

вьюга [vy**oo**ga] snowstorm

Г

г. town/city

газ [gas] gas

газета [gaz**ye**ta] newspaper

газетный киоск [gaz**ye**tni kee-**o**sk] newsagent

газон [gaz**o**n] lawn

галантерея [galantyery**eh**-ya]

haberdashery

галерея [galer**yay**-a] gallery

галстук [gal**stook**] tie, necktie

гараж [gar**ash**] garage

гарантия [gar**a**ntee-ya] guarantee, warranty

гардероб [gardyer**op**] cloakroom

гастроном [gastran**om**] food store

гвоздь m [gvost] nail (in wall)

где? [gdyeh?] where?

где-нибудь [gd**yeh**-neeboot] somewhere; anywhere

где-то [gd**yeh**-ta] somewhere

г-жа [gaspa**J**a] Mrs; Ms; Miss

гигиеническая прокладка [geegee-yen**ee**chyeska-ya prakl**a**tka] sanitary towel/napkin

гид [geet] guide

главный [gl**a**vni] main, principal

гладить/погладить [gl**a**deet/pagl**a**deet] to iron

глаз [glas] eye

глубокий [gloob**o**kee] deep

глупый [gl**oo**pi] stupid

глухой [glooh**oy**] deaf

г-н [gaspad**ee**n] Mr

гнилой [gneel**oy**] rotten

говорить/сказать [gavar**ee**t/ska**za**t] to say; to speak

вы говорите по-... [vi gavar**ee**tyeh pa-...] do you speak ...?

год [got] year

годовщина [gadafsh-ch**ee**na]

anniversary

Голландия [gal-l**a**ndee-ya] Holland

голова [galav**a**] head

головная боль [galavn**a**-ya bol] headache

голодный [gal**o**dni] hungry

голос [g**o**las] voice

голый [g**o**li] naked

гомосексуалист [gomaseksoo-al**ee**st] gay, homosexual

гора [gar**a**] mountain

гораздо [gar**a**zda] much more

гордый [g**o**rdi] proud

гореть/сгореть [gar**ye**t/zgar**ye**t] to burn

горло [g**o**rla] throat

горничная [g**o**rneechna-ya] maid; cleaner

город [g**o**rat] town; city

городской [garadsk**oy**] town, city, urban

горький [g**o**rkee] bitter

горячий [gar**ya**chee] hot

господин [gaspad**ee**n] Mr; Sir

госпожа [gaspa**J**a] Miss; Mrs; Madam; Ms

гостеприимство [gastyepree-**ee**mstva] hospitality

гостиная [gast**ee**na-ya] lounge, living room

гостиница [gast**ee**neetsa] hotel

гость [gost]/**гостья** [g**o**stya] guest (male/female)

государство [gasood**a**rstva] state

готовить/приготовить [gat**o**veet/preegat**o**veet] to cook;

to prepare
готовый [gat**o**vi] ready
град [grat] hail
градус [gr**a**doos] degree
грамматика [gram-m**a**teeka] grammar
грампластинки [gramplast**ee**nkee] records
граница [gran**ee**tsa] border
  за границей [za gran**ee**tsay] abroad
гребная шлюпка [gryebn**a**-ya shly**oo**pka] rowing boat
Греция [gr**ye**tsi-ya] Greece
грипп [greep] flu
гроза [gra**za**] thunderstorm
гром [grom] thunder
громкий [gr**o**mkee] loud
громче [gr**o**mchyeh] louder
грубый [gr**oo**bi] rude; coarse
грудная клетка [groodn**a**-ya kl**ye**tka] chest
грудь f [groot] breast; chest
грузинский [grooz**ee**nskee] Georgian
Грузия [gr**oo**zee-ya] Georgia
грузовик [groozav**ee**k] lorry, truck
группа [gr**oo**pa] group
группа крови [gr**oo**pa kr**o**vee] blood group
грустный [gr**oo**stni] sad
грязное бельё [gr**ya**zna-yeh byely**o**] dirty laundry, washing
грязный [gr**ya**zni] dirty
губа [goob**a**] lip
губная помада [goobn**a**-ya pam**a**da] lipstick

гулять/погулять [gool**ya**t/pagool**ya**t] to go for a walk
густой [goost**oy**] thick

Д

д. house
да [da] yes
давай(те) ... [dav**i**(tyeh) ...] let's ...
давать/дать [dav**a**t/dat] to give
давление в шинах [davl**ye**nee-yeh fsh**i**naн] tyre pressure
давно [davn**o**] long ago; for a long time; long since
дадим [dad**ee**m] we will give
дадите [dad**ee**tyeh] you will give
дадут [dad**oo**t] they will give
даже [d**a**jeh] even
даже если [d**a**jeh y**e**slee] even if
далёкий [dal**yo**kee] far, far away
далеко [daly**e**ko] far, far away
дальше [d**a**lsheh] further
дам [dam] I will give
дама [d**a**ma] lady
Дания [d**a**nee-ya] Denmark
дарить/подарить [dar**ee**t/ padar**ee**t] to give (present)
даст [dast] he will give; she will give; it will give
дать [dat] to give
дача [d**a**cha] house/cottage in the country

дашь [dash] you will give

два [dva] two

двадцатый [dvatsati] twentieth

двадцать [dvatsat] twenty

две [dvyeh] two

две недели [dvyeh nyedyelee] fortnight, two weeks

двенадцатый [dvyenatsati] twelfth

двенадцать [dvyenatsat] twelve

дверь f [dvyer] door

двести [dvyestee] two hundred

двойной [dvinoy] double

дворец [dvaryets] palace

дворник [dvorneek] windscreen wiper; janitor; street cleaner

двухместный номер [dvooh-myesni nomyer] double room

двухразовое питание [dvoohrazava-yeh peetanee-yeh] half board

дебютант [dyebyootant] beginner

деверь [dyevyer] brother-in-law (husband's brother)

девичья фамилия [dyeveechya fameelee-ya] maiden name

девочка [dyevachka] girl (child)

девушка [dyevooshka] girl (young woman)

девяносто [dyevyanosta] ninety

девятнадцатый [dyevyatnatsati] nineteenth

девятнадцать [dyevyatnatsat]

nineteen

девятый [dyevyati] ninth

девять [dyevyat] nine

девятьсот [dyevyatsot] nine hundred

дедушка [dyedooshka] grandfather

дежурная [dyeJoorna-ya] concierge

дежурная аптека [dyeJoorna-ya aptyeka] duty pharmacist

дезинфицирующее средство [dyezeenfeetseeroo-yoosh-chyeh sryetstva] antiseptic; disinfectant

дезодорант [dyezadarant] deodorant

действительно [dyaystveetyelna] really, indeed

действительный [dyaystveetyelni] valid

декабрь m [dyekabr] December

делать/сделать [dyelat/zdyelat] to do; to make

делиться/поделиться [dyeleetsa/padyeleetsa] to share

дело [dyela] matter, business

в самом деле [fsamam dyelyeh] really

как дела? [kak dyela?] how are you?, how are things?

день m [dyen] day

деньги [dyengee] money

день рождения [dyen raJdyenee-ya] birthday

деревня [dyeryevnya] countryside; village

дерево [dyeryeva] tree; wood

из дерева [eez d**ye**ryeva] wooden

держать [dyer**J**at] to hold; to keep; to support

держитесь левой стороны [dyer**J**eetyes l**ye**vi staran**iy**] keep to the left

десятый [dyes**ya**ti] tenth

десять [d**ye**syat] ten

дети [d**ye**tee] children

детская коляска [d**ye**tska-ya kal**ya**ska] pram, baby carriage

детская кроватка [d**ye**tska-ya krav**a**tka] cot

детская порция [d**ye**tska-ya p**o**rtsi-ya] children's portion

дешевле [dyesh**e**vlye] cheaper

дешёвый [dyesh**o**vi] cheap

джинсы [dJ**ee**nsi] jeans

диабетик [dee-ab**ye**teek] diabetic

диета [dee-**ye**ta] diet

дизель m [d**ee**zyel] diesel

дикий [d**ee**kee] wild

директор [deer**ye**ktar] director

дискотека [deeskat**ye**ka] disco

длина [dleen**a**] length

длинный [dl**ee**n-ni] long

для [dlya] for

для вас/меня [dlya vas/ myen**ya**] for you/me

для некурящих [dlya nyekoor**ya**sh-cheeн] non-smoking

дневник [dnyevn**ee**k] diary

днём [dny**o**m] in the afternoon; p.m.

дно [dn**o**] bottom

на дне [na dny**e**h] at the bottom of

до [d**o**] up to, as far as; before; until

доброе утро [d**o**bra-yeh **oo**tra] good morning

добрый [d**o**bri] good; kind

добрый вечер [d**o**bri v**ye**chyer] good evening

добрый день [d**o**bri dyen] good afternoon

довольно [dav**o**lna] quite; fairly

довольно хорошо [dav**o**lna нarash**o**] pretty good

довольный [dav**o**lni] pleased

до востребования [da vastr**ye**bavanee-ya] poste restante, general delivery

договор [dagav**o**r] contract

дождик [d**o**Jdeek] shower

дождливый [daJdl**ee**vi] rainy

дождь m [d**o**sht] rain

идёт дождь [eed**yo**t dosht] it's raining

документ [dakoom**ye**nt] document

долго [d**o**lga] a long time

должен: я/он должен [ya/on d**o**lJen] I/he must

должна: я/она должна [ya/ana dalJn**a**] I/she must

долина [dal**ee**na] valley

дом [dom] house; home

дома [d**o**ma] at home

он дома? [on d**o**ma?] is he in?

доплата [dapl**a**ta] supplement

дорога [dar**o**ga] road

дорогой [darag**oy**] expensive,

dear

дороже [daroJeh] dearer

дорожные работы [daroJni-yeh raboti] roadworks

дорожный чек [daroJni chyek] traveller's cheque/check

досадно [dasadna] annoying

до свидания [da sveedanya] goodbye

доставать/достать [dastavat/dastat] to get, to obtain

достаточно [dastatachna] enough

достать [dastat] to get, to obtain

дочь [doch] daughter

драка [draka] fight

древний [dryevnee] ancient

друг [drook] friend; boyfriend

другой [droogoy] other; another, a different

в другом месте [vdroogom myestyeh] elsewhere

что-то другое [shto-ta droogoy-yeh] something else

думать/подумать [doomat/padoomat] to think

я думаю, что ... [ya dooma-yoo, shto ...] I think that ...

духи [doonee] perfume

духовка [dooнofka] oven

душ [doosh] shower

дым [diym] smoke

дыра [dira] hole

дышать [dishat] to breathe

дядя [dyadya] uncle

E

еврейский [yevryayskee] Jewish

Европа [yevropa] Europe

европейский [yevrapyayskee] European

его [yevo] him; it; of him; of it; his; its

еда [yeda] food; meal

едим [yedeem] we eat

единый билет [yedeeni beelyet] monthly season ticket

едите [yedeetyeh] you eat

едят [yedyat] they eat

её [yeh-yo] her; it; of her; of it; hers; its

ездить [yezdeet] to go (by transport); to ride; to drive; to travel

ей [yay] her; to her; by her

ем [yem] I eat

ему [yemoo] him; it; to him; to it

если [yeslee] if

ест [yest] he eats; she eats; it eats

естественный [yestyestvyen-ni] natural

есть [yest] there is; there are

здесь есть ...? [zdyes yest ...?] is there ... here?

у меня есть ...? [oo myenya yest ...] I have ...

есть/съесть [yest/syest] to eat

ехать/ездить [yeнat/yezdeet] to go (by transport); to ride; to drive; to travel

ешь [yesh] you eat; eat

ешьте [**ye**shtyeh] eat

ещё [yesh-cho] still; another; another one; more

ещё более ... [yesh-cho bolyeh-yeh ...] even more ...

ещё не [yesh-cho nyeh] not yet

ещё одно пиво [yesh-cho adno **pee**va] another beer

Ж

Ж ladies' toilets, ladies' room

жаловаться [**J**alavatsa] to complain

жаль [Jal] pity; it's a pity

как жаль [kak Jal] what a pity

жара [**J**ara] heat

жарить [**J**areet] to fry; to grill

жвачка [**J**v**a**chka] chewing gum

ждать/подождать [Jdat/ pada**J**d**at**] to wait

подождите меня! [pada**J**d**ee**tyeh mye**nya**!] wait for me!

железная дорога [Jel**ye**zna-ya dar**o**ga] railway

железо [Jel**ye**za] iron (metal)

жёлтый [**J**olti] yellow

желудок [Jel**oo**dak] stomach

жена [**J**ena] wife

женат [**J**enat] married (man)

не женат [nyeh **J**enat] single

жених [**J**enee**H**] fiancé; bridegroom

женская одежда [**J**enska-ya ad**ye**Jda] ladies' clothing

женский зал [**J**enskee zal] ladies' hairdresser

женский отдел [**J**enskee ad-**dyel**] ladies' department

женский туалет [**J**enskee too-al**yet**] ladies' toilet, ladies' room

женщина [**J**ensh-cheena] woman

жетон [**J**eton] token

живой [Jiv**oy**] alive; living

живот [Jiv**ot**] stomach; belly

животное [Jiv**o**tna-yeh] animal

жидкость для снятия лака [**J**eetkast dlya snya**tee**-ya laka] nail polish remover

жизнь f [Jiyzn] life

жильё [Jil**yo**] accommodation

жир [Jiyr] grease, fat

жирный [**J**iyrni] greasy, fatty; rich

жить [Jiyt] to live

жить в палатках [Jiyt fpal**a**tkaH] to camp

журнал [**J**oornal] magazine

З

за [za] behind

забавный [zab**a**vni] funny, amusing

заблудиться [zablood**ee**tsa] to lose one's way

заболеть [zabal**yet**] to be ill;

to fall ill; to be sore

забор [zabor] fence

забота [zabota] worry; bother

заботиться/позаботиться о [zaboteetsa/pazaboteetsa o] to take care of

забывать/забыть [zabivat/ zabiyt] to forget

заведующий [zavyedooyoosh-chee] manager

завернуть [zavyernoot] to wrap

зависеть: это зависит [eta zaveeseet] it depends

завод [zavot] factory, plant

завтра [zaftra] tomorrow

до завтра [da zaftra] see you tomorrow

завтра вечером [zaftra vyechyeram] tomorrow night

завтра утром [zaftra ootram] tomorrow morning

завтрак [zaftrak] breakfast

загар [zagar] suntan

загорать/загореть [zagarat/ zagaryet] to get sunburnt, to tan

загораться/загореться [zagaratsa/zagaryetsa] to catch fire

загрязнённый [zagryaznyon-ni] polluted

зад [zat] bottom (of body)

задержка [zadyershka] delay

задние фары [zadnee-yeh fari] rear lights

задний [zadnee] back; reverse

задний ход [zadnee нot]

reverse gear

задняя часть [zadnya-ya chast] back, back part

зажечь [zaJech] to light

зажигалка [zaJigalka] lighter

зажигание [zaJiganee-yeh] ignition

зажигать/зажечь [zaJigat/ zaJech] to light

заказ [zakas] order; reservation

заказано [zakazana] reserved

заказное письмо [zakazno-yeh peesmo] registered mail

заказывать/заказать [zakazivat/zakazat] to order; to book

закат [zakat] sunset

закон [zakon] law

закричать [zakreechat] to shout

закрывать/закрыть [zakrivat/ zakriyt] to close

закрыто [zakriyta] closed

закрыто на ремонт [zakriyta na ryemont] closed for repairs

закрыто на учёт [zakriyta na oochot] closed for stocktaking

закрыть [zakriyt] to close

закурить [zakooreet] to smoke

закуска [zakooska] snack; hors d'oeuvre, appetizer

зал ожидания [zal aJidanee-ya] waiting room; departure lounge

замечательный [zamyechatyelni] remarkable,

wonderful

замок [zam**ok**] lock

замок [**za**mak] castle

замороженный [zamaro**j**en-ni] frozen

замужем [**za**mooJem] married (woman)

не замужем [nyeh **za**mooJem] single

замшевый [**za**mshevi] suede

занавеска [zana**vy**eska] curtain

занимать/занять [zaneem**at**/zan**yat**] to borrow; to occupy; to take up

заниматься/заняться [zaneem**a**tsa/zan**ya**tsa] to occupy oneself with; to study; to begin to

занято [**za**nyata], **занятый** [**za**nyati] engaged, occupied; engaged, busy

занять [zan**yat**] to borrow

запад [**za**pat] west

к западу от [k **za**padoo at] west of

запасной выход [zapasn**oy viy**Hat] emergency exit

запах [**za**paH] smell

запирать/запереть [zapeer**at**/zapyer**yet**] to lock

записная книжка-календарь [zapeesna-ya kn**ee**shka-kalyend**ar**] diary; planner

заплатить [zaplat**eet**] to pay

заполнить [zap**o**lneet] to fill in

запор [zap**o**r] bar; bolt; lock;

constipation

заправочная станция [zap**ra**vachna-ya st**a**ntsi-ya] petrol/gas station; garage

запрещено [zapryesh-chyen**o**] prohibited, forbidden

запчасти [zapch**a**stee] spare parts

запястье [zap**ya**styeh] wrist

зарабатывать/заработать [zarab**a**tivat/zarab**o**tat] to earn

заработок [zar**a**batak] salary

заражение [zaraJ**e**nee-yeh] infection; contamination

заранее [zar**a**nyeh-yeh] in advance

засмеяться [zasmyeh-**ya**tsa] to laugh

засоренный [zas**o**ryen-ni] blocked

застегните привязные ремни [zastyegn**ee**tyeh preevyazn**iy**-yeh ryemn**ee**] fasten seatbelts

застёжка-молния [zast**yo**shka-m**o**lnee-ya] zip

застенчивый [zast**ye**ncheevi] shy

затвор объектива [zatv**o**r abyekt**ee**va] shutter (on camera)

затормозить [zatarmaz**eet**] to brake

защищать/защитить [zash-cheesh-ch**at**/zash-cheet**eet**] to protect, to defend

звать/позвать [zvat/pazv**at**] to call

как вас зовут? [kak vas zav**oo**t?] what's your name?

меня зовут ... [myen**ya** zav**oot** ...] my name is ...

звезда [zvyezd**a**] star

звонить/позвонить [zvan**eet**/pazvan**eet**] to ring; to phone

звонок [zvan**ok**] bell; phone call

здание [zd**a**nee-yeh] building

здесь [zdyes] here

здоровый [zdar**o**vi] healthy; huge

здоровье [zdar**o**vyeh] health

за ваше здоровье! [za v**a**sheh zdar**o**vyeh!] your health!, cheers!

здравствуйте [zdr**a**stvooytyeh] hello; how do you do?

зелёный [zyely**o**ni] green

земля [zyeml**ya**] earth; world; ground

зеркало [z**y**erkala] mirror

зима [zeem**a**] winter

зимой [zeem**oy**] in winter

змея [zmyeh-**ya**] snake

знакомить/познакомить [znak**o**meet/paznak**o**meet] to introduce

знакомиться/познакомиться [znak**o**meetsa/paznak**o**meetsa] to get to know, to become acquainted with, to meet

знать [znat] to know

я не знаю [ya nyeh zn**a**-yoo] I don't know

значить [zn**a**cheet] to mean

что это значит? [shto eta zn**a**cheet?] what does it mean?

золовка [zal**o**fka] sister-in-law (husband's sister)

золото [z**o**lata] gold

зонтик [z**o**nteek] umbrella

зоопарк [za-ap**a**rk] zoo

зрелый [zr**y**eli] ripe

зуб [zoop] tooth

зубная боль [zoobn**a**-ya bol] toothache

зубная паста [zoobn**a**-ya p**a**sta] toothpaste

зубная щётка [zoobn**a**-ya sh-ch**o**tka] toothbrush

зубной врач [zoobn**oy** vrach] dentist

зубной протез [zoobn**oy** prates] dentures

зуд [zoot] itch

зять [zyat] son-in-law

И

и [ee] and

иголка [eeg**o**lka] needle

игра [eegr**a**] game

играть/сыграть [eegr**a**t/sigr**a**t] to play

игрушка [eegr**oo**shka] toy

идея [eed**y**eh-ya] idea

идти/ходить [eet-tee/Had**ee**t] to go (on foot), to walk; to suit

известный [eezv**y**esni] famous

извините! [eezveen**ee**tyeh!] excuse me!, sorry!

извините, пожалуйста [eezveen**ee**tyeh, paJ**a**lsta] excuse me

извиняться/извиниться
[eezveen**ya**tsa/eezveen**ee**tsa] to
apologize
я очень извиняюсь [ya
ochyen eezveen**ya**-yoos] I'm
really sorry
из-за [**eez**-za] because of
изнасиловать [eeznas**ee**lavat]
to rape
икона [eek**o**na] icon
или [**ee**lee] or
или ... или ... [**ee**lee ... **ee**lee ...]
either ... or ...
им [**eem**] him; it; by him; by
it; them; to them
имеется ... [eem**yeh**-yetsa ...]
there is ...
иметь [eem**yet**] to have
имеются ... [eem**yeh**-yootsa ...]
there are ...
ими [**ee**mee] (by) them
имя [**ee**mya] name, first
name
иначе [een**a**chyeh] otherwise
инвалид [eenval**eet**] disabled
иногда [eenag**da**] sometimes
иностранец [eenastr**a**nyets]/
иностранка [eenastr**a**nka]
foreigner (man/woman)
иностранный [eenastr**a**n-ni]
foreign
**институт иностранных
языков** [eensteet**oot**
eenastr**a**nih yazik**ov**] language
school
инструктор [eenstr**oo**ktar]
instructor
инструмент [eenstroom**yent**]
tool; instrument

интересный [eentyer**ye**sni]
interesting
Интернет [eenter**net**] Internet
Интурист [eentoor**ee**st]
Intourist
информация [eenfarm**a**tsi-ya]
information
Ирландия [eerl**a**ndee-ya]
Ireland
искать [eesk**at**] to look for
искренний [**ee**skryen-nee]
sincere
искупаться [eeskoop**a**tsa] to
go swimming
искусственный
[eesk**oo**stvyen-ni] artificial
искусство [eesk**oo**stva] art
Испания [eesp**a**nee-ya] Spain
исполнитель [eespaln**ee**tyel]
executive; performer
использовать [eesp**o**lzavat] to
use
испорченный [eesp**o**rchyen-ni]
faulty; rotten
исторический
[eestar**ee**chyeskee] historical
история [eest**o**ree-ya] history
исчезать/исчезнуть
[eeschyez**at**/eesch**ye**znoot] to
disappear
Италия [eet**a**lee-ya] Italy
итог [eet**o**k] total; result
их [ee**н**] their; theirs; them;
of them
июль m [ee-**yool**] July
июнь m [ee-**yoon**] June

К

к [k] to; towards

к. block

кабинет врача [kabeenyet vracha] doctor's surgery

каблук [kablook] heel

каждый [kaJdi] each; every

каждый день [kaJdi dyen] every day

каждый раз [kaJdi ras] every time

Казак [kazak] Cossack

Казахстан [kazaнstan] Kazakhstan

казачий [kazachee] Cossack

как [kak] like, as

как? [kak?] how?

как дела? [kak dyela?] how are you?, how are things?

календарь m [kalyendar] calendar

камень m [kamyen] stone

камера хранения [kamyera нranyenee-ya] left luggage office, baggage checkroom

Канада [kanada] Canada

канал [kanal] canal; channel

канат [kanat] rope

каникулы [kaneekooli] school holidays

канун Нового года [kanoon novava goda] New Year's Eve

канцтовары [kantstavari] stationery

капля [kaplya] drop

капот [kapot] bonnet, (US) hood

карандаш [karandash] pencil

карий [karee] brown (eyes)

карман [karman] pocket

карта [karta] map; playing card

картина [karteena] painting

картинная галерея [karteen-na-ya galyeryeh-ya] art gallery

картон [karton] cardboard

карточка (бизнесмена) [kartachka (beeznyesmyena)] business card

Каспийское море [kaspeeska-yeh moryeh] Caspian Sea

касса [kas-sa] cash desk; booking office; box office

кассета [kas-syeta] cassette

кассетный магнитофон [kas-syetni magneetafon] cassette recorder

кастрюля [kastryoolya] saucepan

катастрофа [katastrofa] disaster

кататься на коньках [katatsa na kankaн] to skate

кататься на лыжах [katatsa na liyJaн] to ski

католик [katoleek] Catholic

кафе [kafeh] café

кафетерий [kafyeteree] cafeteria

качество [kachyestva] quality

кашель m [kashel] cough

кашлять [kashlyat] to cough

каштановый [kashtanavi] brown, chestnut (hair)

каюта [ka-yoota] cabin

кв., квартира [kvarteera] flat,

apartment

квартирная плата
[kvarteerna-ya plata],
квартплата [kvartplata] rent

квитанция [kveetantsi-ya]
receipt; ticket

кеды [kyedi] trainers

кем [kem] who; (by) whom

кемпинг [kempeenk] campsite

Киев [kee-yev] Kiev

кило [keelo] kilo

километр [keelamyetr]
kilometre

кино(театр) [keeno(-tyeh-atr)]
cinema, movie theater

кинокамера [keenakamyera]
camcorder

кинофильм [keenafeelm] film,
movie

кислый [keesli] sour

кисть f [keest] paintbrush

Китай [keetI] China

кладбище [kladbeesh-chyeh]
cemetery

класс [klas] class

классика [klaseeka] classical
music or literature

классическая музыка
[klaseechyeska-ya moozika]
classical music

классический
[klas-seechyeskee] classical

класть/положить [klast/
palaJeet] to put; to lay

клей [klyay] glue

клейкая лента [klyayka-ya
lyenta] Sellotape®, Scotch
tape®

клиент [klee-yent] client

климат [kleemat] climate

клиника [kleeneeka] clinic

клуб [kloop] club

ключ [klyooch] key

книга [kneega] book

книжечка [kneeJechka] book
of 10 tickets

книжный магазин [kneeJni
magazeen] bookshop,
bookstore

ковёр [kavyor] carpet; rug

когда? [kagda?] when?

когда-нибудь [kagda-neeboot]
at some time; ever; one day

вы когда-нибудь ...? [vi
kagda-neeboot ...?] have you
ever ...?

когда-то [kagda-ta] one day;
some time

кого [kavo] who; (of) whom

код [kot] code

кожа [koJa] skin; leather

кожаный [koJani] leather

койка [koyka] bunk bed

колготки [kalgotkee], колготы
[kalgoti] tights, pantyhose

колено [kalyena] knee

колесо [kalyeso] wheel

количество [kaleechyestva]
quantity

коллекция [kal-lyektsi-ya]
collection

колокол [kolakal] bell

кольцо [kaltso] ring; circle

ком [kom] who; whom

команда [kamanda] team

командировка [kamandeerofka]
business trip

комар [kamar] mosquito

комиссионный (магазин) [kamees-see-**on**-ni (maga**zeen**)] secondhand shop

Коммунистическая партия [kam-mooneest**ee**chyeska-ya **par**tee-ya] Communist Party

комната [**kom**nata] room

компания [kam**pa**nee-ya] company

компостер [kam**po**styer] ticket punch

компьютер [kam**pyoo**tyer] computer

кому [kam**oo**] who; (to) whom

конверт [kan**vye**rt] envelope

кондитерская [kan**dee**tyerska-ya] confectioner's

кондиционирование воздуха [kandeetsi-an**ee**ravanee-yeh **voz**dooнa] air-conditioning

конец [kan**yets**] end

конечно [kan**ye**shna] of course

конечный пункт [kan**ye**chni poonkt] terminus

консервный нож [kans**ye**rvni nosh] tin-opener

консульство [**kon**soolstva] consulate

контактные линзы [kan**ta**ktni-yeh **leen**zi] contact lenses

контролёр [kantral**yor**] ticket inspector

конфета [kan**fye**ta] sweet, candy

концерт [kan**tsert**] concert

концертный зал [kan**tser**tni zal] concert hall

кончать/кончить [kan**chat**/ **kon**cheet] to finish

коньки [kan**kee**] skates

кооператив [ka-apyerat**eef**] co-operative

копейка [kap**yay**ka] kopeck

у меня ни копейки денег [oo myen**ya** nee kap**yay**kee **dye**nyek] I'm broke

корабль m [kar**abl**] ship

корзина [kar**zee**na] basket

коридор [kareed**or**] corridor

коричневый [kar**ee**chnyevi] brown

коробка [kar**op**ka] box

коробка передач [kar**op**ka pyeryed**ach**] gearbox

королева [karal**ye**va] queen

король [kar**ol**] king

короткий [kar**ot**kee] short

короткий путь [kar**ot**kee poot] shortcut

корп., корпус [**kor**poos] block

корь f [kor] measles

косметика [kasm**ye**teeka] make-up; cosmetics

костыли [kastil**ee**] crutches

кость f [kost] bone

костюм [kast**yoom**] suit

который [kat**or**i] which

который час? [kat**or**i chas?] what time is it?

кофта [**kof**ta] cardigan

кошелёк [kashel**yok**] purse, coin purse

кошка [**kosh**ka] cat

кошмар [kash**mar**] nightmare

к перронам [k per-**ron**am] to

the platforms/tracks

к поездам [k pa-yezd**a**m] to the trains

кража [kr**a**ja] theft

край [kr**i**] edge

крайний: по крайней мере [pa kr**i**nyay m**ye**ryeh] at least

кран [kran] tap, faucet

красивый [kras**ee**vi] nice; beautiful; handsome

красить/покрасить [kr**a**seet/ pakr**a**seet] to paint

Красная Площадь [kr**a**sna-ya pl**o**sh-chat] Red Square

краснуха [krasn**oo**на] German measles

красный [kr**a**sni] red

красть/украсть [krast/ookr**a**st] to steal

кредитная карточка [kryed**ee**tna-ya k**a**rtachka] credit card

крем [kryem] cream; butter cream

крем для бритья [kryem dlya breet**ya**] shaving foam

крем для обуви [kryem dlya **o**boovee] shoe polish

крем для снятия косметики [kryem dlya sn**ya**tee-ya kasm**ye**teekee] cleansing cream

Кремль m [kryeml] Kremlin

крепость f [kr**ye**past] fortress; strength

кресло-каталка [kr**ye**sla-kat**a**lka] wheelchair

критическое положение [kreet**ee**chyeska-yeh pala**ј**enee-

yeh] emergency

кричать/закричать [kreech**a**t/ zakreech**a**t] to shout

кровать f [krav**a**t] bed

кровь f [krof] blood

кроме [kr**o**myeh] except

кроме воскресений [kr**o**myeh vaskryes**ye**nee] except Sundays

круглый [kr**oo**gli] round

круиз [kroo-**ee**z] cruise

крутой [kroot**oy**] steep

крыло [kril**o**] wing

Крым [kr**i**ym] Crimea

крыша [kr**i**ysha] roof

крышка [kr**i**yshka] lid

к себе [ksyeb**ye**h] pull

ксерокс [ks**ye**raks] photocopy; photocopier

кто? [kto?] who?

кто-нибудь [kt**o**-neeboot], **кто-то** [kt**o**-ta] someone; anyone

кувшин [koofsh**i**yn] jug

кузен [kooz**e**n], **кузина** [kooz**ee**na] cousin (male/female)

кукла [k**oo**kla] doll

кулинария [kooleenar**ee**-ya] delicatessen

купальная шапочка [koop**a**lna-ya sh**a**pachka] bathing cap

купальник [koop**a**lneek] swimming costume

купаться/искупаться [koop**a**tsa/eeskoop**a**tsa] to go swimming

купе [koop**e**h] compartment

купить [koop**ee**t] to buy

купол [**koo**pal] cupola, dome
курить/закурить
[koor**eet**/zakoor**eet**] to smoke
курс (валюты) [koors (val**yoo**ti)]
exchange rate
куртка [**koo**rtka] jacket;
anorak
кусок [koos**ok**] piece
кухня [**koo**Hnya] kitchen;
cooking, cuisine
кухонная посуда [**koo**Han-na-
ya pas**oo**da] cooking utensils
кухонное полотенце
[**koo**Han-na-yeh palat**yen**tseh] tea
towel

Л

ладно [**la**dna] all right, OK
лак для волос [lak dlya val**os**]
hair spray
лак для ногтей [lak dlya
nakt**yay**] nail polish
лампа [**la**mpa] lamp
лампочка [**la**mpachka] light
bulb
ластик [**la**steek] rubber,
eraser
Латвия [**la**tvee-ya] Latvia
лгать/солгать [lgat/salg**at**] to
lie, to tell a lie
левша [lyef**sha**] left-handed
левый [**lye**vi] left
лёгкие [**lyo**Hkee-yeh] lungs
лёгкий [**lyo**Hkee] light (not
heavy); easy
лёд [lyot] ice
леденец [lyedyen**yets**] lollipop

лезбиянка [lyezbee-**ya**nka]
lesbian
лезвие бритвы [**l**yezvee-yeh
br**ee**tvi] razor blade
лейкопластырь [l**ya**ykapl**a**stir]
plaster, Bandaid®
лекарство [lyek**a**rstva]
medicine, drug
ленивый [lyen**ee**vi] lazy
лес [lyes] forest, wood
лестница [**l**yesneetsa] stairs;
ladder
летать/лететь [lyet**at**/lyet**yet**] to
fly
лето [**l**yeta] summer
летом [**l**yetam] in summer
лечь [lyech] to lie down
ли [lee] question particle
ливень m [**l**eevyen] downpour
лист [leest] leaf
Литва [leetva] Lithuania
литр [leetr] litre
лифт [lift] lift, elevator
лихорадка [leeHar**a**tka] fever
лицо [leets**o**] face
лишний [**l**eeshnee] spare
лишний вес багажа [**l**eeshnee
vyes bagaJ**a**] excess baggage
лоб [lop] forehead
ловить/поймать [lav**eet**/p**i**mat]
to catch
лодка [**l**otka] boat
лодыжка [lad**i**yshka] ankle
ложиться/лечь [laJ**ee**tsa/lyech]
to lie down
ложка [**l**oshka] spoon
ложный [**l**oJni] false
локоть m [**l**okat] elbow
ломать/сломать [lam**at**/slam**at**]

to break

ломтик [**lom**teek] slice

Лондон [**lon**dan] London

лосьон для загара [las**yon** dlya za**ga**ra] suntan lotion

лосьон для снятия косметики [las**yon** dlya sn**ya**tee-ya kasm**ye**teekee] make-up remover

лошадь f [**lo**shat] horse

луна [**loo**na] moon

лучше [**looch**-sheh] better

лучший [**looch**-shi] better; best

  самый лучший [**sa**mi **looch**-shi] the best

лыжи [**liy**Ji] skis

лыжные ботинки [**liy**Jni-yeh bat**ee**nkee] ski boots

лыжный спорт [**liy**Jni sport] skiing

любезный [lyoob**ye**zni] kind, obliging

любимый [lyoob**ee**mi] favourite

любить [lyoob**eet**] to love

любовь f [lyoob**of**] love

люди [l**yoo**dee] people

М

M gents' toilet, men's room; underground, metro, (US) subway

магазин [maga**zeen**] shop

магазин беспошлинной торговли [maga**zeen** byesp**o**shleen-nı tar**go**vlee]

duty-free shop

магнитофонная кассета [magneetafon-na-ya kas**ye**ta] tape, cassette

мазь f [mas] ointment

май [mı] May

маленький [**ma**lyenkee] small; little; short

мало [**ma**la] not much; not many

  мало времени [**ma**la vr**ye**myenee] not much time

мальчик [**mal**cheek] boy

мама [**ma**ma] mum

марка [**mar**ka] stamp; make (of car etc)

марки [**mar**kee] stamps

март [mart] March

маршрут [marshr**oot**] route, itinerary

маршрутное такси [marshr**oot**na-yeh taks**ee**] minibus

масло [**ma**sla] oil

масло для загара [**ma**sla dlya za**ga**ra] suntan oil

мастер [**ma**styer] foreman; expert; hair stylist

матрас [**mat**ras] mattress

матрёшка [mat**ryo**shka] Russian doll

мать f [mat] mother

машина [mashi**y**na] car; vehicle

мебель f [**mye**byel] furniture

медленно [**mye**dlyen-na] slowly

медленный [**mye**dlyen-ni] slow

медовый месяц [my**e**dovi

myesyats] honeymoon
медсестра [myetsyestra] nurse
между [myeJdoo] between
междугородный автобус
[myeJdoogarodni aftoboos]
coach, long-distance bus
междугородный звонок
[myeJdoo-garodni zvanok]
long-distance call
междугородный телефон
[myeJdoo-garodni tyelyefon]
long-distance phone
международные рейсы
[myeJdoonarodni-yeh ryaysi]
international flights
международный
[myeJdoonarodni] international
международный звонок
[myeJdoonarodni zvanok]
international call
международный телефон
[myeJdoonarodni tyelyefon]
international telephone
мелочь f [myelach] small
change
менеджер [menedjer] manager
менее [myenyeh-yeh] less
меньше [myensheh] smaller;
less
меня [myenya] me; of me
у меня [oo myenya] I have
менять/поменять [myenyat/
pamyenyat] to change
мёртвый [myortvi] dead
мест нет [myest nyet] full
места [myesta] seats
местное время [myesna-yeh
vryemya] local time
местность f [myesnast] area

местный звонок [myesni
zvanok] local call
место [myesta] place; seat
на месте [na myestyeh] on the
spot
место для курения [myesta
dlya kooryenee-ya] smoking
area
месяц [myesyats] month
месячные [myesyachni-yeh]
period
металл [myetal] metal
метр [myetr] metre
метро [myetro] underground,
metro, (US) subway
мех [myeн] fur
меха [myeнa] fur shop
механик [myeнaneek]
mechanic
меховая шапка [myeнava-ya
shapka] fur hat
мешать [myeshat] to disturb;
to stir; to mix; to prevent
милиционер [meeleetsi-anyer]
policeman
милиция [meeleetsi-ya] police
миллион [mee-lee-on] million
Минск [meensk] Minsk
минута [meenoota] minute
мир [meer] world; peace
мне [mnyeh] me; to me
многие [mnogee-yeh] many;
many people
много [mnoga] a lot (of);
many; much
мной [mnoy] (by) me
могу: я могу [ya magoo] I can
мода [moda] fashion
модный [modni] fashionable

моё [ma**yo**] my; mine
моего [ma-**yevo**] (of) my; (of) mine
моей [ma-**yay**] my; mine; of my; of mine; to my; to mine; by my; by mine
моём [ma-**yom**] my; mine
моему [ma-**yemoo**] (to) my; (to) mine
может быть [**mo**Jet biyt] maybe
можно [**mo**Jna] one can, one may; it is possible
можно ...? [**mo**Jna ...?] can I ...?
мои [ma-**ee**] my; mine; of my; of mine
моим [ma-**eem**] (by) my; (by) mine; (to) my; (to) mine
моими [mo-**eemee**] (by) my; (by) mine
моих [ma-**ee**н], мой [moy] my; mine
мокрый [**mo**kri] wet
Молдова [mald**o**va] Moldova
молния [**mo**lnee-ya] lightning; zip, zipper
молодой [malad**oy**] young
молодые люди [malad**iy**-eh ly**oo**dee] young people
моложе [mal**o**Jeh] younger
море [**mo**ryeh] sea
мороженое [maro**Je**na-yeh] ice cream
мороз [mar**o**s] frost
морозилка [maraz**ee**lka] freezer
Москва [maskv**a**] Moscow
мост [mosst] bridge

мотор [mat**o**r] engine
моторная лодка [mat**o**rna-ya l**o**tka] motorboat
мотоцикл [matats**ee**kl] motorbike
мочь/смочь [moch/smoch] can, to be able to
мою [ma-**yoo**] my; mine
моя [ma-**ya**] my; mine
муж [moosh] husband
мужская одежда [moosshsk**a**-ya ad**ye**Jda] menswear
мужской зал [mooshsk**oy** zal] men's hairdresser
мужской туалет [mooshsk**oy** too-al**yet**] gents' toilet, men's room
мужчина **m** [moosh-ch**ee**na] man
музей [mooz**yay**] museum
музыка [m**oo**zika] music
музыкальный [mooz**ika**lni] musical
мусор [m**oo**sar] rubbish, trash
мусорный ящик [m**oo**sarni **ya**sh-cheek] dustbin, trashcan
муха [m**oo**на] fly (insect)
мы [miy] we
мыло [m**iy**la] soap
мыть/помыть [miyt/pam**iy**t] to wash
мыть/помыть посуду [miyt/pam**iy**t pas**oo**doo] to do the washing-up
мышь **f** [miysh] mouse
мягкие контактные линзы [m**ya**нkee-yeh kant**a**ktni-yeh l**ee**nzi] **s**oft lenses

мягкий [**mya**нkee] soft
мясной магазин [myasn**oy** magaz**een**] butcher's
мясо [**mya**sa] meat
мяч [myach] ball

Н

на [na] on; at
наберите номер [nabyer**ee**tyeh **no**myer] dial the number
наб., набережная [**na**byerye**л**na-ya] embankment
на вынос [na v**iy**nas] to take away, (US) to go
на себя [na syeb**ya**] pull
наверху [navyerн**oo**] at the top; upstairs
  там наверху [tam navyerн**oo**] up there
над [nat] over; above
  над головой [nad galav**oy**] overhead
надеяться [nad**yeh**-yatsa] to hope
надо [n**a**da] it is necessary; one must; need
  мне надо ... [mnyeh n**a**da ...] I need ...
надоесть: мне надоело ... [mnyeh n**a**da-**ye**la ...] I'm fed up with ...
назад [naz**a**t] back; backwards; ago
  три дня назад [tree dnya naz**a**t] three days ago
название [nazv**a**nee-yeh] name; title

наиболее [na-eeb**o**lyeh-yeh] the most
найти [n**i**tee] to find
накладная [nakladn**a**-ya] invoice
наконец [nakan**ye**ts] at last
налево [nal**ye**va] to the left
наличные: платить наличными [plat**ee**t nal**ee**chnimee] to pay cash
налог [nal**o**k] tax
нам [nam] (to) us
нами [n**a**mee] (by) us
нападать/напасть [napad**a**t/nap**a**st] to attack
напасть [nap**a**st] to attack
написать [napees**a**t] to write
напиток [nap**ee**tak] drink
наполнять/наполнить [napaln**ya**t/nap**o**lneet] to fill
направление [napravl**ye**nee-yeh] direction
направо [napr**a**va] to the right
например [napreem**ye**r] for example
напрокат [naprak**a**t] for hire, to rent
напротив [napr**o**teef] opposite
народ [nar**o**t] people; nation
народная музыка [nar**o**dna-ya m**oo**zika] folk music
нарочно [nar**o**chna] deliberately
наружное [nar**oo**лna-yeh] for external use only
наружный [nar**oo**лni] external; outdoor
нас [nas] us; of us

у нас [oo nas] we have

насекомое [nasyek**o**ma-yeh] insect

насморк [n**a**smark] cold

настольный теннис [nast**o**lni ten-nees] table tennis

настоящий [nasta-**ya**sh-chee] genuine, real

настроение [nastra-**ye**nee-yeh] mood

натощак [natash-chak] on an empty stomach

наука [na-**oo**ka] science

научить [na-ooch**ee**t] to teach

нахальный [naн**a**lni] cheeky, impertinent

находить/найти [naнad**ee**t/ nit**ee**] to find

национальность f [natsi-an**a**lnast] nationality

начало [nach**a**la] beginning

начальник [nach**a**lneek] head, chief, boss

начинать/начать [nacheen**a**t/ nach**a**t] to begin, to start

наш [nash], **наша** [n**a**sha] , **наше** [n**a**sheh] our; ours

нашего [n**a**sheva] (of) our; (of) ours

нашей [n**a**shay] our; ours; of our; of ours; to our; to ours; by our; by ours

нашем [n**a**shem] our; ours

нашему [n**a**shemoo] (to) our; (to) ours

наши [n**a**shi] our; ours

нашим [n**a**shim] (by) our; (by) ours; (to) our; (to) ours

нашими [nash**i**ymee] (by) our;

(by) ours

наших [n**a**shiн] (of) our; (of) ours

нашу [n**a**shoo] our; ours

не [nyeh] not

небо [ny**e**ba] sky

неважно [nyev**a**Jna] it doesn't matter

невероятный [nyevyera-**ya**tni] incredible

невеста [nyev**ye**sta] fiancée; bride

невозможно [nyevazm**o**Jna] it's impossible

не высовываться из окон [nyeh vis**o**vivatsa eez **o**kan] do not lean out of the windows

него [nyev**o**] his; its

у него [oo nyev**o**] he has; it has

недалеко (от) [nyedalyek**o** (at)] not far (from)

неделя [nyed**ye**lya] week

в неделю [vnyed**ye**lyoo] per week

на этой неделе [na **e**ti nyed**ye**lyeh] this week

две недели [dvyeh nyed**ye**lee] fortnight, two weeks

недоразумение [nyedarazoom**ye**nee-yeh] misunderstanding

неё [nyeh-**yo**] her; hers; it; its

у неё [oo nyeh-**yo**] she has; it has

независимый [nyezav**ee**seemi] independent

не за что [ny**e**h za shta] you're

А
Б
В
Г
Д
Е
Ё
Ж
З
И
Й
К
Л
М
Н
О
П
Р
С
Т
У
Ф
Х
Ц
Ч
Ш
Щ
Ъ
Ы
Ь
Э
Ю
Я

welcome, don't mention it

ней [nyay] her; it

некоторые [**nye**katari-yeh] some; a few

не курить [nyeh koor**ee**t] no smoking

нелепый [nyel**ye**pi] ridiculous

нём [nyom] him; it

немедленно [nyem**ye**dlyen-na] immediately

немецкий [nyem**ye**tskee] German

немецкий язык [nyem**ye**tskee yaz**iy**k] German (language)

немного [nyemn**o**ga] a little bit

ненавидеть [nyenav**ee**dyet] to hate

не нырять [nyeh nir**ya**t] no diving

необходимо [nyeh-apнad**ee**ma] it's necessary

не останавливается в ... [nyeh astan**a**vleeva-yetsa v ...] does not stop at ...

неправильный [nyepr**a**veelni] wrong, incorrect

не прислоняться [nyeh preeslan**ya**tsa] do not lean against the door

неприятный [nyepree-**ya**tni] unpleasant

не работает [nyeh rab**o**ta-yet] out of order

не разрешается ... [nyeh razryesh**a**-yetsa ...] do not ...

нервный [**nye**rvni] nervous

нёс [nyos] carried; was carrying; were carrying

несколько [**nye**skolka] several; a few

несла [nyesl**a**] carried; was carrying; were carrying

несли [nyesl**ee**] carried; were carrying

несносный [nyesn**o**sni] intolerable

нести [nyest**ee**] to carry

нет [nyet] no

нет, спасибо [nyet, spas**ee**ba] no, thank you

нет входа [nyet fн**o**da] no entry

нет выхода [nyet v**iy**нada] no exit

не трогать [nyeh tr**o**gat] do not touch

неустойчивый [nyeh-oost**oy**cheevi] changeable; unstable

ни ... ни ... [nee ... nee ...] neither ... nor ...

нигде [neegd**ye**] nowhere

нижнее бельё [n**ee**jnyeh-yeh byel**yo**] underwear

низкий [n**ee**skee] low

никогда [neekagd**a**] never

никто [neekt**o**] nobody

ними: с ними [sn**ee**mee] with them

нитка [n**ee**tka] thread

них [neeн] their; theirs; them

у них [oo neeн] they have

ничего [neechyev**o**], **ничто** [neesht**o**] nothing

но [no] but

Новая Зеландия [n**o**va-ya zyel**a**ndee-ya] New Zealand

новогодняя ночь [navagodnya-ya noch] New Year's Eve

новости [novastee] news

новый [novi] new

новый год [novi got] New Year

с Новым годом! [snovim godam!] happy New Year!

нога [naga] leg; foot

ноготь m [nogat] fingernail; toenail

нож [nosh] knife

ножницы [noJneetsi] scissors

ноль m [nol] zero

номер [nomyer] number; hotel room

номер на двоих [nomyer na dva-een] double room

номер с двумя кроватями [nomyer zdvoomya kravatyamee] twin room

номерной знак [namyernoy znak] number plate

Норвегия [narvyegee-ya] Norway

нормально [narmalna] not bad, OK

нормальный [narmalni] normal

нос [nos] nose

носить/нести [naseet/nyestee] to carry

носки [naskee] socks

носовой платок [nasavoy platok] handkerchief

ночная рубашка [nachna-ya roobashka] nightdress

ночь f [noch] night

спокойной ночи [spakoyni nochee] good night

ноябрь m [na-yabr] November

нравиться [nraveetsa] to like

мне нравится ... [mnyeh nraveetsa ...] I like ...

нуль [nool] zero

нырять/нырнуть [niryat/nirnoot] to dive

О

о [a] about

оба/обе [oba/obyeh] both

обед [abyet] lunch

обёрточная бумага [abyortachna-ya boomaga] wrapping paper

обещать [abyesh-chat] to promise

обижать/обидеть [abeeJat/abeedyet] to offend

облако [oblaka] cloud

область f [oblast] administrative region

облачный [oblachni] cloudy

обмен валюты [abmyen valyooti] currency exchange

обогреватель m [abagryevatyel] heater

обратный адрес [abratni adryes] sender's address

обратный билет [abratni beelyet] return ticket, round-trip ticket

обручён/обручена [abroochon/abroochyena] engaged

А Б В Г Д Е Ё Ж З И Й К Л М Н О П Р С Т У Ф Х Ц Ч Ш Щ Ъ Ы Ь Э Ю Я

(man/woman: to be married)

обслуживание [apslooJivanee-yeh] service

обслуживать/обслужить [apslooJivat/apslooJit] to serve

обувь f [oboof] footwear

общежитие [apsh-chyeJeetee-yeh] hostel

общество [opsh-chyestva] society

объектив [abyekteef] lens

объяснение [abyasnyenee-yeh] explanation

объяснять/объяснить [abyasnyat/abyasneet] to explain

обыкновенный [abiknavyen-ni] usual

обычай [abiychI] custom

обычно [abiychna] usually

овощи [ovash-chee] vegetables

овощной магазин [avash-chnoy magazeen] greengrocer's

огонь m [agon] fire

ограничение скорости [agraneechyenee-yeh skorastee] speed limit

одеваться/одеться [adyevatsa/adyetsa] to get dressed

одежда [adyeJda] clothes

одеколон после бритья [adyekalon poslyeh breetya] aftershave

Одесса [adyesa] Odessa

одеться [adyetsa] to get dressed

одеяло [adyeh-yala] blanket

один [adeen] alone; one

одиннадцатый [adeenatsati] eleventh

одиннадцать [adeenatsat] eleven

одна [adna] alone; one

одно [adno] one

одноместный номер [adna-myesni nomyer] single room

одолжить [adalJeet] to lend

ожерелье [aJeryelyeh] necklace

ожог [aJok] burn

озеро [ozyera] lake

окно [akno] window

около [okala] near; about

октябрь m [aktyabr] October

окулист [akooleest] optician

он [on] he; it

она [ana] she; it

они [anee] they

оно [ano] it

опаздывать/опоздать (на) [apazdivat/apazdat (na)] to arrive/be late; to miss

опасность f [apasnast] danger

опасный [apasni] dangerous

опера [opyera] opera

операция [apyeratsi-ya] operation

опоздать (на) [apazdat (na)] to arrive/be late; to miss

опрокинуть [aprakeenoot] to knock over

оптика [opteeka] optician's

опухший [apooHshi] swollen

оранжевый [aranJevi] orange (colour)

организация [arganeezatsi-ya]

organization

организовать [arganeezavat]
to organize

оркестр [arkyestr] orchestra

оса [asa] wasp

осень f [osyen] autumn, (US)
fall

 осенью [osyenyoo] in the
 autumn, in the fall

осмотр [asmotr] check-up

особенно [asobyen-na]
especially

особняк [asabnyak] detached
house

особый [asobi] special

оставаться/остаться
[astavatsa/astatsa] to stay; to
remain

оставить [astaveet] to leave
behind; to forget

остановиться [astanaveetsa]
to stop

 остановитесь!
 [astanaveetyes!] stop!

остановка [astanofka] stop

остановка автобуса [astanofka
aftoboosa] bus stop

остаток [astatak] rest

остаться [astatsa] to stay; to
remain

осторожно! [astaroJna!] be
careful!; look out!

**осторожно, двери
закрываются!** [astaroJna,
dvyeree zakriva-yootsa!] caution,
the doors are closing!

осторожно, окрашено
[astaroJna, akrashena] wet paint

осторожный [astaroJni]

careful

остров [ostraf] island

острый [ostri] hot, spicy;
sharp

от [ot] from

ответ [atvyet] answer

ответить [atvyeteet] to
answer

ответственный
[atvyetstvyen-ni] responsible

отвечать/ответить [atvyechat/
atvyeteet] to answer

отвратительный
[atvrateetyelni] disgusting

отдел [ad-dyel], **отделение**
[ad-dyelyenee-yeh] department

отделение милиции
[ad-dyelyenee-yeh meeleetsi-ee]
police station

отдельно [ad-dyelna]
separately

отдельный [ad-dyelni]
separate

отдельный номер [ad-dyelni
nomyer] single room

отдохнуть [ad-daHnoot] to
take a rest

отдых [od-diH] holiday,
vacation; rest

отдыхать/отдохнуть
[ad-diHat/ad-daHnoot] to take a
rest

отец [atyets] father

открывалка [atkrivalka]
bottle-opener

открывать/открыть
[atkrivat/atkrit] to open

открытка [atkritka] card;
postcard

открыто [atkr**iy**ta] open

открытый [atkr**iy**ti] open

открыть [atkr**iy**t] to open

отлично! [atl**ee**chna!] excellent!

отличный [atl**ee**chni] excellent

отменять/отменить [atmyen**ya**t/atmyen**ee**t] to cancel

отоларинголог [atalareeng**o**lak] ear, nose and throat specialist

отопление [atapl**ye**nee-yeh] heating

отправитель [atprav**ee**tyel] sender

отправить [atpr**a**veet] to send

отправление [atpravl**ye**nee-yeh] departure

отправлять/отправить [atpravl**ya**t/atpr**a**veet] to send

от себя [at syeb**ya**] push

отъезд [at**ye**st] departure

офис [**o**fees] waiter

официант [afeetsi-**a**nt] waiter

официантка [afeetsi-**a**ntka] waitress; barmaid

очаровательный [acharav**a**tyelni] lovely, charming

очевидец [achyev**ee**dyets] witness

очевидно [achyev**ee**dna] obviously

очень [**o**chyen] very; very much

очень приятно! [**o**chyen pree-**ya**tna!] pleased to meet you!

очередь f [**o**chyeryet] queue, (US) line

стоять в очереди [sta-**ya**t v**o**chyeryedee] to queue, to line up

очки [achk**ee**] glasses, eyeglasses

очки от солнца [achk**ee** at **so**ntsa] sunglasses

ошибиться [ashib**ee**tsa] to be mistaken

я ошибся/ошиблась [ya ash**iy**psa/ash**iy**blas] I've made a mistake (said by man/woman)

ошибка [ash**iy**pka] mistake, error

П

падать/упасть [p**a**dat/oop**a**st] to fall

падать/упасть в обморок [p**a**dat/oop**a**st v**o**bmarak] to faint

пакет [pak**ye**t] packet; parcel; paper bag

палатка [pal**a**tka] tent

палец [p**a**lyets] finger

палец ноги [p**a**lyets nag**ee**] toe

палуба [pal**oo**ba] deck

пальто [pal**to**] coat

памятник [p**a**myatneek] monument

папа [p**a**pa] dad

папироса [papeer**o**sa] Russian non-filter cigarette

пара [p**a**ra] pair; couple

парикмахер [pareekmaнyer] hairdresser

парикмахерская [pareekmaнyerska-ya] barber's, hairdresser's

парилка [pareelka] steam room

парк [park] park

паром [parom] ferry

пароход [paraнot] steamer

партер [parter] stalls

партия [partee-ya] party

парус [paroos] sail

парусная лодка [paroosna-ya lotka] sailing boat

парусник [paroosneek] sailing boat

парусный спорт [paroosni sport] sailing

паспорт [paspart] passport

паспортный контроль [paspartni kantrol] passport control

пассажир [pasaJeer] passenger

Пасха [pasнa] Easter

паук [pa-ook] spider

пахнуть [paннoot] to smell

пачка [pachka] packet; pack; bundle

педаль f [pyedal] pedal

пейзаж [pyayzash] landscape; scenery

пелёнка [pyelyonka] nappy, diaper

пельменная [pyelmyen-na-ya] café selling ravioli

пеницилин [pyeneetsileen] penicillin

пенсионер [pyensee-anyer]

пенсионерка, [pyensee-anyerka] old-age pensioner (man/woman)

пепельница [pyepyelneetsa] ashtray

пер. lane

первая помощь [pyerva-ya pomash-ch] first aid

первый [pyervi] first

первый класс [pyervi klas] first class

первый этаж [pyervi etash] ground floor, (US) first floor

перевал [pyeryeval] pass (mountain)

переводить/перевести [pyeryevadeet/pyeryevyestee] to translate; to interpret

переводчик [pyeryevotcheek] translator; interpreter

переговорный пункт [pyeryegavorni poonkt] communications centre

перед [pyeryed] in front of; just before

передняя часть [pyeryednya-ya chast] front

переезд [pyeryeh-yest] level crossing, (US) grade crossing

перейти [pyeryeh-eetee] to cross

перекрёсток [pyeryekryostak] cross-roads; junction, intersection

перелом [pyeryelom] fracture

переодеться [pyeryeh-adyetsa] to get changed

переполненный

A
Б
В
Г
Д
Е
Ё
Ж
З
И
Й
К
Л
М
Н
О
П
Р
С
Т
У
Ф
Х
Ц
Ч
Ш
Щ
Ъ
Ы
Ь
Э
Ю
Я

[pyeryepolnyen-ni] crowded

перерыв [pyeryeriyf] break; interval

перерыв на обед с ... до ... [pyeryeriyf na abyet s ... do ...] closed for lunch from ... to ...

пересадка [pyeryesatka] change; transfer

пересесть [pyeryesyest] to change (trains etc)

пересылать/переслать [pyeryesilat/pyeryeslat] to forward

переулок [pyeryeh-oolak] lane

переход [pyeryenot] transfer; passage; crossing; underpass, subway

переходить/перейти [pyeryenadeet/pyeryeh-eetee] to cross

переходник [pyeryenadneek] adaptor

перманент [pyermanyent] perm

перчатки [pyerchatkee] gloves

песня [pyesnya] song

песок [pyesok] sand

петь [pyet] to sing

печатный материал [pyechatni matyeree-al] printed matter

печень m [pyechyen] liver

пешеход [pyeshenot] pedestrian

пешеходная зона [pyeshenodna-ya zona] pedestrian precinct

пешеходный переход

[pyeshenodni pyeryenot] pedestrian crossing

пешком [pyeshkom] on foot

пещера [pyesh-chyera] cave

пивной бар [peevnoy bar], **пивнушка** [peevnooshka] bar, beer cellar, pub

пилка для ногтей [peelka dlya naktyay] nailfile

писать/написать [peesat/napeesat] to write

писчебумажный магазин [peesh-chyeboomaJni magazeen] stationer's

письмо [peesmo] letter

питательный [peetatyelni] nutritious

пить/выпить [peet/viypeet] to drink

питьевая вода [peetyeva-ya vada] drinking water

пиццерия [peetseree-ya] pizzeria

пишущая машинка [peeshoosh-cha-ya mashiynka] typewriter

пищевое отравление [peesh-chyevo-yeh atravlyenee-yeh] food poisoning

пл. square

плавание [plavanee-yeh] swimming

плавать запрещается [plavat zapryesh-cha-yetsa] no swimming

плавать/плыть [plavat/pliyt] to swim

плавки [plafkee] swimming trunks

плакат [plak**at**] poster

плакать [pl**a**kat] to cry

пластинка [plast**ee**nka] record

пластмассовый [plasm**a**s-savi] plastic

платите в кассу [plat**ee**tyeh f kas-soo] pay at the cash desk

платить/заплатить [plat**ee**t/ zaplat**ee**t] to pay

платный [pl**a**tni] paid; to be paid for

платок [plat**ok**] headscarf

платформа [platf**o**rma] platform, (US) track

платье [pl**a**tyeh] dress

плащ [plash-ch] raincoat

племянник [plyem**ya**n-neek] nephew

племянница [plyem**ya**n-neetsa] niece

плёнка [pl**yo**nka] film (for camera)

плечо [plyech**o**] shoulder

пломба [pl**o**mba] filling

плоский [pl**o**skee] flat

плохо [pl**o**нa] bad; badly
мне плохо [mnyeh pl**o**нa] I feel ill

плохой [plaн**oy**] bad

площадь f [pl**o**sh-chat] square

плыть [pl**i**yt] to swim

плэйер [pl**a**yer] personal stereo

пляж [pl**ya**sh] beach

по [po] along; according to; on
по-английски [pa-angl**ee**skee] in English

поблагодарить [pablagadar**ee**t]

to thank

побриться [pabr**ee**tsa] to shave

повар [p**o**var] cook

поверить [pav**ye**reet] to believe

поворачивать/повернуть [pavar**a**cheevat/pavern**oo**t] to turn

повредить [pavryed**ee**t] to damage

повторять/повторить [pavtar**ya**t/paftar**ee**t] to repeat

повязка [pav**ya**ska] bandage

погладить [pagl**a**deet] to iron; to stroke

погода [pag**o**da] weather

погулять [pagool**ya**t] to go for a walk

под [pot] below; under; underneath

под. entrance number

подавленный [pad**a**vlyen-ni] depressed

подарить [padar**ee**t] to give (present)

подарок [pad**a**rak] present, gift

подбородок [padbar**o**dak] chin

подвал [padv**a**l] basement

подвозить/подвезти [padvaz**ee**t/padvyest**ee**] to give a lift to

поделиться [padyel**ee**tsa] to share

подержанный [pad**ye**rJan-ni] secondhand

подмётка [padm**yo**tka] sole

подниматься/подняться

[padneematsa/padnyatsa] to go
up

поднос [padnos] tray

подняться [padnyatsa] to go
up

подобный [padobni] similar

подождать [padaJdat] to wait

подойти [paditee] to
approach; to arrive; to
come

подписать [patpeesat] to sign

подпись f [potpees] signature

подросток [padrostak]
teenager

подруга [padrooga] friend;
girlfriend

подтвердить [pat-vyerdeet] to
confirm

подумать [padoomat] to think

подушка [padooshka] pillow

подфарники [patfarneekee]
sidelights

подходить/подойти
[padHadeet/paditee] to
approach; to arrive; to
come

подъезд [padyest] entrance

подъёмник [padyomneek]
ski-lift, chairlift

поезд [po-yest] train

поездка [pa-yestka] journey,
trip

пожалуйста [paJalsta] please

пожар [paJar] fire, blaze

пожарная команда [paJarna-
ya kamanda] fire brigade

пожарный выход [paJarni
viyHat] fire exit

пожелание: с наилучшими

пожеланиями [sna-
eeloochshimee paJelanee-yamee]
best wishes

поживаете: как вы
поживаете? [kak viy
paJivayetyeh?] how are you?

позаботиться o [pazaboteetsa
o] to take care of

позавчера [pazafchyera] the
day before yesterday

позвать [pazvat] to call

позвонить [pazvaneet] to
ring; to phone

поздно [pozna] late; it's late

поздравляю! [pazdravlya-yoo!]
congratulations!

позже [poJ-Jeh] later on

познакомить [paznakomeet] to
introduce

познакомиться
[paznakomeetsa] to get to
know, to become
acquainted with, to meet

поймать [pimat] to catch

пока [paka] while

пока! [paka!] bye!

показывать/показать
[pakazivat/pakazat] to show

покидать/покинуть
[pakeedat/pakeenoot] to leave

по крайней мере [pa krinyay
myeryeh] at least

покрасить [pakraseet] to
paint

покупатель [pakoopatyel]
customer; buyer

покупать/купить
[pakoopat/koopeet] to buy

покупки [pakoopkee]

shopping
идти за покупками [eet-**tee** za pak**oo**pkamee] to go shopping
пол [pol] floor; sex
полдень m [**pol**dyen] midday, noon
поле [**po**lyeh] field
полезный [pal**ye**zni] useful
поликлиника [paleekl**ee**neeka] surgery; medical centre
политика [pal**ee**teeka] politics
политический [palee**tee**chyeskee] political
поллитра [pol-**lee**tra] half a litre
полночь f [**pol**nach] midnight
полный [**pol**ni] full
половина [pala**vee**na] half
  половина второго [pala**vee**na fta**ro**va] half past one
положить [pala**jeet**] to put, to place
полотенце [pala**tyen**tseh] towel
получать/получить [paloo**chat**/paloo**cheet**] to receive
полчаса [polcha**sa**] half an hour
поменять [pamyen**yat**] to change
померить [pam**ye**reet] to try on
помнить/вспомнить [**po**mneet/fsp**o**mneet] to remember, to recall
  я помню [ya **po**mnyoo] I remember

помогать/помочь [pamag**at**/pam**och**] to help
помогите! [pamag**ee**tyeh!] help!
помощь f [**po**mash-ch] help, aid, assistance
помыть [pam**iyt**] to wash
  помыть посуду [pam**iyt** pas**oo**doo] to do the washing-up
помыться [pam**iy**tsa] to wash (oneself)
понедельник [panyed**ye**lneek] Monday
понимать/понять [paneem**at**/pan**yat**] to understand
  я не понимаю [ya nyeh paneem**a**-yoo] I don't understand
понос [pan**os**] diarrhoea
понять [pan**yat**] to understand
поп-музыка [pop-m**oo**zika] pop music
попробовать [pap**ro**bavat] to taste; to try
порт [port] harbour, port
портфель m [part**fyel**] briefcase
порция [**por**tsi-ya] portion
порядок [par**ya**dak] order
  у меня всё в порядке [oo myen**ya** fsyo fpar**ya**tkyeh] fine, I'm OK, everything's OK
посадка [pas**at**ka] landing; boarding; arrival
посадочный талон [pas**a**dachni tal**on**] boarding pass

посещать/посетить [pasyesh-chat/pasyeteet] to visit
послание [paslanee-yeh] message
послать [paslat] to send
после [poslyeh] after
последний [paslyednee] last
послезавтра [poslyezaftra] the day after tomorrow
послушать [paslooshat] to listen (to)
посмотреть (на) [pasmatryet (na)] to look (at); to watch
посольство [pasolstva] embassy
поставить [pastaveet] to put
поставить машину [pastaveet mashiynoo] to park
постараться [pastaratsa] to try
постель f [pastyel] bed
постельное бельё [pastyelna-yeh byelyo] bed linen
постирать [pasteerat] to do the washing
посторонним вход воспрещён [pastaroneem fHot vaspryesh-chon] private, staff only
посуда [pasooda] crockery
посылать/послать [pasilat/paslat] to send
посылка [pasiylka] parcel
потерять [patyeryat] to lose
по техническим причинам [pa tueHneechyeskeem preecheenam] for technical reasons
потолок [patalok] ceiling

потом [patom] then; afterwards
потому что [patamoo shta] because
потребитель [patryebeetyel] consumer
потрясающий [patryasa-yoosh-chee] tremendous
похмелье [paHmyelyeh] hangover
похожий [paHoji] like, similar to
поцеловать [patselavat] to kiss
поцелуй [patseloo] kiss
почему? [pachyemoo?] why?
починить [pacheeneet] to mend, to repair
почки [pochkee] kidneys
почта [pochta] post office; mail
почта до востребования [pochta da-vastryebavanee-ya] poste restante, general delivery
почтальон [pachtalyon] postman, mailman
почти [pachtee] almost
почтовая бумага [pachtova-ya boomaga] writing paper
почтовый индекс [pachtovi eendeks] postcode, zip code
почтовый ящик [pachtovi yash-cheek] letterbox, mailbox
пояс [po-yas] belt
потерять [patyeryat] to lose
пр. avenue
правильный [praveelni] right, correct

правительство [prav**ee**tyelstva] government

православная церковь [pravasl**a**vna-ya ts**e**rkaf] Russian Orthodox Church

правый [pr**a**vi] right

праздник [pr**a**zneek] public holiday

празднование [pr**a**znavanee-yeh] celebration

практичный [prakt**ee**chni] practical

прачечная [pr**a**chyechna-ya] laundry

прачечная-самообслуживани я [pr**a**chyechna-ya-sama-apsl**oo**Jivanee-ya] launderette

пребывание [pryebiv**a**nee-yeh] stay

предварительный заказ [pryedvar**ee**tyelni zak**a**s] reservation

предварительный заказ билетов [pryedvar**ee**tyelni zak**a**s beel**ye**taf] seat reservation

предлагать/предложить [pryedlag**a**t/pryedlaJ**ee**t] to offer, to suggest

предложение [pryedlaJ**e**nee-yeh] offer, proposal

предложить [pryedlaJ**ee**t] to offer, to suggest

предохранитель m [pryedaнran**ee**tyel] fuse

предпочитать [pryetpach**ee**tat] to prefer

председатель m [pryedsyed**a**tyel] chairman

представитель m

[pryetstav**ee**tyel] representative; agent

презерватив [pryezyervat**ee**f] condom

прекрасный [pryekr**a**sni] beautiful; fine; excellent

прелестный [pryel**ye**sni] pretty

преподаватель m [pryepadav**a**tyel] teacher; lecturer

Прибалтика [preeb**a**lteeka] Baltic States

прибыль f [pr**ee**bil] profit

прибытие [preeb**i**ytee-yeh] arrival

привет [preevy**e**t] hello, hi

прививка [preev**ee**fka] vaccination

привлекательный [preevlyek**a**tyelni] attractive

привычка [preev**i**ychka] habit

привязной ремень [preevyazn**oy** ryemy**e**n] seatbelt

приглашать/пригласить [preeglash**a**t/preeglas**ee**t] to invite

приглашение [preeglash**e**nee-yeh] invitation

пригород [pr**ee**garat] suburbs

пригородный поезд [pr**ee**garadni p**o**-yest] local train, suburban train

пригородная касса [pr**ee**garadna-ya k**a**s-sa] ticket office for suburban trains

приготовить [preegat**o**veet] to cook; to prepare

приезд [pree-**ye**st] arrival

А
Б
В
Г
Д
Е
Ё
Ж
З
И
Й
К
Л
М
Н
О
П
Р
С
Т
У
Ф
Х
Ц
Ч
Ш
Щ
Ъ
Ы
Ь
Э
Ю
Я

приезжать/приехать [pree-yezJat/pree-yeHat] to arrive (by transport)

приём посылок [pree-yom pasiylak] parcels counter

приехать [pree-yeHat] to arrive (by transport)

прийти [preetee] to come, to arrive (on foot)

прикурить: у вас есть прикурить? [oo vas yest preekooreet?] have you got a light?

прилёт [preelyot] arrival

пример [preemyer] example

примерно [preemyerna] approximately

принадлежать [preenadlyeJat] to belong

принимать/принять [preeneemat/preenyat] to accept, to take

принтер [preenter] printer

приносить/принести [preenaseet/preenyestee] to bring

принять [preenyat] to accept, to take

природа [preeroda] nature

пристегните ремни [preestyegneetyeh ryemnee] fasten seat belts

приходить/прийти [preeHadeet/preetee] to come, to arrive (on foot)

причал [preechal] quay

причина [preecheena] cause; reason

приятного аппетита!

приятна apyeteeta!] enjoy your meal!

приятный [pree-yatni] pleasant, nice

пробка [propka] plug; traffic jam

проблема [prablyema] problem

пробовать/попробовать [probavat/paprobavat] to taste; to try

проверять/проверить [pravyeryat/pravyereet] to check

прогноз погоды [pragnos pagodi] weather forecast

программа [pragram-ma] programme

прогулка [pragoolka] walk

продавать/продать [pradavat/pradat] to sell

продаётся [prada-yotsa] for sale

продажа [pradaJa] sale; marketing

продажа билетов [pradaJa beelyetaf] tickets on sale

проданный [pradan-ni] sold

продать [pradat] to sell

продукция [pradooktsi-ya] product

проездной билет [pra-yeznoy beelyet] monthly season ticket

проживание с двухразовым питанием [praJivanee-yeh zdvooH-razavim peetanee-yem] half board

проживание с трёхразовым питанием [praJivanee-yeh

stryoн-**ra**zavim peet**a**nee-yem] full board

производство [pra-eez**vo**tstva] production

произнести [pra-eeznyest**ee**] to pronounce

произносить/произнести [pra-eeznas**ee**t/pra-eeznyest**ee**] to pronounce

прокат [prak**at**] rental, hire

прокат автомобилей [prak**at** aftamab**ee**lyay] car rental

прокол [prak**o**l] puncture

промышленность f [pram**iy**shlyen-nast] industry

пропуск [pr**o**poosk] pass; hotel card

проснуться [prasn**oo**tsa] to wake up

проспект [prasp**ye**kt] brochure; avenue

простите [prast**ee**tyeh] excuse me, sorry

простите? [prast**ee**tyeh?] pardon?, pardon me?

простой [prast**oy**] simple

простыня [prastin**ya**] sheet

просьба [pr**o**sba] request

просьба не ... [pr**o**sba nyeh ...] please do not ...

протестант [pratyest**a**nt] Protestant

против [pr**o**teef] against

противозачаточное средство [prateevazach**a**tachna-yeh sr**ye**tstva] contraceptive

прохладный [praнl**a**dni] cool

процент [prats**e**nt] per cent

прочитать [pracheet**a**t] to read

прошлый [pr**o**shli] last

в прошлом году [fpr**o**shlam gad**oo**] last year

на прошлой неделе [na pr**o**shli nyed**ye**lyeh] last week

проявлять/проявить [pra-yavl**ya**t/pra-yav**ee**t] to develop

пруд [proot] pond

прыгать/прыгнуть [pr**iy**gat/pr**iy**gnoot] to jump

прыщик [pr**iy**sh-cheek] spot, pimple

прямо [pr**ya**ma] straight ahead

прямой [pryam**oy**] direct; straight

прямой номер [pryam**oy** n**o**myer] direct dialling

прямой рейс [pryam**oy** ryays] direct flight

птица [pt**ee**tsa] bird; poultry

публика [p**oo**bleeka] audience; public

пуговица [p**oo**gaveetsa] button

пункт [poonkt] point; station; place, spot; centre

пункт скорой помощи [poonkt sk**o**ri p**o**mash-chee] first-aid post

пустой [poost**oy**] empty

путеводитель m [pootyevad**ee**tyel] guidebook

путешествовать [pootyesh**e**stvavat] to travel

путь m [poot] path; way

пчела [pchel**a**] bee

пылесос [pilyes**o**s] vacuum cleaner

пьеса [p**ye**sa] play (theatre)

пьяный [p**ya**ni] drunk

пятка [p**ya**tka] heel (of foot)

пятнадцатый [pyatn**a**tsati] fifteenth

пятнадцать [pyatn**a**tsat] fifteen

пятница [p**ya**tneetsa] Friday

пятно [p**ya**tno] stain

пятый [p**ya**ti] fifth

пять [pyat] five

пятьдесят [pyadyes**ya**t] fifty

пятьсот [pyats**o**t] five hundred

Р

▬

р. rouble

работа [rab**o**ta] job; work

работает с ... до ... [rab**o**ta-yet s ... do ...] open from ... to ...

работать [rab**o**tat] to work

это не работает [**e**ta nyeh rab**o**ta-yet] it's not working

рад [rat] glad

радио [r**a**dee-o] radio

раз [ras] time (occasion)

один раз [ad**ee**n ras] once

разбудить [razbood**ee**t] to wake up

разве? [r**a**zvyeh?] really?

разведён [razvyedy**o**n], разведена [razvyedyen**a**] divorced (man/woman)

развилка [razv**ee**lka] junction; fork (in road)

разговаривать [razgav**a**reevat] to talk

разговаривать с водителем запрещается [razgav**a**reevat svad**ee**tyelyem zapryesh-cha-yetsa] do not speak to the driver

разговор [razgav**o**r] conversation

раздевалка [razdyev**a**lka] changing room

размен [razm**ye**n] change

размер [razm**ye**r] size

разный [r**a**zni] various, different

разочарованный [razachar**o**van-ni] disappointed

разрешается [razryesh**a**-yetsa] it is allowed

разрешать/разрешить [razryesh**a**t/razryesh**iy**t] to let, to allow

разрешение [razryesh**e**nee-yeh] permission; licence

разрешить [razryesh**iy**t] to let, to allow

разумный [raz**oo**mni] sensible

район [r**io**n] district

раковина [r**a**kaveena] sink

ракушка [rak**oo**shka] shell

рана [r**a**na] injury

раненый [r**a**nyeni] injured

рано [r**a**na] early

раскладушка [rasklad**oo**shka] campbed

распаковать (чемодан) [raspakav**a**t (chyemad**a**n)] to unpack

расписание [raspees**a**nee-yeh] timetable, (US) schedule

распродажа [rasprad**a**ʒa] sale

рассказ [r**a**skas] story

рассказать [raskazat] to tell

расслабиться [ras-slabeetsa] to relax

расстояние [ras-sta-yanee-yeh] distance

расстройство желудка [rastroystva Jelootka] indigestion

растение [rastyenee-yeh] plant

расчёска [raschoska] comb

ребёнок [ryebyonak] child; baby

ребро [ryebro] rib

ревматизм [ryevmateezm] rheumatism

ревнивый [ryevneevi] jealous

регистратура [ryegeestratoora] reception

регистрация [ryegeestratsi-ya] check-in; registration

регистрация багажа [ryegeestratsi-ya bagaJa] check-in

регулировщик [ryegooleerovsh-cheek] traffic warden

регулярный рейс [ryegoolyarni ryays] scheduled flight

редкий [ryetkee] rare

резать [ryezat] to cut

резина [ryezeena] rubber

резиночка [ryezeenachka] rubber band

рейс [ryays] flight

река [ryeka] river

реклама [ryeklama] advertisement; advertising

рекламировать [ryeklameeravat] to advertise

рекомендовать [ryekamyendavat] to recommend

религия [ryeleegee-ya] religion

ремень вентилятора [ryemyen vyenteelyatara] fan belt

ремесленные изделия [ryemyeslyen-ni-yeh eezdyelee-ya] crafts

ремонт [ryemont] repair

ремонт обуви [ryemont oboovee] shoe repairs

ремонт сумок [ryemont soomak] bag repairs

ресторан [ryestaran] restaurant

рецепт [ryetsept] prescription; recipe

решать/решить [ryeshat/ryeshiyt] to decide

решение [ryeshyenee-yeh] decision

Рига [reega] Riga

родина [rodeena] native country; home(land)

родители [radeetyelee] parents

родиться [radeetsa] to be born

родственники [rotstvyen-neekee] relatives

Рождество [raJdyestvo] Christmas

с Рождеством! [sraJdyestvom!] merry Christmas!

роза [roza] rose

розетка [razyetka] socket

розовый [rozavi] pink

рок-музыка [rok-moozika] rock music

роман [raman] novel

Россия [ras-see-ya] Russia

рот [rot] mouth

рубашка [roobashka] shirt

рубль m [roobl] rouble

руины [roo-eeni] ruins

рука [rooka] arm; hand

руками не трогать [rookamee nyeh trogat] do not touch

руль m [rool] steering wheel

русская [rooska-ya] Russian

русские [rooskee-yeh] the Russians

русский [rooskee] Russian

русский язык [rooskee yaziyk] Russian (language)

Русь [roos] Russia (historical)

ручей [roochyay] stream

ручка [roochka] handle; pen

ручная кладь [roochna-ya klat] hand luggage, hand baggage

ручной тормоз [roochnoy tormas] handbrake

рыба [riyba] fish

рыбная ловля [riybna-ya lovlya] fishing

рыбная ловля запрещена [riybna-ya lovlya zapryesh-chyena] no fishing

рыбный магазин [riybni magazeen] fishmonger's

рыжий [riyji] red-headed

рынок [riynak] market

рюкзак [ryoogzak] rucksack

рюмка [ryoomka] wine glass

ряд [ryat] row

рядом (с) [ryadam (s)] next to

С

с [s] with

с нарочным [snarochnim] special delivery

сад [sat] garden

садиться/сесть [sadeetsa/syest] to sit down; to get in

салфетка [salfyetka] napkin

самовар [samavar] samovar

самолёт [samalyot] plane

самолётом [samalyotam] by air

самообслуживание [sama-aploojivanee-yeh] self-service

самый [sami] the most

санитарный день [saneetarni dyen] closed for cleaning

Санкт Петербург [sankt pyetyerboork] St Petersburg

сапог [sapok] boot

сауна [sa-oona] sauna

свадьба [svadba] wedding

свежий [svyej] fresh

свёкор [svyokar] father-in-law (husband's father)

свекровь [svyekrof] mother-in-law (husband's mother)

свёрток [svyortak] package

свет [svyet] light

светло- [svyetla-] light (colour)

светофор [svyetafor] traffic lights

свеча [svyecha] candle

свеча зажигания [svyecha zajiganee-ya] sparkplug

свинья [sveen**ya**] pig

свитер [sv**ee**ter] sweater, jumper

свободно [sv**a**b**o**dna] free; vacant; fluent

свободный [sv**a**b**o**dni] free; vacant; fluent

свободных мест нет [svab**o**dnih myest nyet] no vacancies

своё [sva-**yo**], свои [sva-**ee**], свой [svoy], своя [sva-**ya**] my; your; his; its; her; our; their; mine; yours; hers; ours; theirs

свояченица [sva-ya**ch**yeneetsa] sister-in-law (wife's sister)

связываться/связаться (с) [sv**ya**zivatsa/svyaz**a**tsa (s)] to get in touch with

святой [svyat**oy**] holy; saint

священник [svyash-ch**ye**n-neek] priest

сгореть [zgar**yet**] to burn

сделать [zd**ye**lat] to do; to make

сделать пересадку [zd**ye**lat pyeryes**a**tkoo] to change (trains etc)

себе [syeb**yeh**], себя [syeb**ya**] myself; yourself; himself; herself; itself; ourselves; yourselves; themselves

север [s**ye**vyer] north

  к северу от [k s**ye**vyeroo at] north of

Северная Ирландия [s**ye**vyerna-ya eerland**ee**-ya] Northern Ireland

сегодня [syev**o**dnya] today

сегодня вечером [syev**o**dnya v**ye**chyeram] this evening, tonight

сегодня днём [syev**o**dnya dnyom] this afternoon

сегодня утром [syev**o**dnya **oo**tram] this morning

седьмой [syedm**oy**] seventh

сейчас [syaych**a**s] now, at the moment

секретарша f [syekryet**a**rsha] secretary

секретарь m [syekryet**a**r] secretary

секс [seks] sex

секунда [syek**oo**nda] second

семнадцатый [syemn**a**tsati] seventeenth

семнадцать [syemn**a**tsat] seventeen

семь [syem] seven

семьдесят [s**ye**mdyesyat] seventy

семьсот [syems**o**t] seven hundred

семья [syem**ya**] family

сенная лихорадка [s**ye**n-na-ya leeh**a**r**a**tka] hayfever

сентябрь m [syent**ya**br] September

сердечный приступ [syerd**ye**chni pr**ee**stoop] heart attack

сердитый [syerd**ee**ti] angry

сердце [s**ye**rtseh] heart

серебро [syery**e**br**o**] silver

середина [syery**e**d**ee**na] middle

серый [s**ye**ri] grey

А
Б
В
Г
Д
Е
Ё
Ж
З
И
Й
К
Л
М
Н
О
П
Р
С
Т
У
Ф
Х
Ц
Ч
Ш
Щ
Ъ
Ы
Ь
Э
Ю
Я

серьги [syergee] earrings

серьёзный [syeryozni] serious

сестра [syestra] sister

сесть [syest] to sit down; to get in

Сибирь f [seebeer] Siberia

сигара [seegara] cigar

сигарета [seegaryeta] cigarette

сильный [seelni] strong

синий [seenee] blue

синяк [seenyak] bruise

скажите, пожалуйста ... [skaJeetyeh, paJalsta ...] can you tell me ...?

сказать [skazat] to say; to speak

скала [skala] cliff; rock

скандальный [skandalni] shocking

скатерть f [skatyert] tablecloth

сквозняк [skvaznyak] draught

скидка [skeetka] discount

складная детская коляска [skladna-ya dyetska-ya kalyaska] pushchair, (US) stroller

склон [sklon] slope

сковорода [skavarada] frying pan

скользкий [skolskee] slippery

сколько? [skolka?] how much?; how many?

сколько вам лет? [skolka vam lyet?] how old are you?

сколько это стоит? [skolka eta sto-eet?] how much is it?

скорая помощь [skora-ya pomash-ch] ambulance; first aid

скорее [skaryeh-yeh] rather

скорее! [skaryeh-yeh!] quickly!

скоро [skora] soon

скорость f [skorast] speed; gear

скрывать/скрыть [skrivat/ skriyt] to hide

скрыть [skriyt] to hide

скучный [skooshni] boring

слабительное [slabeetyelna-yeh] laxative

слабый [slabi] weak

сладкий [slatkee] sweet (to taste)

слайд [slit] slide (photographic)

слева [slyeva] on the left

следовать [slyedavat] to follow

следующая станция ... [slyedoo-yoosh-cha-ya stantsi-ya ...] next station ...

следующий [slyedoo-yoosh-chee] next; following

в следующем году [fslyedoo-yoosh-chyem gadoo] next year

на следующей неделе [na slyedoo-yoosh-chay nyedyelyeh] next week

следующий день [slyedoo-yoosh-chee dyen] the next day

слепой [slyepoy] blind

слишком ... [sleeshkam ...] too ...

слишком много [sleeshkam mnoga] too much

не слишком много [nyeh sleeshkam mnoga] not too much

словарь m [slovar] dictionary

слово [slova] word

сложный [sloJni] complicated

сломанный [sloman-ni] broken

сломать [slamat] to break

сломаться [slamatsa] to break down

служащий [slooJash-chee] employee

служба [slooJba] service; employment; job; work;duty

служба размещения [slooJba razmyesh-chyenee-ya] reception desk

служебный вход [slooJebni fHot] staff entrance

случай [sloochee] chance

случайно [sloochIna] by chance

случаться/случиться [sloochatsa/sloocheetsa] to happen

слушать/послушать [slooshat/paslooshat] to listen (to)

слышать/услышать [sliyshat/oosliyshat] to hear

смерть f [smyert] death

сметь [smyet] to dare

смешать [smyeshat] to mix

смеяться/засмеяться [smyeh-yatsa/zasmyeh-yatsa] to laugh

смотреть/посмотреть (на) [smatryet/pasmatryet (na)] to look (at); to watch

смочь [smoch] can, to be able to

вы сможете ...? [viy smoJetyeh ...?] will you be able to ...?

он/она сможет [on/ana smoJet] he/she will be able to

смутно [smootna] vaguely

сначала [snachala] first; at first

снег [snyek] snow

СНГ [es-en-geh] CIS

снова [snova] again; once again

сноха [snaHa] daughter-in-law

собака [sabaka] dog

соблюдайте тишину [sablyoodItyeh teeshinoo] please be quiet

собой [saboy] (by) myself; (by) yourself; (by) himself; (by) herself; (by) itself; (by) ourselves; (by) yourselves; (by) themselves

с собой [s-saboy] to take away, (US) to go

соболь m [sobal] sable

собор [sabor] cathedral

собрание [sabranee-yeh] meeting

собственный [sopstvyen-ni] own; proper; personal

Советский Союз [savyetskee sa-yoos] Soviet Union

современный [savryemyen-ni] modern

согласен: я

согласен/согласна [ya saglasyen/saglasna] I agree (said by man/woman)

согласованность расписания [saglasovan-nast raspeesanee-ya] connection

Соединённые Штаты Америки [sayedeenyon-ni-yeh shtati amyereekee] United States

сожаление: к сожалению [k saJaJyenee-yoo] unfortunately

соки-воды [sokee-vodi] fruit juices and mineral water

солгать [salgat] to lie, to tell a lie

солёный [salyoni] salty; savoury; pickled

солнечный [solnyechni] sunny

солнечный ожог [solnyechni aJok] sunburn

солнечный свет [solnyechni svyet] sunshine

солнечный удар [solnyechni oodar] sunstroke

солнце [sontseh] sun

сон [son] dream; sleep

сопровождать [sapravaJdat] to accompany

сорок [sorak] forty

сосед [sasyet], соседка [sasyetka] neighbour (man/woman)

сохранять/сохранить [saнranyat/saнraneet] to keep

социализм [satsi-aleezm] socialism

Сочельник [sachyelneek] Christmas Eve

спальное место [spalna-yeh myesta] couchette

спальный вагон [spalni vagon] sleeping car

спальный мешок [spalni myeshok] sleeping bag

спальня [spalnya] bedroom

спасатель m [spasatel] lifeguard

спасательный пояс [spasatyelni po-yas] lifebelt

спасибо [spaseeba] thank you
  спасибо большое [spaseeba balsho-yeh] thank you very much

спать [spat] to sleep

специальность f [spyetsi-alnast] speciality

спешить [spyesheeyt] to hurry

СПИД [speed] Aids

спина [speena] back (of body)

список [speesak] list

спичка [speechka] match

спокойной ночи [spakoynay nochee] good night

спорт [sport] sport

спортивное оборудование [sparteevna-yeh abaroodavanee-yeh] sports equipment

спортивный центр [sparteevni tsentr] sports centre

справа [sprava] on the right

справедливый [spravyedleevi] fair, just

справка [sprafka] information

справочная [spravachna-ya] enquiries; directory enquiries

справочное бюро [spravachna-yeh byooro] information office

справочный стол [spravachni stol] information desk

спрашивать/спросить [sprashivat/spraseet] to ask

спускаться/спуститься [spooskatsa/spoosteetsa] to go down

спущенная шина [spoosh-chyen-na-ya shiyna] flat tyre

среда [sryeda] Wednesday

среди [sryedee] among

среднего размера [sryednyeva razmyera] medium-sized

средство от насекомых [sryetstva at nasyekomiн] insect repellent

средство против загара [sryetstva proteev zagara] sunblock

срок [srok] period

срочно [srochna] urgent; urgently

срочный [srochni] urgent

СССР [es-es-es-er] USSR

ставить/поставить [staveet/pastaveet] to put

стадион [stadee-on] stadium

стакан [stakan] glass

становиться/стать [stanaveetsa/stat] to become

станция [stantsi-ya] station (underground, bus etc)

станция техобслуживания [stantsi-ya tyeнap-slooJivanee-ya] garage (for repairs), service station

стараться/постараться [staratsa/pastaratsa] to try

старше [starsheh] older

старый [stari] old

стать [stat] to become

стекло [styeklo] glass (material)

стена [styena] wall

стиральная машина [steeralna-ya mashiyna] washing machine

стиральный порошок [steeralni parashok] washing powder

стирать/постирать [steerat/pasteerat] to do the washing

сто [sto] hundred

стоимость [sto-eemast] charge, cost

стоимость международной отправки [sto-eemast myeJdoonarodnay atprafkee] overseas postage

стоить [sto-eet] to cost

стол [stol] table

столкновение [stalknavyenee-yeh] crash

столовая [stalova-ya] dining room; canteen

столовые приборы [stalovi-yeh preebori] cutlery

стоп-кран [stop-kran] emergency cord

сторона [starana] side

сто тысяч [sto tiysyach] hundred thousand

стоянка [sta-yanka] car park, parking lot

стоянка такси [sta-yanka taksee] taxi rank

стоять [sta-yat] to stand
страна [strana] country
страница [straneetsa] page
странный [stran-ni] strange
страх [straн] fear
страхование [straнavanee-yeh] insurance
стрижка [streeshka] haircut
стройный [stroyni] shapely
студент [stoodyent], студентка [stoodyentka] student (male/female)
стул [stool] chair
стыдно: мне стыдно [mnyeh stiydna] I'm ashamed
стюард [styoo-art] steward
стюардесса [styoo-ardesa] stewardess
суббота [soob-bota] Saturday
сувенир [soovyeneer] souvenir
сумасшедший [soomashetshi] mad; madman
сумка [soomka] bag
сумочка [soomachka] handbag, (US) purse
сутки [sootkee] 24 hours, day and night
сухой [sooнoy] dry
сушить [sooshiyt] to dry
схема [sнyema] diagram; network map
сцепление [stseplyenee-yeh] clutch
счастливо оставаться! [sh-chasleeva astavatsa!] good night!; enjoy your stay!
счастливого пути! [sh-chasleevava pootee!] have a good trip!

счастливый [sh-chasleevi] happy
счастье [sh-chastyeh] happiness
к счастью [k sh-chastyoo] fortunately
счёт [sh-chot] bill, (US) check
США [seh-sheh-a] USA
сшить [s-shit] to sew
съесть [syest] to eat
сыграть [sigrat] to play
сын [siyn] son
сырой [siroy] damp; raw
сюрприз [syoorprees] surprise

Т

Т trolleybus or tram stop
та [ta] that; that one
табак [tabak] tobacco
таблетка [tablyetka] pill, tablet
так [tak] so; this way; like this
так! [tak!] well!
так же красиво, как ... [tak jeh kraseeva, kak ...] as beautiful as ...
так как [tak kak] as; since
так себе [tak syebyeh] so-so
также [tagjeh] also
такси [taksee] taxi
таксофон [taksafon] public phone
талия [talee-ya] waist
талкучка [talkoochka] flea market
Таллин [tal-leen] Tallin
талон [talon] ticket

тальк [talk] talcum powder

там [tam] there

там внизу [tam vneez**oo**] down there

таможенная декларация [tamo**J**en-na-ya dyeklar**a**tsi-ya] Customs declaration form

таможенный контроль [tamo**J**eni kantr**o**l] Customs inspection

таможня [tamo**J**nya] Customs

тампон [tamp**o**n] tampon

танцевать [tantsev**a**t] dance

тапочки [t**a**pachkee] slippers

таракан [tarak**a**n] cockroach

тарелка [tar**ye**lka] plate

тариф [tar**ee**f] charge, tariff

Ташкент [tashk**ye**nt] Tashkent

Тбилиси [tbee**lee**see] Tbilisi

твёрдый [tv**yo**rdi] hard

твоего [tva-yev**o**] (of) your; (of) yours

твоей [tva-**ya**y] your; yours; of your; of yours; to your; to yours; by your; by yours

твоему [tva-yem**oo**] (to) your; (to) yours

твоё [tva-**yo**] your; yours

твоём [tva-**yo**m] your; yours

твои [tva-**ee**] your; yours

твоим [tva-**ee**m] (by) your; (by) yours; (to) your; (to) yours

твоими [tva-**ee**mee] (by) your; (by) yours

твоих [tva-**ee**н] (of) your; (of) yours

твой [tvoy] your; yours

твою [tva-**yoo**] your; yours

твоя [tva-**ya**] your; yours

те [tyeh] those

театр [tyeh-**a**tr] theatre

театральная касса [tyeh-atr**a**lna-ya k**a**s-sa] box office

тебе [tyeb**yeh**] you; to you

тебя [tyeb**ya**] you; of you

у тебя [oo tyeb**ya**] you have

телевизор [tyelyev**ee**zar] television, TV set

телеграмма [tyelyegr**a**m-ma] telegram

тележка [tyel**ye**shka] trolley

телекс [t**ye**lyeks] telex

телефон [tyelyef**o**n] telephone

телефон-автомат [tyelyef**o**n-aftam**a**t] payphone

телефонная будка [tyelyef**o**n-na-ya b**oo**tka] phone box

телефонный код [tyelyef**o**n-ni kot] dialling code

телефонный справочник [tyelyef**o**n-ni spr**a**vachneek] telephone directory

тело [t**ye**la] body

тем [tyem] (by) that; (by) that one; (to) those

теми [t**ye**mee] (by) those

тёмный [t**yo**mni] dark

температура [tyempyerat**oo**ra] temperature

тени для век [t**ye**nee dlya vyek] eye shadow

теннис [t**ye**n-nees] tennis

тень f [tyen] shadow; shade

в тени [ftyen**ee**] in the shade

тепло [tyepl**o**] warm; it's warm

тёплый [t**yo**pli] warm

А
Б
В
Г
Д
Е
Ё
Ж
З
И
Й
К
Л
М
Н
О
П
Р
С
Т
У
Ф
Х
Ц
Ч
Ш
Щ
Ъ
Ы
Ь
Э
Ю
Я

термометр [tyermomyetr] thermometer

термос [termas] Thermos® flask

терпеть [tyerpyet] to bear, to stand

терять/потерять [tyeryat/patyeryat] to lose

тесный [tyesni] tight; cramped

тесть m [tyest] father-in-law (wife's father)

тётя [tyotya] aunt

тех [tyeн] those; of those

течь f [tyech] leak

течь [tyech] to flow; to stream; to leak

тёща [tyosh-cha] mother-in-law (wife's mother)

тихий [teeнee] quiet

тише [teesheh] quieter

тише! [teesheh!] quiet!

тишина [teeshina] silence

ткань f [tkan] material

то [to] that; that one

тобой [taboy] (by) you

тогда [tagda] then

того [tavo] (of) that; (of) that one

тоже [toлeh] too; also

я тоже [ya toлeh] me too

той [toy] that; that one; of that; of that one; to that; to that one

толкать/толкнуть [talkat/talknoot] to push

толкнуть [talknoot] to push

толпа [talpa] crowd

толстый [tolsti] fat (adj)

только [tolka] only; just

только по будним дням [tolka paboodneem dnyam] weekdays only

том [tom] that; that one

тому [tamoo] (to) that; (to) that one

тональный крем [tanalni kryem] foundation cream

тонкий [tonkee] thin

тонуть/утонуть [tanoot/ootanoot] to drown

торговый центр [targovi tsentr] shopping centre

тормоза [tarmaza] brakes

тормозить/затормозить [tarmazeet/zatarmazeet] to brake

тот [tot] that; that one

тот же самый [tot лeh sami] the same

тощий [tosh-chee] skinny

трава [trava] grass; herb; weed

традиционный [tradeetsi-on-ni] traditional

традиция [tradeetsi-ya] tradition

транзитная посадка [tranzeetna-ya pasatka] intermediate stop

тратить [trateet] to spend

требовать [tryebavat] to demand

тревога [tryevoga] alarm

третий [tryetee] third

три [tree] three

тридцатый [treetsati] thirtieth

тридцать [**tree**tsat] thirty

тринадцатый [treen**a**tsati] thirteenth

тринадцать [treen**a**tsat] thirteen

триста [**tree**sta] three hundred

трогать/тронуть [**tro**gat/**tro**noot] to touch

тройка [**troy**ka] troika

тронуть [**tro**noot] to touch

тропинка [tra**pee**nka] path

тротуар [tratoo-**ar**] pavement, sidewalk

трубка [**troo**pka] pipe (to smoke)

трубопровод [troobapra**vot**] pipe; pipeline

трудный [**troo**dni] difficult

трусики [**troo**seekee] pants, panties

трусы [troo**siy**] underpants

ту [too] that; that one

туалет [too-al**yet**] toilet, rest room

туалетная бумага [too-al**yet**na-ya boo**ma**ga] toilet paper

туалеты [too-al**ye**ti] toilets, rest rooms

туман [too**man**] fog

туннель m [toon-**nel**] tunnel

тургруппа [toorg**roo**p-pa] tour group

турист [too**reest**] tourist

туристическая поездка [tooreest**ee**cheska-ya pa**yezt**ka] package tour

Турция [**toort**si-ya] Turkey

туфли [**too**flee] shoes

тушь для ресниц f [toosh dlya ryes**neets**] mascara

ты [tiy] you

тысяча [**tiy**syacha] thousand

тюрьма [tyoor**ma**] prison

тяжёлый [tya**zho**li] heavy

тянуть [tyan**oot**] to pull

У

у [oo] at; by; near; with

у них [oo neeh] they have

у вас [oo vas] you have

у тебя [oo tyeb**ya**] you have

у неё [oo nyeh-**yo**] she has; it has

у нас [oo nas] we have

у него [oo nyevo] he has; it has

у меня [oo myen**ya**] I have

у вас есть ...? [oo vas yest ...?] have you got ...?

у меня нет ... [oo myen**ya** nyet ...] I don't have ...

убивать/убить [oobee**vat**/oo**beet**] to kill

убирать/убрать [oobeer**at**/oob**rat**] to take away; to clean

убить [oo**beet**] to kill

убрать [oob**rat**] to take away; to clean

уверенный [oo**vye**ryen-ni] sure

увидеть [oo**vee**dyet] to see

увлажняющий крем [oovlaj**nya**-yoosh-chee kryem] moisturizer

увлекательный [oovlyek**a**tyelni] exciting

угол [**oo**gal] corner

удар [**oo**dar] blow; stroke

ударять/ударить [oodar**yat**/ood**ar**eet] to hit

удача [ood**acha**] luck; success

удивительный [oodee**vee**tyelni] surprising

удлинитель [oodleen**ee**tyel] extension lead

удобный [ood**o**bni] comfortable

удостоверение [oodasta-ver**yen**ee-yeh] certificate

уезжать/уехать [ooyez**jat**/oo**ye**нat] to leave

ужалить [ooj**a**leet] to sting

ужас [**oo**Jas], ужасно [ooJ**asna**] it's awful, it's ghastly

ужасный [ooJ**asni**] awful, terrible, ghastly

уже [ooJ**eh**] already

ужин [**oo**Jin] dinner; supper

ужинать [**oo**Jinat] to have dinner

узкий [**oo**skee] narrow

узнавать/узнать [ooznav**at**/oozn**at**] to recognize

уйти [ooyt**ee**] to go away

указатель поворота m [ookaz**at**yel pav**or**ota] indicator

укладывать/уложить вещи [ook**lad**ivat/oolaJ**eet** vy**esh**-chee] to pack

укол [ook**ol**] injection

Украина [ookra-**ee**na] Ukraine

украсть [ookr**ast**] to steal

укус [ook**oos**] bite

ул., улица [**oo**leetsa] street

на улице [na **oo**leetsyeh] outside; in the street

уличное движение [**oo**leechna-yeh dvee**Je**nee-yeh] traffic

уложить вещи [oolaJ**eet** vy**esh**-chee] to pack

уложить волосы феном [oolaJ**eet** v**ol**asi f**ye**nam] to blow-dry

улучшить [ool**oo**tshit] to improve

улыбаться/улыбнуться [ooli**batsa**/oolibn**ootsa**] to smile

улыбка [ool**iy**pka] smile

улыбнуться [ooliybn**ootsa**] to smile

умелый [oom**ye**li] skilful

умирать/умереть [oomeer**at**/oomyer**yet**] to die

умный [**oo**mni] clever, intelligent

умывальник [oomiv**al**neek] washbasin

универмаг [ooneevyerm**ak**] department store

универсам [ooneevyers**am**] supermarket

университет [ooneevyerseet**yet**] university

упасть [oop**ast**] to fall

упасть в обморок [oop**ast** v**ob**marak] to faint

управляющий [oopravl**ya**-yoosh-chee] manager

уровень масла [**oo**ravyen m**as**la] oil level

уродливый [oor**od**leevi] ugly

урок [oor**ok**] lesson

уронить [ooraneet] to drop
услышать [oosliyshat] to hear
успех [oospyeн] success
  желаю успеха! [Jelayoo
  oospyeнa!] good luck!
успокойтесь ! [oospakoytyes!]
  calm down!
усталый [oostali] tired
устройство [oostroystva]
  device
усы [oosiy] moustache
утонуть [ootanoot] to drown
утро [ootra] morning
  утра [ootra] in the morning;
  a.m.
  в пять часов утра [fpyat
  chasof ootra] at 5 a.m.
утюг [ootyook] iron (for clothes)
ухо [ooнa] ear
уходить/уйти [ooнadeet/ooytee]
  to go away
  уходите! [ooнadeetyeh!] go
  away!
учёт [oochot] stocktaking
учитель m [oocheetyel],
  учительница
  [oocheetyelneetsa] teacher
учиться [oocheetsa] to learn;
  to study
Уэльс [oo-els] Wales
уэльский [oo-elskee] Welsh

Ф

факс [faks] fax
факсимильный аппарат
  [fakseemeelni aparat] fax
  machine

фамилия [fameelee-ya]
  surname
фары [fari] headlights
февраль m [fyevral]
  February
фейерверк [fyay-yervvyerk]
  fireworks
фен [fyen] hairdryer
ферма [fyerma] farm
Финляндия [feenlyandee-ya]
  Finland
фиолетовый [fee-alyetavi]
  purple
фирма [feerma] firm,
  company
флаг [flak] flag
фонарик [fanareek] torch
фонтан [fantan] fountain
фотоаппарат [fata-aparat]
  camera
фотограф [fatograf]
  photographer
фотографировать
  [fatagrafeeravat] to take
  photos
фотография [fatagrafee-ya]
  photograph
Франция [frantsi-ya] France
французский [frantsooskee]
  French
французский язык
  [frantsooskee yaziyk] French
  (language)
фрукты [frookti] fruit
фунт [foont] pound
фуражка [foorashka] cap
фургон [foorgon] van
футбол [foodbol] football
футболка [foodbolka] T-shirt

А
Б
В
Г
Д
Е
Ё
Ж
З
И
Й
К
Л
М
Н
О
П
Р
С
Т
У
Ф
Х
Ц
Ч
Ш
Щ
Ъ
Ы
Ь
Э
Ю
Я

245

футбольное поле [foodb**o**lna-yeh p**o**lyeh] football pitch

X

халат [Hal**a**t] dressing gown

химчистка [Heemch**ee**stka] dry-cleaner

хлеб [Hl**y**ep] bread

хлопок [Hl**o**pak] cotton

ходить [Had**ee**t] to go (on foot), to walk; to suit

хозяин [Haz**ya**-een] owner; host

хозяйственный магазин [Haz**y**lstvyen-ni magaz**ee**n] hardware store

хоккей [Hak**yay**] hockey

холм [H**o**lm] hill

холодильник [Halad**ee**lneek] fridge

холодный [Hal**o**dni] cold

холостяк [Halast**ya**k] bachelor

хороший [Har**o**shi] good

хорошо [Harash**o**] well

хорошо! [Harash**o**!] good!

мне хорошо [mnyeh Harash**o**] I'm well

хотеть [Hat**y**et] to want

я хотел/хотела [ya Hat**y**el/Hat**y**ela] I wanted (said by man/woman)

я хотел/хотела бы ... [ya Hat**y**el/Hat**y**ela bi ...] I would like ... (said by man/woman)

хотим [Hat**ee**m] we want

хотите [Hat**ee**tyeh] you want

хотя [Hat**ya**] although

хотят [Hat**ya**t] they want

хочет [H**o**chyet] he wants; she wants; it wants

хочется: мне хочется ... [mnyeh H**o**chyetsa ...] I feel like ...

хочешь [H**o**chyesh] you want

хочу [Hach**oo**] I want

храбрый [Hr**a**bri] brave

храните в сухом/прохладном/тёмном месте [Hran**ee**tyeh fsooH**o**m/praHl**a**dnam/ty**o**mnam my**e**styeh] keep in a cool/dark/dry place

хранить [Hran**ee**t] to keep; to preserve

хрустящий картофель [Hroost**ya**sh-chee kart**o**fyel] crisps, (US) chips

художник [Hood**o**Jneek] artist, painter

худой [Hood**oy**] thin

худший [H**oo**tshi] worst

хуже [H**oo**Jeh] worse

Ц

царь m [tsar] tsar

цвет [tsvyet] colour

цветная плёнка [tsvyetna-**ya** ply**o**nka] colour film

цветок [tsvyet**o**k] flower

цветочный магазин [tsvyet**o**chni magaz**ee**n] florist's, flower shop

цветы [tsvyet**iy**] flowers

целовать/поцеловать [tselav**a**t/patselav**a**t] to kiss

целый [tseli] whole
цена [tsena] price
центр [tsentr] centre
центр города [tsentr gorada] city centre
центральное отопление [tsentralna-yeh ataplyenee-yeh] central heating
цепочка [tsepochka] chain
церковь f [tserkav] church

Ч

чаевые [cha-yeviyeh] tip
чайник [chIneek] kettle; teapot
чартерный рейс [charterni ryays] charter flight
час [chas] hour; one o'clock
в ... часа [f ... chasa] at ... o'clock
в ... часов [f ... chasof] at ... o'clock
часто [chasta] often
частый [chasti] often
часть f [chast] part
часы [chasiy] watch; clock; hours
часы приёма [chasiy pree-yoma] visiting hours
часы работы [chasiy raboti] opening hours, opening times
чашка [chashka] cup
чаще [chash-cheh] more often
чего [chevo] what; of what
чек [chyek] cheque, (US) check

чековая книжка [chyekava-ya kneeshka] cheque/check book
человек [chelavyek] person
челюсть f [chyelyoost] jaw
чем [chyem] than; what; by what
чём [chyom] what
чемодан [chyemadan] suitcase
чему [chyemoo] what; to what
через [chyeryes] through; across; in
через три дня [chyeryes tree dnya] in three days
чёрно-белый [chorna-byeli] black and white
Чёрное море [chorna-yeh moryeh] Black Sea
чёрный [chorni] black
честный [chyesni] honest
четверг [chyetvyerk] Thursday
четвёртый [chetvyorti] fourth
четверть f [chyetvyert] quarter
четверть часа [chyetvyert chasa] quarter of an hour
четверть второго [chyetvyert ftarova] quarter past one
без четверти два [byes chyetvyertee dva] quarter to two
четыре [chetiyryeh] four
четыреста [chyetiyryesta] four hundred
четырнадцатый [chetiyrnatsati] fourteenth
четырнадцать [chetiyrnatsat] fourteen

Чешская республика
[chyeshska-ya ryespoobleeka]
Czech Republic

чинить/починить [cheeneet/
pacheeneet] to mend

число [cheeslo] date; number

чистить [cheesteet] to clean

чистый [cheesti] clean; pure

читать/прочитать
[cheetat/pracheetat] to read

что [shto] what; that

что-нибудь [shto-neeboot]
anything

что-то [shto-ta] something

чувство [choostva] feeling

чувствовать [choostvavat] to
feel

чувствовать себя [choostvavat
syebya] to feel

чулки [choolkee] stockings

чуть [choot] hardly, scarcely; a
little

чьё: чьё это? [cho eta?] whose
is this?

Ш

шампунь m [shampoon]
shampoo

шапка [shapka] hat (with flaps)

шариковая ручка
[shareekava-ya roochka]
ballpoint pen

шарф [sharf] scarf (neck)

шашлычная [shashliychna-ya]
café selling kebabs

швейцар [shvyaytsar] porter;
doorman

Швейцария [shvyaytsaree-ya]
Switzerland

Швеция [shvyetsi-ya] Sweden

шевелиться/шевельнуться
[shevyeleetsa/shevyelnootsa] to
move; to stir

шезлонг [shezlonk] deckchair

шёл [shol] went; was going

шёлковый [sholkavi] silk

шерсть f [sherst] wool

шестнадцатый [shesnatsati]
sixteenth

шестнадцать [shesnatsat]
sixteen

шестой [shestoy] sixth

шесть [shest] six

шестьдесят [shesdyesyat]
sixty

шестьсот [shes-sot] six
hundred

шея [sheh-ya] neck

шина [shiyna] tyre

широкий [shirokee] wide

шить/сшить [shit/s-shit] to
sew

шкаф [shkaf] cupboard;
wardrobe, closet

школа [shkola] school

шла [shla] went; was going

шли [shlee] went; were going

шло [shlo] went; was going

шляпа [shlyapa] hat

шнурки [shnoorkee] shoelaces

шоколад [shakalat] chocolate

шорты [shorti] shorts

шоссе [shas-seh] highway

Шотландия [shatlandee-ya]
Scotland

шотландский [shatlandskee]

Scottish

штепсельная вилка
[sht**e**psyelna-ya v**ee**lka] plug
(electric)

штопор [sht**o**par] corkscrew

штраф [shtraf] fine

шум [shoom] noise

шумный [sh**oo**mni] noisy

шурин [sh**oo**reen]
brother-in-law (wife's
brother)

шутка [sh**oo**tka] joke

Щ

щётка [sh-ch**o**tka] brush

Э

экипаж [ekeep**a**sh] crew

эластичный [elast**ee**chni]
elastic

электрический
[elyektr**ee**chyeskee] electric

электричество
[elyektr**ee**chyestva] electricity

электричка [elyektr**ee**chka]
suburban train

электронная почта [elyektr**o**n-
na-ya p**o**chta] electronic mail

Эстония [est**o**nee-ya] Estonia

эт. floor

эта [**e**ta] it (is); that; this; this
one

этаж [et**a**sh] floor; storey
первый этаж [p**ye**rvi et**a**sh]
ground floor, (US) first floor

эти [**e**tee] these; those

этим [**e**teem] (by) this; (by)
this one; (to) these

этими [**e**teemee] (by) these

этих [**e**teeн] these; of these

это [**e**ta] it (is); that; this
(one)

этого [**e**tava] (of) this; (of)
this one

этой [**e**t] this; this one; of
this; of this one; to this; to
this one; by this; by this
one

этом [**e**tam] this; this one

этому [**e**tamoo] (to) this; (to)
this one

этот [**e**tat] it (is); that; this;
this one

эту [**e**too] this; this one

Ю

юбка [y**oo**pka] skirt

ювелирные изделия
[yoovyel**ee**rni-yeh eezd**ye**lee-ya]
jewellery

ювелирный магазин
[yoovyel**ee**rni magaz**ee**n]
jeweller's shop

юг [yook] south
к югу от [k y**oo**goo at] south
of

Южная Африка [y**oo**лna-ya
afreeka] South Africa

южный [y**oo**лni] southern

юмор [y**oo**mar] humour

Я

я [ya] I

явиться на регистрацию
[yaveetsa na ryegeestratsi-yoo] to
check in

яд [yat] poison

язык [yaziyk] tongue;
language

Ялта [yalta] Yalta

январь m [yanvar] January

ярлык [yarliyk] label

ярмарка [yarmarka] fair;
market

ярус [yaroos] circle; tier

ясный [yasni] clear; obvious

Menu
Reader:
Food

Essential terms

bread хлеб [Hlyep]
butter масло [masla]
cup чашка [chashka]
dessert десерт [dyesyert]
fish рыба [riyba]
fork вилка [veelka]
glass стакан [stakan]
knife нож [nosh]
main course основное блюдо [asnavno-yeh blyooda]
meat мясо [myasa]
menu меню [myenyoo]
pepper перец [pyerets]
plate тарелка [taryelka]
salad салат [salat]
salt соль f [sol]
set menu комплексный обед [komplyeksni abyet]
soup суп [soop]
spoon ложка [loshka]
starter закуска [zakooska]
table стол [stol]

another ..., please ещё одно ..., пожалуйста [yesh-cho ... peeva, paJalsta]
excuse me! простите! [prasteetyeh!]
could I have the bill, please? счёт, пожалуйста [sh-chot, paJalsta]
I'd like ... (said by man/woman) я бы хотел/хотела ... [ya biy Hatyel/Hatyela ...]

252

абрикос [abreekos] apricot

азу [azoo] small pieces of meat in a savoury sauce

ананас [ananas] pineapple

антрекот [antryekot] entrecote steak

апельсин [apyelseen] orange

апельсиновое варенье [apyelseenava-yeh varyenyeh] marmalade

арахис [araнees] peanuts

арбуз [arboos] water melon

ассорти мясное [asartee myasno-yeh] assorted meats

ассорти рыбное [asartee riybna-yeh] assorted fish

баклажан [baklaJan] aubergine

банан [banan] banana

баранина [baraneena] mutton, lamb

баранина на вертеле [baraneena na vyertyelyeh] mutton grilled on a skewer

баранки [barankee] ring-shaped rolls

бараньи котлеты [baranee katlyeti] lamb chops

батон [baton] baguette

бекон [byekon] bacon

белый хлеб [byeli нlyep] white bread

беф строганов [byef-stroganaf] beef Stroganoff

битки [beetkee] rissoles; hamburgers

битки из баранины [beetkee eez baranini] lamb meatballs

бифштекс [beefshteks] steak

бифштекс натуральный [beefshteks natooralni] fried or grilled steak

блинчики [bleencheekee] pancakes

блинчики с вареньем [bleencheekee svaryenyem] pancakes with jam

блины [bleeniy] buckwheat pancakes, blini

блины с икрой [bleeniy sikroy] blini with caviar

блины со сметаной [bleeniy sa smyetani] blini with sour cream

блюда из птицы [blyooda ees pteetsi] poultry dishes

блюдо [blyooda] dish, course

бородинский хлеб [baradeenskee нlyep] dark rye bread

борщ [borsh-ch] beef, beetroot and cabbage soup

брынза [briynza] sheep's cheese, feta

брюссельская капуста [bryoos-syelska-ya kapoosta] Brussels sprouts

бублик [boobleek] type of bagel

буженина с гарниром [booJeneena zgarneeram] cold boiled pork with vegetables

булки [boolkee] rolls

булочка [boolachka] roll

бульон [boolyon] clear meat soup, bouillon

бульон с пирожками [boolyon

speerashkamee] clear meat
soup served with small
meat pies

бульон с фрикадельками
[boolyon sfreekadelkamee] clear
soup with meatballs

бутерброд [booterbrot]
sandwich

бутерброд с мясом [booterbrot
smyasam] meat sandwich

бутерброд с сыром [booterbrot
s-siyram] cheese sandwich

буханка [boohanka] loaf

ванильный [vaneelni] vanilla

вареники [varyeneekee] curd
or fruit dumplings

варёный [varyoni] boiled

варенье [varyenyeh] jam,
preserve

ватрушка [vatrooshka]
cheesecake

вермишель [vyermeeshel]
vermicelli

вегетарианский [vyegyetaree-
anskee] vegetarian

ветчина [vyetcheena] ham

взбитые сливки [vzbeeti-yeh
sleefkee] whipped cream

винегрет [veenyegryet]
Russian vegetable salad:
beetroot, potatoes, onions,
peas, carrots and pickled
cucumbers in mayonnaise
or oil

виноград [veenagrat] grapes

вишня [veeshnya] sour
cherries

галушка [galooshka]
Ukrainian dumpling

гамбургер [gamboorgyer]
hamburger

гарнир [garneer] vegetables

говядина [gavyadeena] beef

говядина отварная с хреном
[gavyadeena atvarna-ya sнryenam]
boiled beef with
horseradish

говядина тушёная
[gavyadeena tooshona-ya]
stewed beef

голубцы [galooptsiy] cabbage
leaves stuffed with meat
and rice

горох [garoн] peas

горошек [garoshek] peas

горчица [garcheetsa] mustard

горячие закуски [garyachee-
yeh zakooskee] hot starters,
hot appetizers

горячий [garyachee] hot

грейпфрут [graypfroot]
grapefruit

гренки [gryenkee] croutons

гренок [gryenak] toast

грецкие орехи [gryetskee-yeh
aryeнee] walnut

гречка [gryechka] buckwheat

гречневая каша [gryechnyeva-
ya kasha] buckwheat
porridge

грибы [greebiy] mushrooms

грибы в сметане [greebiy
fsmyetanyeh] mushrooms in
sour cream

грибы маринованные
[greebiy mareenovani-yeh]

marinated mushrooms

груша [gr**oo**sha] pear

гуляш из говядины [g**oo**lyash eez gav**ya**deeni] beef goulash

гусь [g**oo**s] goose

десерт [dyes**ye**rt] dessert

джем [djem] jam

дичь [deech] game

домашний [dam**a**shnee] home-made

домашняя птица [dam**a**shnya-ya pt**ee**tsa] poultry

дыня [d**iy**nya] melon

еда [yed**a**] food; meal

ежевика [yeJev**ee**ka] blackberries

жареная рыба [J**a**ryena-ya r**iy**ba] fried fish

жареный [J**a**ryeni] grilled; fried; roast

жареный картофель [J**a**ryeni kart**o**fyel] fried potatoes

жареный на вертеле [J**a**ryeni na v**ye**rtyel-yeh] grilled on a skewer

желе [Jel**ye**h] jelly

жир [Jiyr] lard

жульен [J**oo**lyen] mushrooms or meat cooked with onions and sour cream

завтрак [z**a**ftrak] breakfast

закуска [zak**oo**ska] snack; starter, appetizer

закуски [zak**oo**skee] starters, appetizers

заливная рыба [zaleevn**a**-ya r**iy**ba] fish in aspic

заливной [zaleevn**oy**] in aspic

замороженные продукты [zamar**o**Jen-ni-yeh prad**oo**kti] frozen food

запеканка [zapyek**a**nka] baked pudding; shepherd's pie

запечённый [zapyech**o**nni] baked

зелёный горошек [zyel**yo**ni gar**o**shek] green peas

зелёный лук [zyel**yo**ni look] spring onions

зелёный салат [zyel**yo**ni sal**a**t] green salad

земляника [zyemlyan**ee**ka] wild strawberries

зразы [zr**a**zi] meat cutlets stuffed with rice, buckwheat or mashed potatoes

изделия из теста [eezd**ye**lee-ya ees t**ye**sta] pastry dishes

изюм [eez**yoo**m] sultanas; raisins

икра [eekr**a**] caviar

икра баклажанная [eekr**a** baklaJ**a**nna-ya] mashed fried aubergines with onions and tomatoes

икра зернистая [eekr**a** zyern**ee**sta-ya] fresh caviar

икра кетовая [eekr**a** ky**e**tova-ya] red caviar

индейка [eend**ya**yka] turkey

инжир [eenJ**iy**r] figs

кабачки [kabachkee] courgettes

камбала [kambala] plaice

капуста [kapoosta] cabbage

карп [karp] carp

карп с грибами [karp zgreebamee] carp with mushrooms

картофель [kartofyel] potatoes

картофельное пюре [kartofyelna-yeh pyooreh] mashed potatoes

картофель с ветчиной и шпиком [kartofyel zvyetcheenoy ee shpeekam] potatoes with ham and bacon fat

картофель фри [kartofyel free] chips, French fries

каша [kasha] porridge

каштан [kashtan] chestnut

кебаб [kebap] kebab

кекс [kyeks] fruit cake

кета [kyeta] Siberian salmon

кетчуп [kyetchoop] ketchup

кильки [keelkee] sprats

кисель [keesyel] thin fruit jelly

кисель из клубники [keesyel ees kloobneekee] strawberry jelly

кисель из чёрной смородины [keesyel ees chorni smarodeeni] blackcurrant jelly

кислая капуста [keesla-ya kapoosta] sauerkraut

кислые щи [keesli-yeh sh-chee] sauerkraut soup

клубника [kloobneeka] strawberries

клюква [klyookva] cranberries

колбаса [kalbasa] salami sausage

комплексный обед [komplyeksni abyet] set menu

компот [kampot] stewed fruit in a light syrup; compote

компот из груш [kampot eez groosh] stewed pears

компот из сухофруктов [kampot ees soona-frooktaf] stewed dried fruit

консервы [kansyervi] tinned foods

конфета [kanfyeta] sweet, candy

копчёная колбаса [kapchona-ya kalbasa] smoked sausage

копчёная сёмга [kapchona-ya syomga] smoked salmon

копчёные свиные рёбрышки [kapchoni-yeh sveeniy-yeh ryobrishkee] smoked pork ribs

копчёный [kapchoni] smoked

коржики [korJikee] shortbread

корица [kareetsa] cinnamon

котлета [katlyeta] cutlet; burger; rissole

котлеты по-киевски [katlyeti pa-kee-yefskee] chicken Kiev

котлеты с грибами [katlyeti zgreebamee] steak with mushrooms

кофейный [kafyayni] coffee-flavoured; coffee

краб [krap] crab

крабовые палочки [krabavi-yeh palachkee] crab sticks

красная икра [krasna-ya eekra] red caviar

красная смородина [krasna-ya smarodeena] redcurrants

креветки [kryevyetkee] prawns

крем [kryem] butter cream

кровь: с кровью [s krovyoo] rare

кролик [kroleek] rabbit

кукуруза [kookoorooza] sweet corn

кулебяка [koolyebyaka] pie with meat, fish or vegetables

курица [kooreetsa] chicken

лапша [lapsha] noodles

лесные орехи [lyesniy-yeh aryeHee] hazelnuts

лимон [leemon] lemon

ломтик [lomteek] slice

лососина [lasaseena] smoked salmon

лосось [lasos] salmon

лук [look] onions

майонез [mı-anes] mayonnaise

макаронные изделия [makaron-ni-yeh eezdyelee-ya] pasta

макароны [makaroni] macaroni

малина [maleena] raspberries

мандарин [mandareen] mandarin; tangerine

манная каша [man-na-ya kasha] semolina

маргарин [margareen] margarine

маслины [masleeni] olives

масло [masla] butter; oil

мёд [myot] honey

медовый [myedovi] honey

меню [myenyoo] menu

мидии [meedee-ee] mussels

миндаль [meendal] almonds

моллюски [mal-lyooskee] shellfish

молоко [malako] milk

молочный [malochni] milk; dairy

молочный кисель [malochni keesyel] milk jelly

морковь [markof] carrots

мороженое [maroJena-yeh] ice cream

мороженое малиновое [maroJena-yeh maleenava-yeh] raspberry ice cream

мороженое 'пломбир' [maroJena-yeh plambeer] originally ice cream with candied fruit, but nowadays often just plain vanilla ice cream

мороженое клубничное [maroJena-yeh kloobneechna-yeh] strawberry ice cream

мороженое молочное [maroJena-yeh malochna-yeh] dairy ice cream

мороженое молочное с ванилином [maroJena-yeh malochna-yeh svaneeleenam] vanilla dairy ice cream

мороженое шоколадное [maroJena-yeh shakaladna-yeh] chocolate ice cream

морская капуста [marska-ya kapoosta] sea kale

морские продукты [marskee-yeh pradookti] seafood

мука [mooka] flour

мясной [myasnoy] meat

мясной бульон [myasnoy boolyon] clear meat soup

мясо [myasa] meat

на вертеле [na vyertyelyeh] on a skewer

на вынос [na viynas] to take away, to go

национальные русские блюда [natsi-analni-yeh rooskee-yeh blyooda] Russian national dishes

начинка [nacheenka] filling

обед [abyet] lunch

овощи [ovash-chee] vegetables

овощной [avash-chnoy] vegetable

овощной суп [avash-chnoy soop] vegetable soup

огурец [agooryets] cucumber

огурцы со сметаной [agoortsiy sa smyetani] cucumber with sour cream

окорок [okarak] gammon

окрошка [akroshka] cold soup made with kvas (see p. 268), vegetables and meat

оладьи [aladee] thick pancakes

оливки [aleefkee] olives

омар [amar] lobster

омлет [amlyet] omelette

омлет натуральный [amlyet natooralni] plain omelette

омлет с ветчиной [amlyet svyetcheenoy] ham omelette

орехи [aryehee] nuts

осётр запечённый в сметане [asyotr zapyechoni fsmyetanyeh] sturgeon baked in sour cream

осетрина заливная [asyetreena zaleevna-ya] sturgeon in aspic

осетрина под белым соусом [asyetreena pat byelim so-oosam] sturgeon in white sauce

осетрина с гарниром [asyetreena zgarneeram] sturgeon with vegetables

осетрина с пикантным соусом [asyetreena speekantnim so-oosam] sturgeon in piquant sauce

основное блюдо [asnavno-yeh blyooda] main course

отбивная котлета [atbeevna-ya katlyeta] chop

отварная рыба [atvarna-ya riyba] poached fish

отварной [atvarnoy] boiled; poached

отварной цыплёнок [atvarnoy tsiplyonak] boiled chicken

палтус [paltoos] halibut

панированный [paneerovanni] in breadcrumbs

панированный цыплёнок [paneerovanni tsiplyonak] chicken in breadcrumbs

паштет [pashtyet] pâté; pie

пельмени [pyelmyenee] type of ravioli

первое блюдо [pyerva-yeh blyooda] first course

перец [pyeryets] pepper

персик [pyerseek] peach

петрушка [pyetrooshka] parsley

печёнка [pyechonka] liver

печёный [pyechoni] baked

печенье [pyechyenyeh] biscuit, cookie; pastry

печень трески в масле [pyechyen tryeskee vmasl-yeh] cod liver in oil

пирог [peerok] pie; tart; cake

пирог с повидлом [peerok spaveedlam] jam tart

пирог с мясом [peerok smyasam] meat pie

пирог с яблоками [peerok syablakamee] apple pie

пирожки [peerashkee] pies

пирожки с капустой [peerashkee skapoosti] cabbage pies

пирожки с мясом [peerashkee smyasam] meat pies

пирожки с творогом [peerashkee stvoragam] cottage cheese pies

пирожное [peeroJna-yeh] pastries; cake, pastry

пицца [peetsa] pizza

плавленый сыр [plavlyeni siyr] processed cheese

плов [plof] pilaf

повидло [paveedla] jam

под белым соусом [pat byelim so-oosam] in white sauce

поджаренный [padJaryen-ni] grilled; fried

поджаренный хлеб [padJaryen-ni Hlyep] toast

под майонезом [pad mi-anezam] in mayonnaise

подсолнечное масло [patsolnyechna-yeh masla] sunflower oil

пожарские котлеты [paJarskee-ye katlyeti] minced chicken patties

помидор [pameedor] tomato

пончики [poncheekee] doughnuts

порция [portsi-ya] portion

почки [pochkee] kidneys

приправа к салату [preeprava k salatoo] salad dressing

простокваша [prastakvasha] natural set yoghurt

пряник [pryaneek] gingerbread

пряность [pryanast] spice

птица [pteetsa] poultry

рагу из баранины [ragoo eez baraneeni] lamb ragout

рагу из говядины [ragoo eez gavyadeeni] beef ragout

рак [rak] crayfish

рассол [ras-**sol**] pickle

рассольник [ras-**sol**neek] meat or fish soup with pickled cucumbers

ржаной хлеб [rᴊan**oy** Hlyep] rye bread

рис [rees] rice

ромштекс с луком [**rom**shteks sl**oo**kam] rump steak with onions

ростбиф с гарниром [**rost**beef zg**ar**neeram] roast beef with vegetables

рубленое мясо [**roo**blyena-yeh m**ya**sa] minced meat

рубленые котлеты [**roo**blyeni-yeh katl**ye**ti] rissoles

рулет [rool**yet**] meat and potato roll; swiss roll

рулет из рубленой телятины [rool**yet** eez **roo**blyenı tyel**ya**teeni] minced veal roll

русская кухня [**roo**ska-ya k**oo**ʜnya] Russian cuisine

рыба [**rı**yba] fish

рыбные блюда [**rı**ybni-yeh bl**yoo**da] fish dishes

рыбный [**rı**ybni] fish

ряженка [**rya**ᴊenka] fermented baked milk, similar to thick yoghurt

салат [sal**at**] lettuce; salad

салат зелёный [sal**at** zyel**yo**ni] green salad

салат из картофеля [sal**at** ees kart**o**fyelya] potato salad

салат из лука [sal**at** eez l**oo**ka] spring onion salad

салат из огурцов [sal**at** eez ag**oor**ts**of**] cucumber salad

салат из помидоров [sal**at** ees pameed**o**raf] tomato salad

салат из помидоров с брынзой [sal**at** ees pameed**o**raf zbr**ıy**nzı] tomato salad with sheep's cheese

салат из редиски [sal**at** eez ryed**ee**skee] radish salad

салат из яблок [sal**at** eez **ya**blak] apple salad

салат мясной [sal**at** myasn**oy**] meat salad

салат с крабами [sal**at** skr**a**bamee] crab salad

салат столичный [sal**at** stal**ee**chni] potato salad with meat, carrots, peas and mayonnaise

сало [s**a**la] salted pork fat, sliced and eaten with rye bread (Ukrainian)

самообслуживание [sama-apsl**oo**ᴊivanee-yeh] self-service

сандвич [s**a**ndveech] sandwich

сардельки [sard**el**kee] thick frankfurters

сардины [sard**ee**ni] sardines

сардины в масле [sard**ee**ni vm**a**slyeh] sardines in oil

сахар [s**a**ʜar] sugar

свежий [sv**ye**ᴊi] fresh

свёкла [sv**yo**kla] beetroot

свинина [sveen**ee**na] pork

свинина жареная с гарниром [sveen**ee**na ᴊar**ye**na-ya zg**ar**neeram] fried pork with vegetables

свинина с квашеной капустой [sveen**ee**na skv**a**sheni kap**oo**sti] pork with sauerkraut

свиной [svee**noy**] pork

свиные отбивные [sv**ee**niy-yeh atb**ee**vniy-yeh] pork chops

с гарниром [zgarn**ee**ram] with vegetables

селёдка малосольная [syel**yo**tka malas**o**lna-ya] slightly salted herring

сельдь [syeld] herring

сёмга [s**yo**mga] salmon

скумбрия горячего копчения [sk**oo**mbree-ya gar**ya**chyeva kapchy**e**nee-ya] smoked mackerel

скумбрия запечённая [sk**oo**mbree-ya zapyech**o**na-ya] baked mackerel

сладкий [sl**a**tkee] sweet

сладкое [sl**a**tka-yeh] dessert, sweet course

слива [sl**ee**va] plum

сливки [sl**ee**fkee] cream

сливочное масло [sl**ee**vachna-yeh m**a**sla] butter

с майонезом [smi-an**e**zam] with mayonnaise

сметана [smy**e**tana] sour cream

солёное печенье [sal**yo**na-yeh pyech**ye**nyeh] savoury biscuits

солёные огурцы [sal**yo**ni-yeh ag**oo**rts**iy**] pickled cucumbers

солёные помидоры [sal**yo**ni-yeh pameed**o**ri] pickled

tomatoes

солёный [sal**yo**ni] salty; savoury; salted; pickled

соль [sol] salt

солянка [sal**ya**nka] spicy soup made from fish or meat and vegetables; stewed meat and cabbage with spices

сосиски [sas**ee**skee] frankfurters

соус [s**o**-oos] sauce

спаржа [sp**a**rja] asparagus

с рисом [s r**ee**sam] with rice

стерлядь [st**ye**rlyat] small sturgeon

студень [st**oo**dyen] meat jelly; galantine; aspic

судак [s**oo**dak] pike-perch

судак в белом вине [s**oo**dak vby**e**lam veen-**yeh**] pike-perch in white wine

судак жареный в тесте [s**oo**dak ja**r**eni fty**e**styeh] pike-perch fried in batter

суп [s**oo**p] soup

суп из свежих грибов [s**oo**p ees sv**ye**jiн greeb**of**] fresh mushroom soup

суп картофельный [s**oo**p kart**o**fyelni] potato soup

суп-лапша с курицей [s**oo**p lapsh**a** sk**oo**reetsay] chicken noodle soup

суп мясной [s**oo**p myasn**oy**] meat soup

суп с грибами [s**oo**p zgreeb**a**mee] mushroom soup

суп томатный [s**oo**p tam**a**tni] tomato soup

с хреном [sнryenam] with horseradish sauce

сыр [siyr] cheese

сырник [siyrneek] small cheesecake; cottage cheese pancake or fritter

сырой [siroy] raw

творог [tvarok] cottage cheese

телятина [tyelyateena] veal

телячьи отбивные [tyelyachee atbeevniy-yeh] veal chops

тесто [tyesta] pastry; dough

тефтели с рисом [tyeftyelee sreesam] meatballs with rice

тмин [tmeen] thyme

томатный соус [tamatni so-oos] tomato sauce

торт [tort] cake, gateau

травы [travi] herbs

треска [tryeska] cod

тунец [toonyets] tuna fish

тушёный [tooshoni] stewed

укроп [ookrop] dill

уксус [ooksoos] vinegar

устрицы [oostreetsi] oysters

утка [ootka] duck

уха [ooнa] fish soup

фаршированная рыба [farshirovan-na-ya riyba] stuffed fish

фаршированные помидоры [farshirovan-ni-yeh pameedori] stuffed tomatoes

фаршированный [farshirovan-ni] stuffed

фасоль [fasol] French beans; haricot beans

филе [filyeh] fillet

фирменные блюда [feermyen-ni-yeh blooda] speciality dishes

фисташки [feestashkee] pistachio nuts

форель [faryel] trout

фрикадельки [freekadyelkee] meatballs

фрикадельки из телятины в соусе [freekadyelkee ees tyelyateeni vso-oosyeh] veal meatballs in gravy

фруктовое мороженое [frooktova-yeh maroлena-yeh] fruit ice cream

фрукты [frookti] fruit

харчо [нarcho] Georgian thick, spicy mutton soup

хлеб [нlyep] bread

холодной [нalodni] cold

холодные закуски [нalodni-yeh zakooskee] cold starters, cold appetizers

хорошо прожаренный [нarasho praлaryen-ni] well-done

хрен [нryen] horseradish

хрустящий картофель [нroostyash-chee kartofyel] crisps, (US) chips

цветная капуста [tsvyetna-ya kapoosta] cauliflower

цыплёнок [tsiplyonak] chicken

цыплёнок в тесте [tsiplyonak

ft**ye**styeh] chicken in pastry

цыплёнок по-охотничьи
[tsipl**yo**nak pa-a**н**otneechee]
chicken chasseur

цыплёнок 'табака' [tsipl**yo**nak
taba**ka**] Georgian chicken
with garlic, grilled or fried

цыплёнок фрикасе [tsipl**yo**nak
freekas**eh**] chicken fricassee

чахохбили [cha**н**o**н**b**ee**lee]
Georgian-style chicken
casserole

черешня [cher**yesh**nya] sweet
cherries

чёрная смородина [ch**o**rna-ya
smar**o**deena] blackcurrants

черника [chyern**ee**ka]
bilberries

чёрный перец [ch**o**rni p**ye**ryets]
black pepper

чёрный хлеб [ch**o**rni **н**l**ye**p]
black bread, rye bread

чеснок [chyesn**o**k] garlic

чечевица [chyechyev**ee**tsa]
lentils

шашлык [shashl**iy**k] kebab

шашлык из баранины
[shashl**iy**k eez bar**a**neeni] lamb
kebab

шашлык из свинины с
рисом [shashl**iy**k ees sveen**ee**ni
sr**ee**sam] pork kebab with
rice

шницель [shn**ee**tsel] schnitzel

шницель с яичницей
глазуньей [shn**ee**tsel sya-
eeshneetsay glaz**oo**nyay]
schnitzel with fried egg

шоколад [shakal**at**] chocolate

шпинат [shpeen**at**] spinach

шпроты [shpr**o**ti] sprats

щи [sh-chee] cabbage soup

щука [sh-ch**oo**ka] pike

эскалоп [eskal**o**p] escalope

эскимо [eskeem**o**] choc-ice

яблоко [**ya**blaka] apple

яблочный пирог [**ya**blachni
peer**o**k] apple pie

язык [yaz**iy**k] tongue

яичница [ya-**ee**shneetsa] fried
egg; omelette

яичница болтунья [ya-
eeshneetsa balt**oo**nya]
scrambled eggs

яичница глазунья [ya-
eeshneetsa glaz**oo**nya] fried
eggs

яйцо [y**i**ts**o**] egg

яйцо вкрутую [y**i**ts**o** fkroot**oo**-
yoo] hard-boiled egg

яйцо всмятку [y**i**ts**o** fsm**ya**tkoo]
soft-boiled egg

яйцо под майонезом [y**i**ts**o**
pad mi-an**e**zam] egg
mayonnaise

Menu Reader:
Drink

Essential terms

beer пиво [**pee**va]
bottle бутылка [boot**iy**lka]
brandy коньяк [kan**yak**]
coffee кофе **m** [**ko**fyeh]
cup чашка [**chash**ka]
fruit juice фруктовый сок [frook**to**vi sok]
gin джин [djin]
gin and tonic джин с тоником [djin st**o**neekam]
glass стакан [sta**kan**]
  (wine glass) бокал [ba**kal**]
milk молоко [mala**ko**]
mineral water минеральная вода [meenyer**al**na-ya va**da**]
red wine красное вино [**kra**sna-yeh vee**no**]
soda (water) газированная вода [gazeer**o**van-na-ya va**da**]
soft drink безалкогольный напиток [byezalkag**o**lni nap**ee**tak]
sugar сахар [**sa**Har]
tea чай **m** [chI]
tonic (water) тоник [**to**neek]
vodka водка [**vo**tka]
water вода [va**da**]
whisky виски [**vee**skee]
white wine белое вино [**bye**la-yeh vee**no**]
wine вино [vee**no**]
wine list карта вин [**k**arta veen]

another beer, please ещё одно пиво, пожалуйста [yesh-ch**o**
  adn**o pee**va, paJ**a**lsta]
a cup of tea, please чашку чая, пожалуйста [**chash**koo cha-ya,
  paJ**a**lsta]
a glass of ... стакан ... [sta**kan**]

абрикосовый сок [abrek**o**savi sok] apricot juice

Акашени [akash**e**nee] Georgian red wine

апельсиновый сок [apyels**ee**navi sok] orange juice

аперитив [apyere**tee**f] aperitif

Арарат® [arar**a**t] brandy from Armenia

армянксий коньяк [arm**ya**nskee kan**ya**k] Armenian brandy

бальзам [balz**a**m] alcoholic herbal drink flavoured with honey and fruit

безалкогольный напиток [byezalkag**o**lni nap**ee**tak] soft drink

безо льда [byezal**d**a] without ice

без сахара [byes s**a**Hara] without sugar

белое вино [b**ye**la-yeh veen**o**] white wine

Белый Аист® [b**ye**li a-eest] brand of cognac

Боржоми® [barJ**o**mee] brand of mineral water

брют [br**yoo**tt] dry, brut

вермут [v**ye**rmoot] vermouth

вино [veen**o**] wine

виноградный сок [veenagr**a**dni sok] grape juice

виски [v**ee**skee] whisky

вишнёвый сок [veeshn**yo**vi sok] cherry juice

вода [vad**a**] water

водка [v**o**tka] vodka

водка Зубровка® [v**o**tka zoobr**o**fka] bison grass vodka

водка Лимонная® [v**o**tka leem**o**n-na-ya] lemon vodka

водка Московская® [v**o**tka mask**o**fska-ya] brand of vodka

водка Охотничья® [v**o**tka aH**o**tneechya] hunter's vodka flavoured with juniper berries, ginger and cloves

водка Перцовка [v**o**tka pyerts**o**vka] pepper vodka

водка Старка® [v**o**tka st**a**rka] apple and pear-leaf vodka

водка Столичная® [v**o**tka stal**ee**chna-ya v**o**tka] brand of vodka

газированная вода [gazeer**o**van-na-ya vad**a**] fizzy water

газированный [gazeer**o**van-ni] fizzy

горилка [gar**ee**lka] Ukrainian vodka

Гурджани [goordJ**a**nee] Georgian dry white wine

грузинское вино [grooz**ee**nska-yeh veen**o**] Georgian wine

джин [djin] gin

джин с тоником [djin st**o**neekom] gin and tonic

заварка [zav**a**rka] strong leaf tea brew to which boiling water is added

А
Б
В
Г
Д
Е
Ё
Ж
З
И
Й
К
Л
М
Н
О
П
Р
С
Т
У
Ф
Х
Ц
Ч
Ш
Щ
Ъ
Ы
Ь
Э
Ю
Я

267

игристое вино [eegreesta-yeh veeno] sparkling wine

какао [kaka-o] cocoa
карта вин [karta veen] wine list
квас [kvas] kvas – non-alcoholic drink made from fermented bread and water
кефир [kyefeer] sour yoghurt drink
Киндзмараули [kindzmara-oolee] Georgian red wine
кисель [keesyel] thickened fruit juice drink
клюквенный морс [klyookvyen-ni mors] cranberry drink
Кока-Кола® [koka-kola] Coca-Cola®
коктейль [kaktayl] cocktail
компот [kampot] fruit syrup drink with pieces of fresh or dried fruit
коньяк [kanyak] brandy
кофе [kofyeh] coffee
кофе по-турецки [kofyeh pa-tooryetskee] Turkish coffee
кофе с молоком [kofyeh smalakom] coffee with milk
красное вино [krasna-yeh veeno] red wine
креплёное вино [kryeplyona-yeh veeno] fortified wine
кумыс [koomiys] fermented drink made from mare's milk

лёд [lyot] ice; ice cubes

ликёр [leekyor] liqueur
лимон [leemon] lemon
лимонад [leemanat] lemonade

Массандра [mas-sandra] Crimean fortified wine
минеральная вода [meenyeralna-ya vada] mineral water
молоко [malako] milk
Московское® [maskofska-yeh] brand of bottled light ale
Мукузани [mookoozanee] Georgian red wine

напитки [napeetkee] drinks
напиток [napeetak] drink
Нарзан® [narzan] brand of mineral water
настойка [nastoyka] liqueur made from berries or other fruit

пиво [peeva] beer
пиво Балтика® [peeva balteeka] brand of bottled beer
пиво Жигулёвское® [peeva Jigoolyofska-yeh] brand of bottled beer
пиво Очаковское® [peeva achakofska-yeh] brand of bottled beer
пиво Тверское [peeva tvyersko-yeh] dark beer
полусладкий [palooslatkee] medium-sweet
полусладкое вино [palooslatka-yeh veeno]

medium-sweet wine
полусухое вино [poloosooно-yeh veeно] medium-dry wine
полусухой [poloosooноy] medium-dry
Пепси® [pepsee] Pepsi®
портвейн [portvyayn] port-style drink

растворимый кофе [rastvareemi kofyeh] instant coffee
ром [rom] rum

Саперави [sapyeravi] Georgian red wine
сахар [saнar] sugar
светлое пиво [svyetla-yeh peeva] lager
сладкий [slatkee] sweet
сладкое вино [slatka-yeh veeno] dessert wine
сливки [sleefkee] cream
с молоком [smalakom] with milk
сок [sok] juice
со льдом [saldom] with ice
с сахаром [s-saнaram] with sugar
столовое вино [stalova-yeh veeno] table wine
сухой [sooноy] dry

томатный сок [tamatni sok] tomato juice
травяной чай [travyaноy chi] herbal tea

Фанта® Fanta®

Цинандали [tsinandalee] Georgian dry white wine

чай [chi] tea
чай с лимоном [chi sleemonam] lemon tea
чёрный кофе [chorni kofyeh] black coffee

шампанское [shampanska-yeh] champagne

яблочный сок [yablachni sok] apple juice

А
Б
В
Г
Д
Е
Ё
Ж
З
И
Й
К
Л
М
Н
О
П
Р
С
Т
У
Ф
Х
Ц
Ч
Ш
Щ
Ъ
Ы
Ь
Э
Ю
Я